One Baby Step at a Time

Seven Secrets of Jewish Motherhood

One Baby Step at a Time

Seven Secrets of Jewish Motherhood

Chana (Jenny) Weisberg

Urim Publications
Jerusalem • New York

One Baby Step at a Time: Seven Secrets of Jewish Motherhood
by Chana (Jenny) Weisberg

Printed at Hemed Press, Israel. First Edition.
ISBN-13: 978-965-524-001-6
ISBN-10: 965-524-001-0
Urim Publications
P.O. Box 52287, Jerusalem 91521 Israel

Lambda Publishers Inc.
3709 13th Avenue Brooklyn, New York 11218 U.S.A.
Tel: 718-972-5449 Fax: 718-972-6307, mh@ejudaica.com

www.UrimPublications.com

This book is dedicated to the people who enabled and inspired me to write this book — my five beloved and extraordinary children. How can I possibly thank all of you enough for making me your mother?

CONTENTS

ACKNOWLEDGEMENTS

I feel so thankful to Hashem for surrounding me with the special people who enabled me to write this book.

Thank You for my teachers, Rebbetzins Talia Helfer and Yemima Mizrachi, whose weekly classes have transformed me and the way I mother my children.

Thank You for the sisters Yikrat Friedman and Noga Hullman, for Yikrat's weekly transcriptions of Rebbetzin Yemima's classes, and for Noga's collection of inspirational readings. Without Yikrat and Noga's efforts to stay inspired and to inspire women in our community, this book would look very different.

Thank You for Shlomit Wolff, who insisted one morning as we dropped our daughters off at nursery school that what women really need is a book that talks about bringing spirituality and inspiration into our daily lives as mothers.

Thank You for my community: the women of Nahlaot, Kol Rina Synagogue, Nishmat, and www.JewishPregnancy.org.

Thank You for my publisher, Tzvi Mauer of Urim Publications, for his ongoing support and publication of books for the benefit of Jewish mothers.

Thank You for Rabbi David Sperling, who provided advice on several important questions about this book.

Thank You for Caroline Bass, Aviva Yoselis, Elana Greenspan, Rachel Oppenheim, Chana Mason, Sara Esther Crispe, and Noga Hullman, who provided encouraging and insightful feedback and editing advice.

Thank You for Alit Sedley, who gave my book a title.

Thank You for my parents, Gladys and Matthew Freedman, and the rest of the Freedman and Weisberg families who shower my family and me with so much love and encouragement.

Thank You for my precious children, who are the greatest joy of my whole life.

And above all, thank You for my husband, Joshua, the best friend I've ever had, and the best person I've ever known.

INTRODUCTION

TURNING INTO A MOTHER

A FEW WEEKS AGO we hosted one of my husband's best friends from college and his wife who were visiting Israel, and then last week we received a sweet email from them. In the email, the wife quoted the traditional American folk song, "Simple Gifts":

> *When we find ourselves in the place just right,*
> *It will be in the Valley of Love and Delight....*
> *to turn, turn, will be our delight*
> *till by turning, turning we come round right.*

The author of this email had no idea that this was one of my favorite songs when I was a young girl. And she had no idea just how much it meant to me when she suggested that Josh and I, living an Orthodox Jewish life in Jerusalem, had found our very own "place just right." I agreed with her from the bottom of my heart.

But I did not always feel this way. Like many women who are mothers today, when I graduated from college just over a decade ago, my education had prepared me to do just about whatever I wanted – for a career in diplomacy, or in academia, or anything else I could have dreamed. I envisioned a life spent crashing through glass ceilings.

But when I became a mother five years after my college graduation, I realized that the education I had received had prepared me for every possible job, career, or calling in life... except one.

I wrote the essays in this book between the years 2002 and 2005 about the joys and hardships of my abrupt transition from being a full-time student to being the mother of three children under the age of four. In this book, you will see me trying my hardest to figure out how to be a good mother and manage a home despite a distinct lack of parenting and domestic skills, and in the shadow of the tension caused by the terrible Intifada that claimed over a thousand Jewish lives. An intensive, sink-or-swim course under less than ideal conditions in Jewish Motherhood 101.

I wrote many of these essays in order to send them out to the several hundred women on the mailing list of www.JewishPregnancy.org, a popular website that I created in 2001. Within a few hours of sending out these Jewish Pregnancy Updates, as I called them, emails started pouring in from list members in North America, Australia, Israel, South Africa, and the UK. The mothers on the list reacted strongly to what I had written. I had made them cry, or I had spoken about an idea that had really inspired them, or I had, they insisted, gotten something entirely wrong. Their letters made me realize that writing honestly about my life as a very well-intentioned and often bewildered young mother provided a lot of much-needed validation and encouragement for other women, as well as an opportunity for all of us to think about and discuss issues that are central to our mothering lives.

In the end, it has taken the crash course in Jewish motherhood described in this book for me to understand fully the American folk song that I sang along with all the other fourth graders at Friends School in Baltimore. This is because it describes exactly what you will see me doing a lot of in the coming pages: turning my heart around and around and around in search of a place just right. Just as the rotation of the Earth causes night and day simply by changing our perception of the light of the sun, so too, I realized that I can often turn darkness to light by simply moving and changing and turning myself.[1] Turning my heart to God for help and guidance during difficult times, turning to teachers and other mothers in order to become more skilled and inspired as a mother, and learning to look inward and turn around the way I think and see the world in order to make my life easier and better.

---

[1] Rebbetzin Yemima Mizrachi, lecture on *Parshat Ki Tetze*, September 13, 2005.

The Rebbetzins and the Seven Secrets

The challenges that you will see me facing in the coming pages are close to universal for mothers of young children, but the specific ways in which I have coped are unique in some ways to the Jerusalem community of Nahlaot that I have called home for the past decade. This is because of the great influence on my life of two Nahlaot teachers whose insightful and innovative ideas on Jewish womanhood and mothering have left a big mark on the homes and hearts of many young mothers here. It is these two teachers who, in their classes as well as by their personal example, have introduced me over the years to "Seven Secrets of Jewish Motherhood."[2]

The first teacher is Rebbetzin Talia Helfer of Jerusalem's Sanhedria neighborhood. Rebbetzin Talia was born in Rehovot into a family of religious Holocaust survivors, and when she married and moved to Jerusalem she devoted herself to mothering a large family. Fifteen years ago, she began teaching classes in various Jerusalem neighborhoods on the essence of the Jewish woman and mother.

Rebbetzin Talia has taught thousands of students over the years, and I have had the privilege of attending her classes on parenting in Nahlaot for the past three years.[3] In her weekly lectures, Rebbetzin Talia emphasizes the importance of using encouragement and enthusiasm to bring about children's cooperation in the home as well as in their education towards the performance of *mitzvot*. I hope that what I write about the tremendous benefit I have received from Rebbetzin Talia's classes will inspire all the women who read this book to seek out helpful parenting classes in their own communities.

---

[2] These rebbetzins did not discuss the seven secrets systematically in their lectures. Rather, they are ideas and themes that I picked up from several years of attending their classes. Therefore, please bear in mind that while the wisdom of Rebbetzins Talia and Yemima is the lifeblood of this book, any errors I have made in applying their teachings or relating them in the coming pages are entirely my own.

[3] This class is based on the book *Ohel Yaakov ve-Leah* by Rabbi Menachem Shlanger (Netanya: 1998).

The second teacher is Rebbetzin Yemima Mizrachi, who grew up in Jerusalem in a religious, French-speaking family and graduated with a degree in law from Hebrew University. Her family encouraged her to excel intellectually and professionally, and it was only when she married and became a mother that she started looking to Judaism, and specifically to the teachings of great Hasidic rabbis, as a way to infuse spirituality into her everyday life as a wife, mother, and Jewish woman.

In recent years, Yemima has found her calling not in law but rather in passing on these teachings to her hundreds of students around Jerusalem, among them the many Nahlaot mothers who fight over seats at her weekly class on the Torah portion. Every week, she provides practical advice based on Torah sources about how we can bring more inspiration and spirituality into our lives as Jewish mothers.

The Interviews

The last section of this book contains seven interviews with religious mothers from the Jerusalem area: English-speaking mothers and Israeli mothers, stay-at-home mothers and working mothers, *Haredi*[4] mothers and modern Orthodox mothers, mothers of eleven and mothers of one. These women talk honestly about the challenges they have faced raising young children, and I sincerely hope that their stories will provide some comfort and validation, whether on days when a mother goes to bed with her heart in her socks because she yelled at her four-year-old who then cried himself to sleep, or on the days when a first-time mother of a three-month-old feels like a candidate for the FBI's Most Wanted List because she realizes that she has never been so terribly miserable and lonely in her whole life.

In other words, if there is any conclusion I have come to after speaking with so many mothers while writing this book, it is that motherhood inevitably contain aspects that are downright tough for every woman who ever carries a newborn baby through the hospital's sliding door and over the threshold of her own home. May the knowledge that we are not alone in our struggles provide some comfort, and may it mean that we learn to forgive

---

[4] *Haredi* is the term used in Israel to mean ultra-Orthodox.

our own foibles and to love ourselves at least a fraction as much as God loves us for all the good things we mothers do around the clock for so many people. As the Talmud states, "'Praiseworthy is the person who… gives charity at all times.' Is it really possible to constantly give charity? Our Sages explain that this refers to those who care for their young children."[5]

To this same end, I have included inspirational readings which I have called "Blah-Buster Tidbits" between the essays and interviews,[6] so that as we go about our days tying shoelaces, peeling oranges, and searching for that ever-disappearing left glove, we will not fall into the trap of feeling that we are, in fact, dedicating our lives to matters of little importance. By the time you put down this book, I pray that you will be able to smile at the truth (and not only the silliness) of the statement: "Mothers are changing the world, one diaper at a time."

As I conclude this introduction, I am thinking about the stereo that we perched on top of a high bookshelf so that it would be safe from curious little hands when we brought it home from the store four years ago. This means that for the past four years, whenever I have wanted to listen to music or to put on a tape for my daughters, I have had to stand on top of a rickety wooden chair and feel around for the control buttons that are too

---

[5] Babylonian Talmud, *Ketubbot* 50a. It sounds a bit strange to say that taking care of our children is an act of charity. But it's true. In the Talmudic era, parents were only required to provide basic food, clothing, and shelter for their children, and only until the age of six! The Bialer Rebbe explains that a mother's constant and watchful care of her young children, even over the age of six, is one of the most admirable acts of charity possible. He writes, "If one goes above and beyond the bare necessities by generously providing for all of his children's needs, then this is an admirable form of charity. This is certainly the case with the righteous women, who cheerfully and enthusiastically provide for their children, trying to make their lives pleasant and enjoyable. They fulfill much more than their responsibility.… They forgo their own peace and comfort for the good of their beloved children. They sacrifice themselves, body and soul. Therefore, their reward is greater than anyone can imagine." (From *The Merit of Righteous Women* by Rabbi Ben Tsion Rabinowitz, the Bialer Rebbe [Jerusalem: 2003], 402).

[6] Many of these inspirational readings were collected by friend Noga Hullman. I sincerely thank her for sharing them with me and with the readers of this book.

high for me to see on the top of the stereo. This also means that I usually press the wrong buttons a few times, rewinding when I want to fast-forward, pausing when I want to start, and turning on the radio when I want to listen to a CD. And then, the other day as I was feeling around the dusty top of the stereo and pressing all of the wrong buttons, I noticed a remote control coated with dust that we must have placed next to the stereo when we brought it back from the store. I took the remote control down, went to the kitchen to find two batteries to insert into it, and bingo, I was able to turn on the tape, rewind the tape, increase the volume, turn on the radio instead, all while standing on the ground, the rickety wooden chair parked safely at the table.

I pray with all of my heart that learning and implementing the seven secrets described in this book will do for you what finding that forgotten remote control did for me. I pray that this book will dust off some tried-and-true insights and advice and place them into our hands so that we will all be able to spend less time confused and frustrated while groping around in the dark and pressing all of the wrong buttons as we try our best to raise our beloved children. May this book validate our experiences at the same time that it inspires us and empowers us to make Jewish motherhood a bit easier and smoother, infusing our mothering lives with more happiness and holiness.

A Note on Translations

Hebrew terms appear frequently throughout the book. While providing an accompanying translation for every single Hebrew word is disruptive for readers who know Hebrew, I also want the book to be accessible to women who know little or no Hebrew. The compromise I have reached is that I have translated more difficult Hebrew words when they first appear in a chapter, but not when they appear again in that same chapter. There is also a glossary of Hebrew words at the end of the book.

STEP ONE

LEARNING TO VALUE OUR MOTHERING ACCOMPLISHMENTS

WHEN I WAS IN HIGH SCHOOL and college, I thought that it was fine for a woman to pursue motherhood as a side dish to her career, but certainly not as the main course of life. I believed that women who did so were oppressed, unfulfilled, or, at best, woefully unliberated.

When motherhood and home became the spaghetti and meatballs of my life a few years later, I had to learn from scratch how to value the way I was spending my days. In the coming essays and excerpts, you will read how I, as well as other mothers, have learned to ignore the Betty Friedan-quoting women's studies professors who refuse to evacuate our brains and have chosen, alternatively, to turn up the volume on what the Torah has to say about the importance of mothering – for the future of our children and that of the Jewish people, and for our own personal and spiritual growth as well.

BLAH-BUSTER TIDBIT

Restocking Our Spiritual Tool Box

by Pessy Leah Lester[1]

Being a wife and mother is hard work, harder than any job I've ever had. As a young mother, I felt the truth of that old saying, "Man's work is from sun to sun, but a woman's work is never done." I was running so fast just to stay in one place. I thought the day would never end.

Over time I gained valuable home management skills from friends, relatives, role models, and counselors. I also gleaned valuable advice from books and magazines. These helpful hints included such things as menu planning, play groups with neighbors, shopping lists, writing it all down, the portable phone, getting as much cleaning and babysitting help as you can, and making time for yourself.

But even after getting organized physically, I still wasn't able to get through the day happily. These management tools may help organize your day, but if you don't have a good attitude towards [managing a home and raising a family], then all the tools, techniques, menus, and lists won't help organize you body and soul.

I used to resent the amount of work I had to do at home. I thought that being a mother meant I would be eternally doomed to loads of dirty laundry, tied to the stove with a ball and chain, and forever changing diapers. But that's not necessarily the case. I realized I could be the kind of wife and mother I choose to be. I could be a happy mother or a miserable mother; it is merely a matter of attitude. An older and experienced mother in my community with a dozen or so children once told me, "You can get through the day laughing or crying. It's easier (and nicer) to laugh."

…Well beyond physical help and management skills, most women today in their early childbearing years also need a mental and spiritual toolbox. I used to pride myself on how well I could fix things around the house and looked fondly upon the box of tools my father assembled for me before I went to college. But I came to realize that my mental tool kit was bare, so I started to assemble some suggestions and reminders to keep me going, one baby step at a time.…

---

[1] Lester, Pessy Leah. "Getting through the Day." *Natural Jewish Parenting* (Fall 1996): 27–28. Pessy Leah Lester is a writer and mother in Chicago, Illinois.

Mindful Motherhood

Four Tools for the Prevention
of Emotional Orphans

When I was a student at Bowdoin College in Maine just over a decade ago, I had a few friends who were education majors. I would tell them that I would never want to be a teacher, since I was certain that whatever I would be doing in the world, it would be something big – involving nationwide policies, working in Congress, or (this was my real dream) influencing and ultimately saving the whole entire world. In my sophomore year of college, Thomas Pickering, a Bowdoin graduate who was at the time the US Ambassador to the United Nations, came to speak with the undergraduates. I don't remember a thing he said. I only remember how inspired I was by his presence and how he represented the fulfillment of my highest possible aspiration – that one day, many years later, I would stand at the podium in that same auditorium and be the kind of person that college students would also dream to become.

To this end, I majored in Russian and in political science and became fixated on the Soviet Union. I traveled many times to Russia, memorized the intricate hierarchy of the Soviet government, and spent hundreds of hours watching the Soviet news via satellite with a notebook balanced in my lap to mark down new vocabulary words. I thought that after graduation I would work for the Foreign Service or the State Department, or something like that, and climb my way up. Well, needless to say, my life has followed a very different path from the one I had envisioned for myself.

My life as a mother is not only not big; it is absolutely microscopic. My life centers not around shaping countries, regions, or even cities, but rather around my teensy-weensy daughters and watching them grow, ever so slowly, into infinitesimally more grown-up human beings, And this process is often as slow and as thankless for long stretches of time as sitting and waiting on Friday afternoon for a ten-liter pot of chicken soup to boil.

This week, Rebbetzin Yemima Mizrachi reminded us in her class on the weekly Torah portion that the Torah says that Abraham died when he was "*zaken ba ba-yamim*" (Genesis 24:1), which literally means "old and coming with days." The *Sefat Emet* explains that the phrase "coming with days" refers to the fact that when we die, each one of our days will come along with us to Heaven in order to testify as to whether we got the fullest potential out of every day or whether we just let the Heaven-sent opportunities in our lives slip through our fingers. The *Sefat Emet* explains that Abraham's days came with him when he died and testified that he had succeeded in finding the point of light hidden in each and every day, the mini-mission from God for that particular day – to give charity that Thursday, to preach monotheism to a nomadic tribe the following Sunday, and so on.[1]

In some ways, "coming with days," getting the most out of every moment, has become much easier since I've become a mother. With my writing in the mornings, for example, I know that I have exactly two and a half, maybe three hours of writing until my baby wakes up, so I am efficient. I don't make phone calls in the middle, I don't even run downstairs for an apple despite my rumbling belly. I write as though I am half-way through a final exam and there is only half an hour left to go. This is in comparison with the dreamy distraction with which I used to write my college papers: taking a break to go to the Student Union to buy a package of Doritos, or to skim an unrelated article in a journal from which I was quoting.

The same is true when I attend my weekly class on the books of Ezra and Nehemia. Early every Thursday morning, I take my baby to a babysitter, take my kids to nursery school and kindergarten, and, boy, do I enjoy that morning of Torah study. You can't even compare the intensity of that enjoyment with when I was single and spent a few years learning Torah every day for the entire day. All Thursday morning I am sitting on the edge

---

[1] *Sefat Emet,* Hayyei Sara, on Genesis 24:1.

of my seat, utterly fascinated, afraid to miss a single word. And I spend the rest of the week thinking about the class and telling my husband about all the amazing things I learned about the Persian Empire and the construction of the Second Temple during those four short hours.

I was also in a "coming with days" mode last Thursday when my mother-in-law, who is visiting for a few weeks, offered to watch the kids so that my husband and I could go to Tel Aviv for the night. This is the first time in five years that we have gone anywhere overnight totally on our own, and the intensity with which we enjoyed each other's company and appreciated the treat of this rare solitary outing was off the charts. We walked on the beach and then through the market, pointing out all the ways in which our neighborhood market in Jerusalem is superior to the one in Tel Aviv, and then stopped at a restaurant where they served our meal in old frying pans, and we talked and joked and had the greatest time. We used to go to Tel Aviv once every few months when we were dating and newly married. It was also fun, but you can't even compare the fun we had then with the fun we had on this trip. This was eat-the-chicken, lick-the-bone-clean, and suck-out-the-marrow fun.

On the other hand, there are ways in which "coming with days" is infinitely harder for me now that I am a mother – in particular, when I come back from my brief getaways at the computer, in class, and to Tel Aviv, and find myself face-to-face with my children. On my worst days, I am eating lunch with my two-year-old and reading a magazine, my kids are in the living room and I am cleaning the kitchen, my four-year-old is telling me about her day, and I am telling her to wait just one moment while I make a phone call.

I am not saying that I aspire to be totally focused on my children at all times when they are home. It is important that my children develop patience and learn to respect my need to engage in activities during the day that are not connected to them, such as filling the dishwasher, returning a call from a friend, or saying my morning prayers. What I am referring to is getting into a mothering pattern where I am never really with my children even when I am with them. At times, I can go through a whole day of motherhood and realize that there was not even a ten-minute span during which I was totally tuned in and listening to each one of my children. Ten minutes for each child during which I was fully focused on what I am trying to accomplish as a mother – in my life's mission as educator, role model, and spiritual guide for my children.

The following are ideas that I have collected from teachers, books, and friends that I maintain at all times in my brain's glove compartment for frequent emergency retrieval. These reminders have helped me (on my good days) to maintain an inspired "coming with days" mentality – meaning a present mommy, a mommy on a mission, a mommy I can feel proud of being.

Reminder # 1: Before You Know It, They'll Be Grown Up

I find it helpful to remind myself that the intensely demanding period of mothering young children is crucial to our children's development and is over far too quickly. I am the worst kind of mother when I focus on the eternity of hours and minutes that I will spend taking care of children in the coming decades. When I am in this mode, I approach my days as obstacles to get through with as little effort as possible, each and every day a stretch of supermarathon through rural, frostbitten northern Ohio.

Something I do to pull myself out of this uninspired, distracted state is to think about the amount of weekday hours I actually spend with my kids. Even as a stay-home mother, I figured out that between nursery school and time spent with Dad, I spend only fifteen hours a week with my two older girls.

The first time I realized this, it was quite an eye-opener to realize that I have only fifteen hours with my daughters over the course of the week to educate them, to hear what they have on their minds, to actively get *nachas* from these amazing girls who far exceed my wildest pre-motherhood dreams. And this knowledge makes me really focus on getting as much mothering into those few hours as possible – making an effort to consciously enjoy their company while we are together instead of ignoring them the whole afternoon while I peel carrots and rearrange the fridge.

If I'm maintaining the right frame of mind, then I find it much easier to give my children my full attention, giving them my mind and heart, and not only a head that nods and a mouth that exclaims "Wow!" to their stories while my mind is wandering around the outer stratosphere. When I am in a present and mindful state and Tiferet* reminds me with wide-open eyes about the volunteer at the zoo who wrapped the boa constrictor around her neck and told her the tragic life story of the bird with the broken wing, then I find I am able to really listen to what she is saying, while remembering what an incredible thing it is that *Hashem* gave me a daughter who is so curious and enthusiastic about the world around her.

Another thing that I remind myself is something that our parenting class teacher, Rebbetzin Talia Helfer, told us – that these few years of baby and toddlerhood followed by nursery and elementary school are the time when mothers can have the most influence on their children in terms of values, education, and love of Judaism. She reported from her own personal experience as the mother and grandmother of a large clan: "Before you know it, they'll be home less and less – playing at friends' houses, going off to high school, and then getting married. While they are little is your chance to make a difference in their lives!"

Mental snapshots can also be a helpful tool. If, let's say, I'm eating lunch with my kids and I'm in a blah, distracted mood, I find it incredibly helpful to take a mental picture of us sitting there, in order give myself a self-administered mega-dose injection of *nachas*. This causes me to realize something along the lines of, "Wow, this is a truly incredible moment. What a wonderful thing it is to have this quiet time together with Tiferet and Nisa, just the three of us schmoozing and eating tuna sandwiches on whole-wheat pita for lunch."

Or, at other times, I imagine a snapshot of my husband and me sitting on the sofa by ourselves in thirty years, sort of happy to have earned a few decades of relative rest and quiet, but also sad – missing all the little people

---

* Throughout this book, I will use pseudonyms for my children in order to protect their privacy.

who used to share the house with us, the way they used to sit on our laps during Shabbat dinner and never failed to give us something to laugh about.

Reminder # 2: Connect Mundane Mothering Moments with Long-Term Goals (i.e., Secrets of the Madwoman Mutterer)

Rebbetzin Yemima taught us this week that when the Israelites were running away from the Egyptians, the Torah says, "The desert closed in on them" (Exodus 14:3). Yet the same verse can also mean, "Speech closed for them" (*midbar* read as *medaber*). When our ancestors were in Egypt, and when each one of us finds herself in her own personal *Mitzrayim* (literally meaning closed-in, narrow straits)[2] – in depression, anger, fear, powerlessness, despair – then we can often release ourselves from this difficult situation by opening our mouths and speaking to God.[3]

Yemima says, "The Israelites did not have time to breathe, they were working so hard. They didn't even have time to sigh! Their mouths were closed, and so was their connection with God. Today we are in a similar situation to those slaves in Egypt. We spend our days so fully occupied with work, children, school, the dishes, and the laundry, that we can barely lift up our heads to breathe. Also our husbands are working at slave labor of various kinds. And, for many of us, our ability to speak is essentially in exile. We don't have the strength to pray and to request, to speak from our hearts with those around us and with God." So the ticket out of Egypt is to speak, to just talk to God while we're going about our days, from the depths of our hearts – or even about whatever little splinter of a thing is under our skin at the moment.

Yemima also taught us that the word *mitzvah* is related to the word *tzavta*, or together, because when we do a *mitzvah*, we form a team with God. Therefore, one of the best, most effective times to engage in this spontaneous prayer is when we are involved in performing a commandment, and the truth is that it is pretty hard to catch us Jewish mothers involved in

---

[2] If vowelized differently, Mitzrayim (Egypt) can be read as Metzarim (straits or a narrow place).

[3] *Likutei Moharan* 66:4.

anything else. It's a *mitzvah* to do anything involved in taking care of children, taking care of our homes, or even making money in order to support our families. You holy pregnant women are the best, since you are at all times fulfilling God's first command in the history of the universe, "Be fruitful and multiply!" This means you could be sleeping, or getting a manicure, or even just standing in line at the post office, and you are in a constant state of *mitzvah*, a starting player on God's All-Star team.

Therefore, I often find myself muttering like a madwoman – when I'm making ponytails in the morning, I call out: "*Hashem*, please help Nisa to stop biting the other kids in nursery school." Or, when I'm folding laundry, I plead: "*Hashem*, please help Dafna to get to sleep earlier so that she won't be so tired and grouchy in the morning."

Any program without clear goals, whether in education, marketing, or self-improvement, will get far off track or flop altogether. The same is true about a family. Spontaneous prayer is the main way in which I stay in touch with my goals, so that I don't lose my days in a morass of nonstop demands and details unfocused by my ultimate dreams and aspirations for my children and for the kind of mother I hope to be.

Two thumbs up for madwoman muttering – it makes the time fly, makes your life better, and I can personally testify that it truly works wonders.

Reminder #3: Recognize Your Mothering Accomplishments

If I actually had become the Ambassador to the UN (even though, today, the image of myself in a power suit with a briefcase instead of in a spit-up spotted denim jumper with a diaper bag over my shoulder seems impossibly ridiculous), my days would have been marked by accomplishments such as successful meetings with the dictators of small African countries, convincing interviews with CNN, and maybe even an occasional promotion to head a subcommittee or two.

But as a mother, my natural tendency is, unfortunately, to let my day flow uncharted from the first diaper change of the day to the last peanut butter sandwich for tomorrow's lunch packed away five minutes past my bedtime. Let's look at the year 2001, for example. That was a year during which I did not give birth, that I was not pregnant, that I was home with baby Tiferet. In short, I remember absolutely nothing about the year 2001. It is a year during which I am certain that I nursed Tiferet thousands of times, washed thousands of dishes, and brushed thousands of little teeth. It is a year that has absolutely disappeared into a black hole somewhere behind my cerebellum.

In more recent years, I have been combating this life-disappearing-into-black-holes phenomenon through my writing. I dedicate a morning to describing a certain struggle, a difficulty, a fleeting mothering victory, and that makes it real for me. It makes me feel that within the blur of pregnancies, births, and mothering that the last six years of my life has been, that there is form and shape and, even, on occasion, a bit of progress.

To give you an example, I have been struggling with a terrible problem for the past year and a half. My three-year-old loves her baby sister so much that she constantly wants to pick her up and carry her around. The problem is that, from time to time, the three-year-old remembers that she also hates the baby a little bit, so she drops her. That means that the baby is hysterical whenever her sister picks her up, since she is so terribly afraid that this will be one of the few times when she is dropped.

I am also a nervous wreck whenever the older sister is holding the baby, since the baby screams, not without justification, and I am scared for her. I have been at a total loss about what to do. Telling the older sister never to pick up her sister is not a good solution, since almost all the time the three-year-old is very good with the baby, and I do so want them to learn to get along. I asked a bunch of older, more experienced mothers and parenting experts about what to do, and I prayed a lot for a solution. Then, last week, I realized that it had been weeks since this pick up the baby till she screams scenario had played itself out.[4] I don't know when it stopped, or why —

---

[4] As I edit this essay for inclusion in this book, three years after it was written, I feel differently from the way I did when I wrote it. Since the birth of our newest baby, at the urging of the mother of seven from Mea Shearim who shared my hospital room, we have made it family policy that the older children never hold the baby except for ten minutes each on Shabbat. Maybe when the baby is a year old I will feel differently, but at the moment I am amazed by how easily my

whether I finally followed the right advice or whether my kids simply grew out of it, but I realized that these two girls now play very nicely together and that their interactions don't stress me out like they used to.

This was something that turned every afternoon of my life into a stress-fest for a year and a half, and yet it disappeared with absolutely no fanfare. I mentioned this transformation to my husband in passing over plates of lasagna and felt a bit happy about it for a moment or two. But there was no real recognition for something that, for me, was way up there as an all-time success and a revolution in my brief but intense mothering career.

This is why Dr. Miriam Adahan suggests that mothers should make a point of commending themselves for a job well done. You got everyone to bed without losing your cool, you managed to clean the kitchen even though you are tired and pregnant, you taught your toddler to identify her nose as well as her bellybutton, then you should commend yourself with a note, an ice cream cone, or just a nice silent word to yourself (and your husband?) on your accomplishment. Because the fact of the matter is that if you don't give yourself a bit of recognition for a job well done, nobody will. And my way of commending myself is that I write about it, as I just did here, and it makes me feel that on occasion I'm doing something right.

Teacher Leah Golomb gave me another idea about how to commend ourselves for our teensy daily accomplishments. She told me that when she was engaged to her husband, she and her friend Dina stood together as Dina set out the white cloth she was going to use to make Leah's wedding dress. Dina took the scissors in her hand, and as she cut into the fabric she declared, *"Le-shem mitzvat hakhnasat kallah"* ("In honor of the *mitzvah* of marrying off the bride"). Leah describes how this simple statement moved her so much that it brought tears to her eyes, seeing how Dina's declaration transformed the mundane tasks of cutting and sewing and embroidering into *mitzvot,* infusing Dina with awareness of the holiness and greater purpose of what she was doing.

---

older girls accepted this new rule and how much less stressful it has made my mothering life.

And we as mothers can do the same thing in order to appreciate the bigness of the small acts of our mothering lives. As I walk to pick up Dafna from kindergarten, I can say, "*Le-shem mitzvat gemilut hasadim*" ("In honor of the *mitzvah* of performing acts of lovingkindness"). As I fry up scrambled eggs for dinner for the third time this week, I can whisper into the frying pan, "*Le-shem mitzvat ve-ahavta le-re'akha kamocha*" ("In honor of the *mitzvah* of loving your neighbor as yourself"). As I sew a button onto Tiferet's favorite Shabbat dress, I can declare to everybody in my household, "*Le-shem yihud Kudsha Brikh Hu u-Shekhinteh*" ("In order to unite the Holy One with the Divine Presence") – the mystical result of every good deed we perform.

Sounds silly? Probably. Will it work? It does for me. This is one of the best ways I have found to remain present throughout my day, and constantly (or at least occasionally) aware of the importance of the smallest acts of mothering kindness.

Reminder #4: Time Spent with Children Is a Luxury

Most of the mothers I know are married, stable financially (or at least managing to keep a roof over their heads and food on the table), and able to invest a good part of their day in being loving mothers towards their children. It's in this kind of environment that it's probably easiest to take the simple pleasures of motherhood for granted. Recently, though, I've been hearing some things that have made me realize that the normalcy that I take for granted is far from normal. A recent study on the modern family from Yale University,[5] for example, reported that just over a hundred years ago there was a huge increase in babies born out of wedlock among Christians in Europe, which resulted in a sort of large-scale state-sponsored policy of infanticide.

In 1850 in Vienna, for example, half of all babies were born out of wedlock, which meant that almost all those babies were given away to orphanages, where about sixty percent were expected to die as a result of

---

[5] Kertzer, David, et al., eds. *The History of the European Family*. Yale Publications, 2003.

substandard conditions. In France during the same period, nursing was thought to be very damaging to the mother's health, so the majority of babies were sent out for the first year of their lives to be nursed by poorer women. The problem was that these poorer women lived in drafty, unsanitary houses, and as a result, forty to sixty percent of these wet-nursed babies ended up dying. The writer of the study quips about how this served as a way to limit population growth despite the high birth rate. Beyond horror.

Then this week I met a social worker who works with prostitutes in Berlin. There are tens of thousands of these prostitutes, who are often mothers from Southeast Asia and the former Soviet Union, who leave their families behind in order to earn money to support them. Often, these women think they are coming to Berlin to work as waitresses or nannies, but then are forced into prostitution. Others know they will be working as prostitutes, but do not realize that they will be confined to their rooms, beaten, and cheated out of the money they earn by their pimps.

When the social worker talks with these women, she offers them the possibility of asylum in a safe house or the opportunity to press charges against the traffickers who misled and abused them. But what these prostitutes fear most of all is being deported by the German authorities, and the hunger and terrible poverty that await them and their children if they return home empty-handed.

And there are the heartbreaking stories with which we are all too familiar: the poor mother who has to place her child in unreliable day care from morning till night so that she can work in order to make ends meet, the millions of women who are never able to have children, or who never get married despite years of searching. Not to mention the millions of tragic deaths every year from hunger and AIDS – in 2004 more than five million children died of malnutrition and 500,000 children died of AIDS, which has already left fifteen million children orphaned of one or both parents.

From the little, secluded world that I call home, my life feels extraordinarily run-of-the-mill. But it's really not ordinary at all. A happy, healthy child and a happy, healthy mother who is able to take care of her child are increasingly becoming deviations from the norm, almost a freak of nature.

In short, the best advice I got on preventing our children from becoming emotional orphans was from the rabbi of our synagogue, Rabbi Aaron Leibowitz. He said that if you look closely at the prophets in the Bible, you realize that they focus less on predicting the future than on seeing what's happening in the present in a clear way – seeing what God wants them to be doing at that very moment, as well as that action's long-term impact on the Jewish people. So, I bless all of you mothers that we should always be able to see the present clearly, to see the opportunities for educating our children Jewishly and connecting with them that are hidden in each of our mothering days, as well as the long-term impact of these days on us, on our children, and on the future of the Jewish people. And please bless me too that I should always remember that even though my college will absolutely never invite me back to address the undergraduates, that what I am doing with all these days of mothering is in fact very, very big.

BLAH-BUSTER TIDBIT

Gentle Words

by Elizabeth Applebaum[1]

I came across a black-and-white picture of a mother holding her baby. Below was this quote from author W. M. Thackeray: "Mother is the name for God on the lips and in the hearts of little children."

… I think of this many times during the day, and always when my children seem to be most trying. It reminds me that what I say to each one of them matters. It reminds me that my praise will nourish them, and that a thoughtless comment can wound them for days. It reminds me that for this short time their father and I are the center of their universe.

I don't want God to ignore me. I don't want Him to be short-tempered with me, or impatient…. I need Him to hear my prayers, to watch over me, to comfort me when I ache and forgive me when I err. I don't want God to leave me when I am awake late at night and cannot sleep and whisper into the silence, "I'm afraid." That is when, most of all, I need Him to be there for me.

The other night Yitzhak, still wide awake at 10:15, crawled out of his little bed and walked into the den where I was resting. He was rubbing his hand across his eyes, coming fresh out of the dark into a room stained by the harsh lights of television.

It had been one of those days, and I had phone calls to return and floors to mop and laundry to put away and dishes to wash. Yitzhak said, "I'm afraid."

"Come here," I said.

Then I pulled him to me – his soft hair falling on my cheek, his warm legs resting against my own – and I held him close like that, making my arms a nest for his tiny body, deep into the night.

---

[1] Applebaum, Elizabeth. "Gentle Words." *Natural Jewish Parenting* 9 (Spring, 2000): 12. Elizabeth Applebaum is a mother and writer from Oak Park, Michigan.

Love Is Not a Luxury[1]

My daughter comes home hungry from kindergarten; I feed her. My toddler is crying; I pick her up and cuddle with her on the sofa. My third-grader rushes in from the playground with a skinned knee; I smear on some antibiotic cream, cover it with an adhesive bandage, and seal it with a kiss.

If you were to glance over the list of mothering tasks that I perform over the course of an average day, you might think that I am totally replaceable. Bring in a conscientious babysitter, an average (or even below-average) short-order chef and maid, and a sympathetic nurse for emergencies, and my children would be no worse off.

For fifty years, the Israeli kibbutz movement tried to do just that. Kibbutz children ate healthy meals in a communal dining hall, were cared for after school by devoted and carefully-trained kibbutz members, and slept in a communal "children's house" equipped with a state-of-the-art intercom for children to alert the kibbutz member on duty if they had a bad dream in the middle of the night.

The results were tragic. Dozens of academic studies of kibbutz children have revealed that more than half of them have grown up into adults who suffer from trauma and serious psychological disorders.

The diagnosis? Severe lack of love.

Rabbi Lawrence Kelemen, a Harvard-educated scholar of education and author of the acclaimed bestseller *To Kindle a Soul: Ancient Wisdom for Modern Parents and Teachers* (2001), details how the intangible emotion of love and the close relationship it creates between parents and their children influences children dramatically and permanently.

Rabbi Kelemen quotes a multitude of academic studies that demonstrate that a parent's love is a basic prerequisite for healthy human development. More than their IQs, their friends, or the schools we send them to, in the

---

[1] This article originally appeared on Aish.com, a leading Judaism website.

end it is our love for our children and our ability to express that love that will ultimately make them or break them.

A newborn horse or kitten, for example, can walk shortly following birth. But in order to reach the level of self-sufficiency that most animals have at birth, human beings require an additional nine months outside of the womb.

In 1998, Dr. Michael Orlans, a founding executive board member of the American Psychotherapy Association, explained that during these nine months the most important factor in the brain's development is "interactive routines between caregiver and infant."

Or, as Rabbi Kelemen explains, "Children do their final 'wiring' when we love them."

The impact of our love on our children's development, expressed through the attention and affection we provide them, does not grow less when our babies grow into toddlers and children and adolescents. Our children continue to crave the sense of security and confidence (known as "secure attachment") cultivated by a parent's careful attention to their needs whether that attention is provided by giving a bottle of warm milk to your toddler, reading to your six-year-old, or hanging up the phone so that you can hear all about your child's adventures at school.

Providing the high quantity and quality of attention that children need is time-consuming, demanding, and often requires a thorough reshuffling of priorities.

It's also worth it. Quality attention is one of the most important gifts you will ever give your child.

Current research at leading universities confirms that children raised by parents who are sensitive and attentive to their needs are more than six times as likely to avoid serious psychological disorders in later life. They are twice as likely to grow up into adults with high self-esteem. They are also more likely to be independent, confident, and emotionally thriving adults.

Send One Your Love

The next ingredient in creating healthy children is affection: the hugs, the kisses, the adoring looks that express just how much you love your child.

Mounting research has shown that children who are raised in an affectionate family environment are more likely to grow up to be caring, empathetic, and giving people. They are thirty percent more likely to get married and to stay married. Most striking of all, psychologist Joan McCord, former President of the American Society of Criminology, was able to predict with awe-inspiring ninety-two percent accuracy whether a child would grow up to be a criminal based exclusively on the level of affection that a given child had received from his mother.

As Rabbi Kelemen concludes from all of these findings, "Love is not a luxury. Taken together, the basic ingredients of love – attention and affection – might constitute the single most important factors in human development."

The most remarkable research findings presented in *To Kindle a Soul* relate to the long-term health consequences of parental love. In the 1950s, researchers at Harvard University asked students to rate their parental relationships as "very close," "warm and friendly," "tolerant," or "strained and cold." Thirty-five years later, researchers discovered that an astounding one hundred percent of people who had rated their relationship with their parents as "strained and cold" were suffering from critical health conditions such as severe heart disease, intestinal ulcers, and alcoholism. This is in contrast with only forty-seven percent of the people who described their relationships with their parents as "very close" or "warm and friendly." The research team concluded that feeling loved by one's parent promotes life-long immune function and good health.

So the next time you pick up your crying baby, make spaghetti with meatballs for your children, or bandage a skinned knee and seal it with a kiss, remember that you are doing something of tremendous importance. These minor, daily expressions of parental love, attention, and affection have major long-term positive impact.

It's true that you will never list these parenting responsibilities on your CV, brag about them to your colleagues or even to your fellow mothers on the park bench. But the moments, days, and years that you devote to your children are among the most important of your life.

They are certainly the surest investment you will ever make, with the highest possible return: a thriving human being.

BLAH-BUSTER TIDBIT

Mother Theresa and the Jewish Mother

by Gila Manolson[1]

Homemaking suffers from an absence of income and public recognition. Yet neither of these indicates spiritual worth. A top basketball star earns several million dollars a year, while those who saved lives during the Holocaust received no reimbursement. Nor do homemakers. The most meaningful jobs don't come with a salary (or at least not a significant one). Nor do they necessarily make one famous. As Rabbi Nachum Braverman… once wrote, Mother Theresa may have won the Nobel Prize for caring for the sick, dirty and helpless in Calcutta, but millions of unsung homemakers worldwide do the same in their own homes….

The story is told (*Bava Batra* 10b) of a Sage whose son nearly died and had a vision of the next world before returning to this one. When asked what he had seen there, he said, "I saw a world upside down. The upper was below and the lower was above."

His father replied, "You saw a clear world."

The World of Truth is the opposite of this world. In the World to Come, so much of what society esteems counts for nothing, while spirituality, nurturing, and all else we dismiss mean everything. The same will be true in the Messianic era, history's "next world." The role of women is to bring the values of the future into the present.

---

[1] Gila Manolson, *Head to Heart: What to Know before Dating and Marriage*. Michigan: 2002, 95–96. Gila Manolson is also the author of *The Magic Touch* and *Inside/Outside*. She is a popular international lecturer who lives in Jerusalem with her husband and children.

THE HEROINE IN EVERYWOMAN

RIGHT AFTER I GOT MARRIED eight years ago, I temped for four months as a secretary at the Jewish National Fund. I was a college graduate with high hopes for a rewarding and high powered career. But I was terrified that as a new immigrant to Israel who was still unsure of my Hebrew and the ins and outs of Israeli culture, and as a graduate of a small college that no one in the Middle East has ever heard of, that this four-month stint was a confirmation that I would spend the rest of my life at the bottom of the professional ladder.

I have never felt as humiliated in my whole life as I felt that summer. I thought over and over about how everyone was looking at me, and thinking that I *was* a secretary – that my potential and my intelligence were such that I had found my true calling in answering phone calls, photocopying, and editing inane form letters. My boss, a Mexican rabbi who was a terribly sweet teddy bear of a man, bore the brunt of my anger and frustration. It did not help my mood that I was an extremely poor secretary, saving letters to wannabe tree-planters in Uruguay in random computer folders titled "XL2m7," totally overwhelmed by the modest list of tasks I had to complete, and growling, "I already have too much to do" if my boss so much as moved towards my desk with a piece of paper in hand.

I would think over and over about how I had always hoped I would have some impressive career, and look at me, I was such a failure that I couldn't even *collate* properly! What was left for me to do if I couldn't even do this? Spend the rest of my life collecting shekels and handing out toilet paper in the bathroom at the Tel Aviv central bus station?

The reason I'm writing about all this is because what got me through that terrible summer was a book I read by Natan Sharansky called *Fear No Evil* about the nine years he spent in Soviet prisons between 1977 and 1986 because of his request to emigrate to Israel.[1]

---

[1] Sharansky, Natan. *Fear No Evil.* New York: 1988.

What inspired me the most about Sharansky's story was how, despite the nine years that guards, prison officials, and interrogators mocked and harassed him, despite the solitary confinement with no contact with the outside world for months and years at a time, despite being told over and over that if he continued to deny the charges against him that his life would be in danger, despite all this he never stopped knowing that the whole Soviet empire, the world's largest superpower, was, in his words, a "kingdom of lies." He and his wife Avital never stopped believing that they, two idealistic young people, knew the truth in their hearts – that they should have the right to live as Jews, and that they should have the right to move to the homeland of every Jew – Israel.

While it might sound ridiculous (and it *is* ridiculous, come to think of it), I also felt like I, at the JNF, was facing a "kingdom of lies." People (or, in retrospect, voices in my head) would tell me over and over that I would never amount to anything, that going through this humiliating experience was just a preparation for the rest of my life that would be one huge whopper of a disappointment. My dream to live a life in which I would really help people, improve the world, and use and develop my talents, would never come to pass. But I would tell myself over and over that if Natan and Avital Sharansky could stand up to the whole Soviet Union, I can stand up to the JNF, or at least the way that working as a secretary at the JNF made me feel about myself.

It has been about ten years since that terrible summer, during which I hadn't given much thought to the Sharanskys. And then, last week, I showed up at a weekly class that I've seen advertised for years in my shul bulletin. When I arrived, I found a seat among about a hundred grandmothers and great-grandmothers in pastel suits and pearls. I was wondering who the speaker would be when a middle-aged woman walked in, her hair covered by a simple brown headscarf on top of a kind, round face and deep chocolate brown eyes. Our excited hostess declared, "We are honored today to host Mrs. Avital Sharansky, the woman who, along with her husband, defeated the Soviet Union. This is the couple who single-handedly defeated Communism!" Tears came to my eyes to finally see this great woman in person, and for the next hour I had to remove my glasses again and again to wipe the tears that flowed from my eyes as she told her life story in halting English, clearly speaking from the bottom of her heart.

Avital told us about what it was like growing up in a small village in Siberia, not even knowing she was Jewish until her older brother had to fill in his nationality on his Soviet identity card when he turned sixteen. Her parents wanted him to take advantage of their connections with the local Communist officials and write that he was Russian, but he said, "No, I am a Jew!" And young Avital, only fourteen years old, stood beside him and piped in, "Yes, and I am a Jew too!" even though Avital did not even know what a Jew was.

Very slowly, over the next few years, she began questioning the atheism in which she had been raised, despite the first Soviet astronaut's mocking assurance to the world in the late 1960s: "I went up into the heavens, and there definitely wasn't anybody up there." Avital moved to Moscow to study in university and dabbled in Eastern religions and Christianity, but those religions didn't speak to her. And then, one day she was reading an illegal *samizdat* collection of Jewish writings that she had received from a friend (that, if found, would have earned her seven years in jail), and the last article was about the participants in the Leningrad trial – a group of young Jews who in 1970 were sentenced to death for trying to hijack a plane to bring them to Israel.

The end of the article described how a young woman Avital's age, who was a defendant in the trial, called out something as she was led out of the courtroom. But Avital couldn't read what she'd said, since it was written in strange, squiggly letters that Avital thought were probably Sanskrit. Avital, already in her twenties, was unsure where Israel was even located in the world, so she went to find Israel on a map, but could barely see it, since it was so small that the name "Israel" was written out in the Mediterranean.

A few weeks later, some of Avital's friends told her in hushed voices that they had found an elderly man who, would you believe it, still remembered the Hebrew alphabet! So she went with her friends to the apartment of this man who lived right outside of Moscow, and once inside they pulled down all the curtains and put the chain on the door. The man taught them the Hebrew letters and explained to them, "These are the letters with which the Holy One created the Universe," and Avital explained, "And at that moment, it was as though half of the Soviet Union just collapsed. This man was telling us that God actually did exist, and not only that, that He created the world in a language that it was illegal to even study in the Soviet Union." Avital understood that learning Hebrew was the way to free herself of the lies, emptiness, and hypocrisy of Soviet society.

She returned several times to this old man to learn more Hebrew, and realizing that the Leningrad Trial defendant's last words were written in Hebrew, she brought the article to her teacher to see what they meant. And do you know what this young woman had said? The phrase that had empowered her to risk her life, to take on the whole Soviet Union, was taken from King David: "*Im eshkahekh, Yerushalayim, tishkah yemini,*" "If I forget you, Jerusalem, may my right hand lose its cunning"[2] – the verse recited at every Jewish wedding throughout history to express a Jew's longing to return to the Holy Land.

Soon after, someone invited Avital to come to the Moscow synagogue on Shabbat, not to go inside and hang out with all the KGB agents hiding behind prayer books, but rather to stay outside to meet with all the young Jews who gathered there every week. The first time Avital went was a gray, snowy, awful October morning in 1973, but when she arrived, she was amazed to find hundreds of young people standing outside the synagogue speaking and discussing something with a lot of excitement. Every now and then, someone would run away and then rush back, and announce, "We've crossed the Suez Canal!" and then a few minutes later, "We're right outside Damascus!" Avital had not even known that there was a war taking place in the Middle East, but these young people, despite years of Communist education that tried to drive into their brains over and over that anyone in their right mind would rather be a "Soviet" than a Jew, felt as though they were also soldiers in the battle for Israel's survival that was reaching its conclusion at that moment – the Yom Kippur War.

---

[2] Psalms 137:5.

Avital was in awe of all these young people who were so unafraid, who just kept on talking and laughing when the KGB came to photograph them, undeterred by the threats that they would lose their jobs or would be sent to the Gulag if they continued to associate with "Zionists." She had never seen anybody like them in her whole life, and she sensed that this was what Israelis were like as well. She envisioned a country filled with brave people like her new companions, grasping a Bible in one hand, and a hoe in the other.

Avital met her future husband for the first time outside of the Moscow synagogue. Within several weeks they were engaged. They married the night before Avital left on a plane to leave for Israel, not long before Natan was sent to prison for the next decade.

From Israel, Avital traveled to many countries, meeting with world leaders, being interviewed by the press, and coordinating demonstrations. She and her husband were separated for nine years – nine years during which Avital fought tirelessly for Natan's release from prison.

This past Shabbat afternoon, I kept looking at this woman and asking myself what I would have done if I had been in her situation. Where would I have found the strength, the depth of belief to do what she did after growing up in the house of idealistic Communist Party members, at the age of twenty unfamiliar with even the most basic Jewish concepts? Where did her strength come from?

All of this has been an extremely long introduction to tell you about how this has been a very hard week in Israel. Last week, a thirty-four-year-old mother named Tali Hatuel, in her eighth month of pregnancy, was driving with her four young daughters when an Arab walked up to their car and shot each of them twice in the head, leaving the young father bereft of his whole family, wishing only that it could have been himself instead of them.

Last week, the image of this beautiful mother holding her little girls with their bright innocent smiles hung over me day after day. I would go to sleep and see their faces, and wake up and see the husband sobbing with his head in his hands. There was nothing I could do to bring back his family, and since, for better or worse, I'm not a political person, I wasn't sure what to do. I didn't write up a petition, and I didn't go to a demonstration, and I didn't write an enraged letter to the prime minister making one point or another. I just stayed home and took care of my children and cleaned my house and prayed a bit and felt very, very sad.

And then, for some reason, that Shabbat afternoon, listening to Avital Sharansky, I felt the darkness this attack had brought on start to lift. Remembering how this brave couple had brought the Soviet Union to its knees gave me a seed of hope that the Jewish people would also one day be redeemed from this terrible enemy we face day after day, from a group of people who brainwashed a young man to believe that by murdering a pregnant woman and her four daughters, he was doing something that would make God happy.

And then, after Shabbat, we went to our shul's bonfire for Lag ba-Omer. On the way there, Josh ran down the hill with Tiferet roaring with laughter on his shoulders, and I trailed behind with Nisa fast asleep in the baby carriage and Dafna at my side crooning "Bar Yohai." By the time we arrived, there were about fifty little kids there toasting marshmallows, sitting on their mommies' laps, and running around chasing balls. I remembered back to when we moved to Nahlaot eight years ago, and Rachel and James were the only couple in the whole shul who had been married long enough to have two little children. And since then, there have been so many weddings and births and kiddushes and brits in our community that I keep my freezer stocked with casseroles and my closet stocked with baby blankets at all times, just in case I need to make a meal or give a present at a moment's notice.

And I know that for the women in my community, motherhood is often a struggle. Pregnancy is often very difficult, and birth is always very hard to go through and then to recover from, and then raising kids is often filled with serious challenges and unsuspected landmines just when you think that everything is going smoothly. While it is totally obvious, it only really occurred to me while I was watching all of our children at the bonfire that it is solely because of the self sacrifice and hard work of all these Jewish mothers around me who become pregnant and raise children that the Jewish people continues to exist at all.

Without the fanfare-free work of Jewish mothers in Jerusalem, Toronto, Sydney, and everywhere, the Jewish people would disappear within a generation or two no matter how many millions of dollars the UJA raises or how many thousands of pages of gemara our rabbis learn, or how many dozens of state-of-the-art planes Israel buys to protect our borders. Seeing all these young couples and children, and knowing that ours is a Jewish community that sprang up from nothing, brought some further comfort from the tragedy of the previous Sunday. I saw how we will continue doing what Jewish mothers have always done – creating and nurturing life in the face of death.

In my class on the books of Ezra and Nehemia, we read how Nehemia inspired the few Jews who returned from the Babylonian exile to repair the protective wall around Jerusalem even though they were surrounded by enemies who threatened war against them if they continued to build. Nehemia explained to the people that by building the wall, they were protecting the lives of their wives and children from future attack. Then he divided the people in half – half to build the wall, while the other half stood guard with their weapons, ready to fight if their enemies decided to make war against them.[3]

When I learned this, I thought of the Jewish people in our times. How there are people who stand guard, who are prepared to fight our enemies as soldiers, or activists, or politicians. And there are those of us, like the mothers at that Lag ba-Omer picnic, who spend our whole lives building – making homes, raising children, and building families and communities.

Since I heard of the inhuman murder of the Hatuel family, four women in our community have given birth. At the kiddush for one of the new babies this past Shabbat, I went up to the baby's great-grandmother, an impressive and noble woman who was born in Holland, and wished her a big *mazal tov*. She said to me with tremendous pride, "You know, this is my fifteenth great-grandchild." And the great-grandmother, who is not an

---

[3] Nechemia 4:13.

observant woman, continued, "Not long ago a very religious woman told me that I am forbidden by Jewish tradition to state the number of grandchildren and great-grandchildren I have. But," and her voice took on the slightest tremor, "I told her that as a person who lost seventy of her family members in Auschwitz, I think that I am entitled to count my great-grandchildren. Don't you?"

It is the quiet heroism, faith, and self-sacrifice that God invested in Jewish mothers that enables us to continue to exist as a people, and that has meant that the Jewish people has outlived all of the great and mighty empires that tried over and over to be rid of us – the Roman Empire, the Greek Empire, Nazi Germany, the Soviet Union. Maybe Avital Sharansky is less of an exception, less of an aberration from the norm, than a representative of the strength hidden in all Jewish mothers, which we express in large part by having babies and loving them, wiping their runny noses, and raising them to be better people and proud Jews despite the odds.

BLAH-BUSTER TIDBIT
A Mother's Ever-Evolving Mission

Rebbetzin Nechama Greisman[1]: "What is success?... Success means knowing who you are and what you are supposed to be doing, and then doing it."

Author Sarah Shapiro[2]: Someone once said to me: if you want to find your mission in life, just look around. You'll see your mission. Is it a pile of dishes? A child needing attention? A neighbor who is alone, a relative in need? Is there something you want to write, or cooking to do? Does the water bill have to be paid this morning?

Perhaps, at this particular moment, it's attending to that hidden problem in your life – the one not many people know about – which constantly requires that you develop all your powers of self-discipline, kindness, patience, and faith.

---

[1] Rabbi Moshe Miller, ed. *The Nechama Greisman Anthology: Wisdom from the Heart.* Jerusalem: 2000, 136.

[2] Shapiro, Sarah. *A Gift Passed Along.* New York: 2002, 80. Sarah Shapiro is the author of *Growing with My Children: A Jewish Mother's Diary; Don't You Know It's a Perfect World?*; the *Our Lives* anthologies and, most recently, *Wish I Were Here* (Shaar). She writes regularly for publications in Israel and the United States and teaches writing workshops in Jerusalem.

SITTING IN MY OWN GARDEN

WHEN I WAS A CHILD, I was a television addict, watching about five hours of TV a day. It's been fifteen years since I've lived in a house or dorm with a TV, but still, the moment I'm in a hotel room or somewhere else with a TV, I am immediately addicted again. I am like an alcoholic who can't even say a *le-haim* after kiddush lest he get pulled in again.

So now, it is a huge value for me to raise my own children without a TV. But the other day, I was wondering whether TVs are really as bad as all that. There are many educational programs on TV (what a sad thing to have a child grow up without Sesame Street!), it's free babysitting if I need to take a nap or cook for Shabbat, and how will I ever be able to really become part of Israeli society when TV is such a central aspect of Israeli culture? Anyway, I grew up watching huge amounts of TV, and I turned out OK.

But when I thought about it more, I realized that the main thing that bothers me about TV is how it makes everything else outside of our humble little lives look so incredibly fantastic. That spunky, funny, bright little girl in that family on that show looks like she has the greatest possible life! If only I looked as good in a bathing suit as the lady in that Coke commercial (not even one stretch mark), I would have the greatest possible life! Look at that newscaster. If only I were as smart as she is, had as small a nose as she does, had hair as blond as she has, I would have the greatest possible life! Television is made up of millions of fast and furious images of charismatic, glamorous, perma-grinned people, and I find that even watching a bit of it gets me into a mode where my life looks drab, dull and unsatisfying by comparison. As though other people eat at four-star restaurants every night while I eat, day after day, those double-wrapped kosher airplane meals manufactured somewhere in Queens.

And now, after many years without TV watching, I frequently catch myself feeling that *my* life really is the greatest. I live in Jerusalem (and we even own a house here)! I've got three incredible kids! My husband is out of this world (and he even has a job)! I love my neighborhood! I love being Jewish and keeping the Torah! When I was about twenty, I went to get my eyes examined and I realized that I needed glasses. I put them on, and the world was suddenly so bright and colorful, so utterly amazing, that I felt a deep sense of loss, wondering for how many years I had been walking around unable to see how incredibly beautiful the world is around me. And that was the same switch that happened when I stopped watching TV: from longing for someone else's life to seeing the richness and vividness of my own.

But then again, I have moments when I get into TV mode, when I begin to covet the lives of other people. It's interesting that I have almost never coveted the life of a person that I know well. Once I know a person well enough to know her name, I already know her well enough to see that I would not trade my own personal challenges for hers – for her painful skin condition, or her sadness, or for her four children under the age of four. I'll keep my own challenges, thank you very much. At least I'm used to them.

But I do still get into my longing, coveting, TV mode when I see people in other religious communities who seem to have everything so good. This coveting mode was at its height about a year or two ago, when I went through a huge mothering crisis. I was postpartum, and a bit depressed and constantly stressed around my three teensy kids who were always fighting, and the nursery school teacher kept on calling me about my three-year-old who was beating up all the other children, and keeping my house clean felt like trying to sweep a clean path through the desert. I felt like I was drowning in my life.

My only respite from my seemingly impossible life was my walks on Saturday morning to the other side of Bar Ilan Street, to the *Haredi*[1] neighborhoods of Givat Moshe, Kiryat Belz, Mattersdorf, and beyond. Every week, I would go to see all the mothers in their shoulder-length wigs,[2]

---

[1] Ultra-Orthodox.

[2] According to Jewish law, married women are required to cover their hair, and they are permitted to do so with wigs. In Israel, women who wear wigs are generally ultra-Orthodox.

high heels, and suits, walking so calmly with their six perfectly dressed and coiffed children, none of whom ever seemed to cry or have a tantrum. The mothers never looked tired, even though, judging from their children's ages and their little basketball-sized bellies, they had been pregnant pretty much uninterruptedly for the last five years.

And I would think, if only, if only…. If only I had been born into a religious family, if only I lived in a religious neighborhood, if only my husband wore a black hat or, better yet, a *streimel*,[3] if only I wore a wig and could spend my Shabbat mornings sitting on my porch reading Psalms like these women who peer down at me so serenely as I walk by. Then, I would really have the greatest life… then my life would be as easy, as happy, as fully satisfying as theirs.

At the end of those two hours, I would come back to my own house – to the soccer court just outside our windows with the shirtless neighborhood boys kicking around the ball and yelling curses at one another, to my own children who were still in pajamas, to my own table that needed to be set for lunch – and I would think: if only, if only….

But even more than the *Haredim*, I would dream about the settlers, the religious Zionists who believe so strongly in the Jews' right to the land of Israel that they move to the settlements on the other side of the Green Line. Here were real heroes. Whenever I would see the settler mothers driving by in their cars with the foggy inch-thick windows, or walking to a demonstration looking so stoic and determined alongside their bleached-blond children – their skin baked brown from years spent leaping from one hilltop in Samaria to the next, I would stop and stare and wish that their life could also be mine. I saw these women with their Israeli Hebrew and their perfectly rolled *resh*es, who work the night shift as emergency room nurses and still raise eight children and keep spotless houses. I saw how they know all the old patriotic songs, every corner of every hike in the Negev, all the slang and military acronyms that I will never figure out. I would never be as Israeli, as strong, as perfect as these women.

---

[3] A fur hat worn on the Sabbath and holidays by Hasidic men.

And then again, it is wrong for me to be writing about all of this in the past tense. Today, I still stop to stare longingly and count the plaid-shirted boys and tight-two-braided girls walking alongside their Yiddish-speaking mother who passes me on the sidewalk, and my heart still swells as I turn to watch the settler family walking by me on the way downtown to buy new sandals.

But, today, I see these women a bit differently from the way that I used to. Or at least I have started seeing myself a bit differently in relationship to them. This past Saturday, instead of going to shul, I went for the first time in over a year on one of my old walks. And as I walked through Geula, and then crossed over Bar Ilan to the land of the *Haredi* children in poofy satin dresses and pressed white shirts and their thin fashionable mothers in suits walking with them to meet their *tatty* at shul, I felt the same feelings as always – of longing, and of nostalgia for something I never had.

But as I walked and walked and walked, seeing family after family, I realized that my life has gotten easier over the past two years because of certain external factors (my children are now a bit older, and I've started getting more help from my husband and from babysitters and cleaning ladies so that I can cope). But just as important as these external factors has been a lot of work that I've done on the inside – on my mindset and the way I see my life and my role as a Jewish mother.

Most of this change in mindset has come as a result of the classes I attend – from Rebbetzin's Talia's showing us week after week that motherhood is not just a default pursuit for the woman who comes home from work or who does not have a job. For Rebbetzin Talia, motherhood is a vocation that is more important than any other, that we must view as our primary mission and profession in life. She has taught me to see myself – not the way my upstairs neighbor, the graduate student, does when she passes me on her way to the university with a laptop in hand, and I am on my knees on the sidewalk buckling a paint-spattered sandal, but rather the way *Hashem* sees me at that moment, performing yet another act of kindness for this little person He entrusted to my care.

Rebbetzin Yemima has also taught me countless ways to elevate the daily floor-sweeping, diaper-changing, skinned-knee-kissing grind from drudgery into a *mitzvah*. The other day, for example, I was cleaning the kitchen after Shabbat. This usually takes me an hour or two, and in the past it has been a chore that I have hated and resented so much that it has almost brought me to tears. But this Saturday night, I felt myself getting pulled down into bitterness, and right away I began praying as Rebbetzin Yemima taught me to do – that I should make my house clean so that my children and husband will love their home, so that it will be a cozy and orderly place that we will always be eager to come back to. And I almost instantly snapped out of my bitterness and felt so happy to clean my own kitchen – what a nice kitchen it is, how wonderful I will make it look.

And on another night, I had to make a few special meals – for a young mother in our community who is very sick, for a mother who is pregnant and on bed rest, and for another mother who just gave birth. And instead of feeling anxious about all the time I was losing on all this domestic drudgery, as I would have a few years ago, I spent the whole time praying as Rebbetzin Yemima teaches us to: praying that the soup for Sara would help her to have a full recovery, that Avigail should have a healthy pregnancy and give birth to a healthy baby, and that Efrat should have so much strength to take care of her newborn and have a speedy recovery from her birth. I just prayed the whole time, which inspired me and made me feel the specialness and holiness of the work I was doing.

So as I went on my walk this Shabbat, I realized that if two years ago my husband had started wearing a *streimel* and moved us to the middle of Kiryat Belz, it would not have made my life better. And if he had started carrying an M-16 and moved us to a hilltop south of Hebron to raise goats and make organic cheeses, that would not have fixed the things in my life that really needed fixing.

What needed and needs fixing is me – my heart, my guts, and my perspective on my role as a mother. It is true that moving to a certain community can provide more or less guidance in fixing our lives. Maybe a certain rebbe or *rosh yeshiva* or teacher in a certain community can provide more useful guidance than the leaders and dominant voices of another section of society. But on that walk, instead of thinking of all these other people who have it so good, I looked back and wondered how I would have ever overcome my own personal challenges and miseries, how I would have ever gotten that little bitter voice inside my head under control without the guidance of the teachers in my own neighborhood. I wondered how I would have managed without Yemima, without Rebbetzin Talia's parenting classes, without all the mothers on the park benches watching each others' children growing up, and trading advice and mothering stories and ideas for making things easier.

The other day I was walking up Bezalel Street, which is something I have done at least a few hundred times, and for the first time ever I noticed an incredible thing – about a hundred flower pots arranged by the side of the street like a memorial garden or a flower shop. So I crossed over, and saw a middle-aged woman in a sweatsuit sitting silently among the flowers. When I asked her if the flowers were hers, she nodded, and when I asked if they were new, she said that she had had these flowers here for at least ten years, but that in the past cars had been parked in front of them, so no one noticed them. "And why did you plant them?" I asked. She shrugged, and looked down proudly at her flowers, and said "No reason. But they're pretty, aren't they?"

Isn't this a good idea? To spend some time (and what day is better than today?) sitting and thinking and taking pride in our own personal gardens (the sweat-suit is optional), thinking about our families, our homes, our communities. Maybe sometimes we can look into someone else's garden, and we can learn from them as well – to plant something new, to prune something, to weed something out, to water a certain plant more, or to move it so that it can receive more direct sunlight. But these are our gardens, and it's up to us. No need to worry, though – we've got the rest of our lives to make them bloom.

STEP TWO

LEARNING TO LET GOD HELP YOU OUT

RABBI SHIMSHON DAVID PINKUS[1] tells a story about a doctor working one night in his hospital's intensive care unit. At the beginning of his shift, the doctor's supervisor told him that because of a staff shortage, he would be the lone doctor on duty that night. "As long as everyone stays asleep," the supervisor explained, "you should be fine. But," he added, "if one of the patients wakes up, he will make noise and wake up the other patients. And then you will have a big problem on your hands. If that happens, you must call me on the emergency phone so that I can send in reinforcements immediately."

The doctor spent several uneventful hours on the ward until one of the patients woke up right before dawn. The patient started to cry out in pain, and before long all the patients were awake. The doctor ran from bed to bed, trying to calm all the patients down and working frantically to care for all their urgent needs. But in the end, despite his tremendous efforts, one of the patients died.

Soon after this happened, the doctor was taken to court for negligence. The indignant doctor pleaded his case to the judge, and said that on that terrible night he had displayed rare medical acumen as well as great self-sacrifice. But the judge shook his head and said, "Who said that you had to

---

[1] Rabbi Shimshon David Pinkus, *Elul: Ani Le-Dodi ve-Dodi Li*. Yad Shimshon, audio recording. Rabbi Pinkus zt"l was a *rosh yeshiva* and rabbi of the town of Ofakim in the Negev. In additional to being a tremendous scholar, he was a popular lecturer and author of many books. Rabbi Pinkus died in a tragic car accident in 2001 together with his wife and daughter.

manage on your own? Your supervisor explained that if the situation became too difficult, you must call for help."

Rabbi Pinkus explains that this story is a metaphor for the difficulties we face in our lives and how we must turn to God for help through prayer.

All of the essays and readings in this chapter are about turning to God when the challenges, stresses, and hardships of motherhood force us to pick up the red phone and place an emergency call to our Supervisor.

BLAH-BUSTER TIDBIT

Mother Blues

by Drora Matlofsky[1]

Half past six time to get up Moda Ani[2] Benny get up he isn't getting up Eky get dressed she isn't getting dressed Hannah'le's crying goodbye Eky hello Hannah'le here's your bottle time to daven[3] breakfast will I be able to do the dishes today will I be able to do the laundry will I be able to do the floor what's for lunch here they are back again Eky doesn't like the food Shirel's crying Hannah'le spilled the juice will they let me do the dishes will they let me rest Benny's home he's fighting with Eky Hannah'le fell off the chair she's crying here's the phone oh no it's that guy again what's for dinner I can't get dinner ready with four children in the kitchen will you please get out they're fighting Shirel's crying the neighbor's complaining there's the phone again I burned the toast come and eat supper they're not coming I said come Shirel is crying because there is no peanut butter say Birkat ha-Mazon[4] say it properly please once there were three little goats who lived on the mountain Mary Poppins snapped her fingers now go and brush your teeth with your new toothbrush now get into bed they won't go to bed Shimon's home he puts the radio on there has been another terrorist attack I think Benny I told you to get into bed what mitzvos did you do today yes you can have a drink but just one Shema Yisrael[5] why are you crying just one more song good night Shimon I should clean the house but I'm too tired I should put the laundry away I should do the ironing I should write to my mother I don't know what to say to her

I should write my novel I should

Good night. Shema Yisrael.

Half past six time to get up Moda Ani Benny get up he isn't getting up....

---

[1] Author Drora Matlofsky's work has been published in *Horizons* magazine, *Yated Neeman,* and many other Jewish publications. She was born in France and lives with her husband and children in Jerusalem.

[2] The prayer recited upon awakening in the morning.

[3] Pray.

[4] The prayer recited after eating a meal containing bread.

[5] The prayer recited before going to sleep at night.

CRYING WITH OUR CHILDREN

EVERY YEAR RIGHT BEFORE PASSOVER, the women's yeshiva where my husband teaches organizes a trip for all of the students and teachers to the Golan Heights. When we went a few years back, the kids had gone crazy on the bus and I had gotten all stressed out, and it had just seemed impossible, so we didn't go again for a few years. But this year, my husband said, "We're going, and I'll take care of the kids on the bus." So we went, and on the bus I sat next to Dafna and showed her on the map how we would follow the Jordan River up to the Sea of Galilee, and she asked a lot of questions about the different fruit trees and towns that we passed on the drive up. And Tiferet was amazed into silence by the sheep and occasional camel clustered by the Bedouin tents on the mossy sand dunes. And Nisa fell fast asleep on my sleeping husband's lap, and I felt so happy to be able to go with everybody on this big adventure.

And once we started the hike in the northern Golan Heights, we walked along an incredibly beautiful stream. It was the kind of gushing, waterfall-y stream that only someone in Israel's dry climate could get excited over – where even the teensiest pond with a few malnourished goldfish is justification to set up a national park.

The hike led us alongside huge rocks that had been carved out by the stream over thousands of years, so ninety-five percent of the hike consisted of going from one pile of boulders to the next pile of boulders, trying to figure out where to find a foothold and a handhold, and then, several times, trying to figure out how to cross the stream without falling off the few slippery rocks that led across it. I absolutely loved the hike, my kids did too, and reaching the end was exhilarating.

The only problem was that while we were hiking we couldn't really enjoy the incredible scenery since we had to spend the entire time going from one challenge to the next, focusing only on each little pile of boulders and rocks we had to climb over, and never looking up. It was like going through a hundred separate obstacle courses set up in a row without stopping.

The next day, all the other teachers with little kids joined us. We went on a long hike which was really easy, walking down a path that led through gently rolling, Kermit-green hills. The kids ran around looking at the hordes of caterpillars and in search of the wild boars that the guide had assured us were around there somewhere. And I just spent the whole time talking with the students and other mothers, looking around, breathing deeply, and gazing into the distance towards snowcapped Mount Hermon, just thinking about what an unbelievable thing it is that I, Chana Weisberg, am able to live in the land of Israel.

Over Shabbat, I found myself thinking over and over about these two hikes until I realized I was thinking about them because of how they reminded me of two distinct ways that I find myself living my life. I have a tendency – maybe all mothers do – to go through life like the hike on the first day. We go from activity to activity – from giving our kids Cheerios to taking them to kindergarten to going to buy yogurt to going to check our emails. We don't see beyond the immediate task we are involved in, and if we do see beyond it, it is maybe to see the whole day, or maybe, if we are really organized, to see our whole week – all the steps that will lead me from today until Shabbat, for example.

But there are times, rare moments when I am able to see my life as a whole, like the way I looked into the distant landscape on the second hike, looking far into decades to come, to think of what I am really aiming for, what I want to accomplish in life as a mother and a human being.

And that is the case at this rare moment in my mothering life because next year Dafna is going into first grade, and we have to choose a school for her right after Passover (which is also why I've been hyperventilating pretty much non-stop for the last two weeks). I am now forced to ask myself almost constantly what I truly value. I look at Dafna and try to figure out what I dream for her, the way I hope she will live and be at the age of thirty. A friend of mine with older children smiled and nodded knowingly when I told her about our school dilemma. She said, "Oh, I remember! It is so hard to choose. You feel like you're deciding your child's future, and… well, the truth is – you are."

Another friend who is a teacher said something very different. She said, "You know, there are three iron rules in successfully educating a child – prayer, prayer, and prayer." This was also the theme of Rebbetzin Yemima's class this week in which she quoted Rabbi Shimshon Pinkus, who asks what it means when the Passover Haggadah says, "'Our hard labor' – this means the children." And no, Rabbi Pinkus explains, it's not giving them baths, chasing after them to get them to brush their teeth, and cleaning up their mess after they go to sleep. The hard labor the Haggadah is talking about is all the praying we do for our children, and the crying we do for them.

This teacher and Yemima reminded me that the other rare moment of my life when I glance up from the moment-to-moment, boulder-to-boulder approach to motherhood is when I pray every day for my children as a part of my morning blessings. While part of what I request in these prayers changes over time, as the girl who finally stops wetting her bed gets an ear infection that we just can't seem to get rid of, there is also a standard, unchanging prayer for each of my children that has stayed the same for years. Every morning I pray that I will raise my little girls to Torah, *huppah,* and *ma'asim tovim* – to grow up to love the Torah, to stand one day under the wedding canopy with a man they love, and to perform acts of kindness for those around them – for their own families, for their communities, and possibly beyond.

In other words, I am praying for things that will only happen twenty or thirty years from now, and that's very good. This long-term focus keeps my head above the tantrums that give me palpitations, above the corn flakes that Nisa poured this morning all over the newly washed floor, and even helps a bit to keep my head above this stressful decision over choosing a first grade for Dafna. Prayer keeps my eyes focused and my feet walking towards the Promised Land lying just beyond the horizon – a place and time when I, God willing, will be the mother of daughters who have grown into happy and confident mothers who are good people and good Jews.

This morning somebody gave me some money to distribute to needy families in my community before Passover. I thought it would be easiest to do this after I drop my kids off at nursery school and kindergarten so that I could give out the money more quickly on my own. But then I realized that I want my girls to also be involved in this act of charity in the hope that my daily prayer that they should grow up to do acts of kindness will come true.

Prayer also means recognizing, on a daily basis, that not everything is in my hands. Prayer means that I am leaving a space between all of my mothering efforts for *Hashem*'s input so that He can guide me and my children in the right direction – so that He can work miracles.

And what about this crying that Rabbi Pinkus says we are supposed to be doing? There is a famous story about the Hafetz Hayyim, one of the leading rabbis of the late nineteenth and early twentieth centuries, who found his mother's book of Psalms many years after her death. Already an old man, he began to kiss it and cry over it. When his students looked surprised by his behavior, he said, "Do you know how many tears my mother, of blessed memory, poured onto this book of Psalms? Every morning she would pray and cry that her son should be a good and faithful Jew. It is only in her merit and in the merit of all those tears that I became a rabbi at all."

Yesterday, while I was in a taxi, I saw that the driver had a miniature computer that enabled him to see his own taxi driving along as if he were watching himself from an airplane, moving little by little along the correct route leading him to his ultimate destination. I thought about how we mothers desperately need this same feedback for our own lives, to see ourselves making slow but certain progress towards our destination within what so often appears to be a vast, decades-long gridlock of mundane mothering moments.

Thank You, *Hashem*, for the gift of prayer – which keeps us progressing along the right path even without the benefits of cutting-edge satellite-enabled technology. So what do you all think about pledging two minutes a day to pray for our children? Two minutes a day to open our mouths and pray for the impossibly stubborn child, the terribly sad child, the chronically sick child, as well as the happy, confident child who we desperately hope will stay that way. To spend two minutes every day standing up on a high hill and looking down at our lives and our children's lives, to get a good look at the destination we are heading for, and to keep walking towards it with our children, hand in hand.

BLAH-BUSTER TIDBIT

The Challenge of Prayer

by Rabbi Lawrence Kelemen[1]

According to the Jewish tradition, anyone who is responsible for others, anyone who has been given a precious trust, is obliged to pray for them. A Rabbi must pray for his community, a teacher must pray for his students, and, how much more so, a parent must pray for his children.

This is not easy advice to accept. Although belief in God is widespread in the West, few people feel comfortable actually articulating requests for God's help except under the most dire circumstances....

Our challenge is to feel the same sense of urgency (as when death approaches) on a daily basis, to recognize that the most valiant efforts we muster really are not sufficient to safeguard the well-being of our children. The more one knows about the world our children inhabit and about the complexities of human personality, the more one appreciates the traditional Jewish emphasis on prayer. The more we understand the task before us, the more reasonable it seems to ask God for help.

Rebbetzin Yemima Mizrachi: "If you are angry at someone (i.e., your friend, child, husband), that is a sign that they urgently need your prayers. Our children make us angrier than anyone else can – because they are the people most in need of our prayers."

---

[1] Rabbi Lawrence Kelemen, *To Kindle a Soul* (New York: Targum/Leviathan Press, 2001), 67.

Praying My Way to Nursery School

Our rabbis teach us that God really created everything on the first day of Creation, and during the rest of that first week of creating the world God was essentially reaching into His pocket in order to take out the ready-made sun, wildebeest, and firmament in order to put them into their appropriate places in the universe. Our Rabbis teach us that there were only two things that were not fully completed when God placed them into the world: human beings and grass. Which leaves us with the strange question: What's the real connection between me and a blade of grass?

In her class this week, Rebbetzin Yemima Mizrachi quoted Rashi,[1] who explains that the grass was sitting right underneath the ground, just waiting and waiting for the first person to come into existence in order to pray for the first rain.[2] The grass's potential was only fulfilled through our prayer, and that is what we have in common with the grass growing all around us.

Human beings are not created perfect either. Our Rabbis teach us that whenever you are lacking something in your life – and every single person, by definition, is lacking something: happiness, a spouse, a child, peace of mind – it is very likely because God is waiting for you to pray. What you are looking for is, possibly, just underneath the ground, waiting to sprout right up if you will just open your mouth and heart to the One who created you.

A few months ago, a friend was telling me that she has no idea how mothers survive without prayer. And for me also, prayer has proven itself to be an incredibly useful tool. At least once a day, when the kids are in a big fight, or someone's being impossibly stubborn, or I generally have absolutely no idea what I am supposed to do next, I stop, close my eyes, take a deep breath, and pray that God will help me out of the abyss I have dug myself into.

---

[1] Rabbi Shlomo Yitzhaki (known as Rashi, 1040–1105 CE) is the foremost Jewish biblical commentator.

[2] Rashi on Genesis 2:5.

Who knows? Maybe this is just a Jewish mother's version of Benjamin Franklin's trick of counting to ten before speaking when you're angry – but whether it's just that it calms me down, or that God really intervenes to show me just the right way to lift myself back up to level ground, the important thing is that it works. Day after day, when I put my problems in God's hands, it works mothering miracles.

I am writing about all of this today because I had a terrible morning with my kids that made me cry and despair of my abilities as a mother. The morning was rocky from the very beginning. Tiferet, who in addition to being adorable and having a heart of gold is as stubborn as a three-year-old, couldn't find anything that she wanted to wear. The problem was that she only agrees to wear clothing that matches my clothing (imagine what a relief it was to discover this after months and months of her apparently random refusals to put on any clothing I offered) and this morning I was wearing a red skirt, and the only skirts we have for her are denim and light green. Oy! A red dress? No way! A blue skirt with red flowers? You've got to be kidding! I actually considered changing my clothes, but maintaining my last remaining ounce of maternal dignity, I called in reinforcements in the form of my husband, and he figured out how to get her dressed.

Breakfast went well, and I thought we were back on the right track. My parenting class teacher, Rebbetzin Talia Helfer, mentioned recently that pretty much the most important thing we do all day is get the kids off to school in a good mood, even though this is also, in my limited experience, just about the hardest thing we do the whole day. To clarify, getting them off to school isn't so incredibly hard, but managing to get them to school in a good mood is.

Anyway, I thought we were doing just fine, leaving the house earlier than we have ever left – at 7:30 AM just in time for 7:45 opening time. I was proud of my decision to go to bed and wake up an hour earlier, and how that was helping me to get my kids off with so much newfound joy and efficiency. And then, Tiferet declared that she was going to push the baby in her carriage all the way to nursery school located about a mile away. A year of wasted mornings flashed before my eyes when she said that, since when she pushes the baby, it takes about three times longer than when I do it. I knew I needed to take a firm stand to save my few free hours to work in the mornings.

I told her, "Great. You push until the street, and then *Eema* will do it." That worked fine until we got to the street, and I said, "Great job! Now *Eema* does it so we get to nursery school on time." And then Tiferet pulled her sit-down-in-the-middle-of-the-sidewalk-and-not-budge-in-protest trick. My other kids respond well to run-of-the-mill encouragements to get them out of behavioral dead-ends and blackouts – a little sticker placed on their shirt, a promise to write a note for their teacher about how good they had been earlier, a cookie, a bit of active listening and a well-placed "You look angry" work like a charm.

My other kids let me off easy, but my Tiferet's not like that. When she sits down and won't move, there is absolutely nothing I can do. At first I kept on walking and left her behind for five minutes. She just sat there. Then I sent Dafna back with a cookie. Dafna came back without the cookie and also without Tiferet. Then I walked back to where she sat, and felt sorry for her, and laughed like it was all a big joke, and offered her my hand. And she just sat there. So I dragged her by the arm, screaming and kicking and scratching me, passing a few mothers on the way and wondering why I am the only one who has this hard a time.

And the whole time I was praying. "God, I can't do this without Your help. I have no idea how to deal with this. I am at the end of my rope. Please help me to get my little girl to walk." I can't say that my praying got her to walk; she still kicked and bit me. But it did enable me to deal with her calmly, without anger, even though I felt the anger welling up in my throat and threatening to burst my dam. With prayer, I was able to distance myself from how she was acting, and stay calm as I carried her.

Then I said, "Tiferet, you want to push the carriage all by yourself?" OK, an admission of total defeat. No go. She had upped her stakes, and I had no idea what to do. She sat down again, and then I pulled her and she screamed some more.

Then, a block later, I heard someone calling out, "What's the matter?" It was Tiferet's old babysitter, Ruti, who is one of a few surrogate grandmothers my children thankfully have in this country (all of our relatives live in North America). When I told Ruti what had been going on, clearly exasperated, she knew just what to do. She ran into her house, and handed Tiferet a whole container of candy-cake decorations. Tiferet snapped out of her bad mood instantly, and walked along the sidewalk with a big smile on her face as she ate her candies.

Then, of course, Dafna started crying and staged her own sit-in, because all the candies Tiferet handed her fell on the ground first because she couldn't fit her fingers into the narrow bottle, so Dafna wanted to take her own candies. Ruti's neighbors were already looking down the street at me to get another good look at the mother who couldn't get her kids happily to nursery school with a whole container of cake decorations as good mood ammunition.

And I just prayed and prayed, "*Hashem*, just get me one more block to nursery school. Just help me so this will all be behind me." I took the candies away, and told the kids that they would have to work out a solution that they could both agree on before I would give them back the candies – but they were both too far gone for any of my parenting book tricks. The next few minutes are a blur. Did I give the candies back? Did I yell at them, and they took a few more steps? I truly don't remember.

We managed to get to the big set of steps leading down to Bezalel Street, right across from Tiferet's nursery school, and I was just praying and praying that *Hashem* would help me to keep my cool so that I would be able to figure out how to get my girls to walk the next fifty yards to the nursery school's entrance. I pushed the carriage down the steps, and an elderly Ethiopian Jewish man who didn't know a word of Hebrew helped me to take the carriage down. Then, he pointed to Tiferet sitting once again at the top of the steps, indicating that he would watch the carriage, and I could go up and carry her down the steps. So I carried her down. I was still praying, when Shuli, Tiferet's teacher, walked down the stairs behind us. She whispered something into Tiferet's ear. Tiferet smiled and took Shuli's hand, and they walked off to nursery school together as if nothing had happened.

The next few blocks to Dafna's kindergarten, I probably would have cried if Dafna hadn't been with me. I felt so awful, like a total failure. How hard is it to get your three-year-old to nursery school? And even that I can't do. Usually this special time walking together with Dafna is one of the highlights of my day – she tells me about this girl who got in trouble when she put her feet on the table during lunch, and that girl who gave out hairclips with ribbons at her birthday party. But this morning I wasn't in the talking mood. I felt defeated and down, as though I had been left behind, squished in a giant's footprint.

After I left Dafna at kindergarten, I cried a while on the way home, felt really, really sorry for myself, and tried to figure out why everything had been so all-around awful when I had tried to be so good. And then I started switching my head around, trying to think of ways in which the morning had not been a total failure. I thought about how prayer had enabled me to stay calm, so that I didn't scream at Tiferet like I probably would have a few months ago. Also, I thought of all the help I'd gotten on the way: Ruti's help right in the nick of time, the appearance of the Ethiopian man at just the moment that I needed someone to watch my carriage next to the busy street, her teacher showing up to take her the rest of the way.

I've just finished reading Hillary Clinton's book *It Takes a Village*,[3] and as I cried a few last tears of frustration I thought of how blessed I am that of all the villages in the world, that this is the one I call home. I thought about how I live in a place where friends and teachers and total strangers help me out so much with my children when I'm in a jam, even if lots of times the only help I get from them is that as fellow Jews I know that they love my children a little bit too.

And then I remembered something that Rebbetzin Talia taught us this week. She told us that *Rosh Hodesh*, the first day of every Hebrew month, is a special holiday for women because *Hodesh* is related to the word for renewal,

---

[3] Clinton, Hillary Rodham. *It Takes a Village and Other Lessons Children Teach Us.* New York: 1996.

hidush, and as Jewish mothers God has given us the special ability to constantly renew and recreate ourselves. A mother can say to herself, "I've always been a grouchy, critical mother, and my kids had better get used to it." Or, with the power of *hidush*, a mother can look at her watch and say, "Until this moment in my life I have been a grouchy, critical mother, but as of today, March 16th at 3:45 PM, I'm starting over. From this moment on I'm going to be a different kind of mother for my children! I need to change, and I can change."

That was what I thought about as I walked home today. I looked at my watch and decided that that morning, up until that minute, 8:42 AM, I had been a mother who was convinced that she is a hopeless failure who would never figure out how to deal with this three-year-old she loves so much. And I took a deep breath and prayed to *Hashem* that from that moment on I would be different and that He would help me to be a confident, optimistic mother when I go to pick up Tiferet this afternoon. And I wiped the last tears into my cheek with my palm and felt my heart lighten, and I believed that with *Hashem*'s help, it really might be true. I believed that things really might be better that afternoon.

In general, as a mother, I have good days and not-so-good days. I have days when I feel like my life and family are an advertisement for motherhood, and days when I am so frustrated and discouraged that I wonder if things will ever get easier. And on those days, I thank God for the ability to turn to Him – so that I am no longer stuck, no longer alone, no longer helpless. So that I can look at my watch and look towards the future – recreating myself day after day with God's help.

BLAH-BUSTER TIDBIT

Praying with Rebbetzin Yemima

When I first started becoming observant fifteen years ago, I loved keeping Shabbat, learning Torah, and observing the holidays. I also didn't mind keeping kosher, wearing long skirts, or any of the other new mitzvot that I took on. But, for years, every time I sat with a prayer book in my hands, my mind started wandering to distant locales. I felt it was so pointless, as though the Creator of the World couldn't care less that I was reciting these boring, archaic words to Him.

When I became a mother and started studying with Rebbetzin Yemima Mizrachi, she revolutionized my attitude toward prayer. Every week, over and over, she implores her students to pray, and in particular, to discover the power of spontaneous prayer. It is in Rebbetzin Yemima's merit that prayer has become a staple in the daily lives of hundreds of mothers, including mine.

The following selection is a quotation from one of Yemima's weekly classes:

> Rabbi Volbe explains that we are making a big mistake when we think that prayer is a monologue. You think that you are speaking to the wall, that nobody hears and that nobody will answer either. This is why you don't pray when things are tough, and instead of speaking with the Master of the Universe you prefer to call your mother, your neighbor, or your friend. But Abraham shows us over and over that when we speak with God, we are always engaged in a dialogue.
>
> Parenting expert Rachel Arbus writes that the smartest thing you can do when you are in a situation surrounded by question marks is to stop everything, lift your eyes to Heaven, and ask, "God, what do I do now?" If you really listen, you will receive your answer. Suddenly, you will have clarity.
>
> The Piasetzner Rebbe explained another idea that amazed me, and that gave me a tremendous urge to pray. He wrote that God answers prayer by sending you immediate relief. You won't hear Him speaking to you. Rather, God will reveal Himself in what happens after you pray. When you really pray, notice the relief that

you feel afterwards. If you think that this relief comes from you, as in, "I feel better now that I got everything off my chest," you are mistaken. This alleviation doesn't come from you, but is rather the direct response of God to your prayer. This is how God answers you, by sending you patience, happiness, and strength.

The amazing idea here is that prayer is answered on the spot, at that very moment. This knowledge provides a desire to pray that is impossible to describe.

MITZVAH MORSELS

Tomorrow marks the one-week anniversary of my girls' return to nursery school and kindergarten after an all-too-long summer vacation. On the first day of school, Dafna and Tiferet appeared at the foot of my bed at five in the morning asking me to help them get dressed. And I didn't even mind sitting up in the predawn darkness to help Dafna tug on her socks and to help Tiferet tie the back of her dress, since I was just as excited as they were.

For the first few days back at school, the kids only go in for two or three hours each day, so on that first day by the time I got home from leaving everyone off and got Nisa to sleep, I had exactly one hour to sit at the computer. With a big smile, for the first time since June I opened up the book that I'd been thinking about all summer. And after fifty wonderful minutes of writing, I wrote an email to my husband at work with the subject line "Happy Mommy Haiku." In it, I wrote:

The kids are away

The computer is all mine

Peace and happiness

We are now already a week and a half into the month of Elul, the month that is traditionally dedicated to soul-searching in preparation for the High Holidays next month. Jewish mysticism teaches that for this whole month "the King is in the field," meaning that God is right down here with us, closer than at any other time of the year, waiting to help us turn our lives around for the better in time for the judgment of Rosh ha-Shana.

Most years, Elul is totally lost on me – the concept of repentance looming so large above me that, despite my best intentions to do what God wants from me, I give up on soul searching as quickly as I would an equally well-intentioned effort to swallow a watermelon whole. This year, however, only a few minutes into the month of Elul, I had a jarring experience that helped me to get into the Elul spirit.

Just after sunset of Rosh Hodesh, the first day of Elul, my husband and I were getting ready for our weekly date (an absolute, no-excuses-accepted requirement for all married couples who would like to remain happily married couples). The babysitter had just come, we were still rushing around putting kids to bed, and our sixteen-month-old, Nisa, was climbing up and down the stairs as per usual, when I heard a bonk-bonk rhythm that belonged more on a snare drum than on my staircase. I started running, and Nisa was at the bottom of the stairs, screaming, blood trickling out of her mouth.

When I picked her up, I could see that one of her teeth had been knocked out of place. I tried to call my mother in Baltimore, who is a doctor, and when she didn't answer, I called an acquaintance who is a dentist. There was nothing I could do, she said, except to take Nisa to a dentist the following day for an X-ray.

I felt beyond awful. Just the day before, Nisa had fallen in the park, and bitten her tongue so that it had started bleeding. What kind of mother takes such terrible care of a child that her mouth bleeds two days in a row? And what kind of mother still has not ordered a carpet for her stairs to cushion falls? And what kind of mother lets her toddler climb up and down the stairs just because she screams if she finds herself behind a locked safety gate? Well, not an especially good one.

That night and much of the next day I was in a daze, a blue funk, sort of vegetable-like. I would have stayed in bed the whole day if I could have done so. It was an awful thing to feel so guilty, but worse than that it was awful to get such a shocking reminder that no matter how careful I try to be, it is not careful enough. Parenting a young child means that a little person you would take a bullet for is wandering around, as oblivious to danger as the baby crawling on the conveyer belt in the old Disney cartoon. It is as though your heart has sprouted legs and is strolling around, unprotected by ribs, outside of your body – in danger even when you delude yourself into thinking that your child is safe behind your double-locked front door.

And then, the day after the fall, in the mid-afternoon, I remembered to pray for the first time since Nisa had fallen, to turn to God and ask that He help my daughter and me, and that He keep my children safe. And would you believe that these twenty seconds of recognition of my powerlessness versus *Hashem*'s omnipotence transported me, without benefit of twister, from black-and-white Kansas to Technicolor Munchkinland? All it took was twenty seconds of recognizing that even if I'm fairly powerless, the God who watches over my family and me is not.

And I realized that this recognition, this turning (the Hebrew word for repentance, *teshuva*, literally means returning to God) is what Elul is all about. It means recognizing that no matter how much we would like to believe that we maintain control through planning, and protecting, and organizing – and it is certainly crucial to make our best effort – God is really the One in control when push comes to shove.

In light of this trauma-turned-catharsis, this year I am trying not to forget about Elul. I have been helped immensely in this goal by Rebbetzin Yemima's class last week, which could have been called titled "*Teshuva* for the Repentantly Challenged."

Rebbetzin Yemima explained that in preparation for the High Holidays, this Elul we should not attempt to go on a crash diet, cutting out all of the shmutzy things we do and think all too often. This will never work; since during the month of Heshvan following the High Holidays we will gain six pounds from bingeing on all the bad deeds of which we deprived ourselves during Elul and Tishrei. What she suggests instead, in accordance with the teachings of the great Rabbi Yehezkel Levinstein, is that we choose instead to take on two minuscule good deeds to focus on for the forty days from the first day of Elul until Yom Kippur – one a commandment that involves how we treat other people and the other a commandment that relates to how we serve God.

Yemima gave us a few suggestions. For example, if you can't stand your mother, then every morning for the next forty days when you see her grimacing, just-sucked-on-a-lemon face, you will flash her a pleasant smile and say, "Good morning, Mother dearest, did you sleep well?" Or, every time you say a blessing, you will really focus on the word "*Baruch*," what it really means that God is blessed.

So, I have taken on two bite-sized mitzvah morsels of my own. Firstly, I am trying to say one blessing a day with total concentration, and the blessing I have chosen is the one we say in the morning, "Blessed are You God, Our Lord, King of the Universe, Who opens the eyes of the blind." The first day, I focused on the meaning of "Blessed," the second day on the word "You," and before long I was saying the whole blessing, focusing on my deeper interpretations of each word. As Yemima explains, these microscopic efforts might seem insignificant, but in the end, each tiny mitzvah will naturally lead to many other good deeds, like a metropolis of dominos flattened by a flick of your index finger. Now, for example, since I have really thought about the meaning of the words in this one blessing, then, for the whole rest of the day I have a deeper understanding of the words like "*barukh*" and "*olam*" that appear in all blessings.

Also, for the interpersonal mitzvah, I have determined to be really nice to my husband when he comes home from work. I know. This should be so easy. I haven't seen my soul mate the whole day, so what could be easier than giving him a big smile, and offering him a cup of lukewarm apple juice when he walks in the door? But, in reality, the scene at 6 PM in our house is more often along the lines of the following: exhausted mother fighting with beyond exhausted three-year-old because three-year-old was kicking grouchy five-year-old, whose hair has just been pulled by teething one-year-old. In the middle of that, for me to speak civilly with my husband when he walks in the door, and offer him something to drink, and not just growl, "Take the baby! I'll be upstairs lying down" is the opposite of easy – it's as hard as a diamond.

This is especially true since, as Yemima frequently points out,[1] it is infinitely easier to be nice to strangers than to our own family members. If, for example, in the middle of this 6 PM scene, you stopped by, I would smile, and ignore the fighting, and be very polite. But with our own families, we feel no need to cover up our true feelings. We let it all hang out. But, letting it all hang out has its time and place in a marriage, Yemima says, and

---

[1] The Maharal of Prague, *Netiv Ahavat Reah.*

6 PM in the doorway when your husband comes home is definitely not that time and place.

In conclusion, blessings to all of you holy Jewish mothers for a meaningful Elul, full of little good deeds that will lead to bigger and bigger ones.

BLAH-BUSTER TIDBIT

A Mother's Meditation on Gratitude

from *Mother Nurture: A Mother's Guide to Health
in Body, Mind, and Intimate Relationships*[1]

Set aside some quiet time during which you can reflect on some of the many things you could be thankful for. As a starting point, you might read the passage below to yourself or out loud, adapting it to your situation as you like.

Thank You, God. There really is so much to be thankful for.

I am grateful for my children, for the delight and love they bring, for the sweet smell of their hair and the soft touch of their skin. For the first time they smiled at me or walked into my arms. For the meaning they bring to life. For receiving my love and lessons. For being their own persons, for giving me their own love and lessons. Having them at all is a miracle, and the rest is details.

I appreciate myself. For the love I have given my children, all the diapers changed, all the dishes done. For the long hours I've worked, the hoops I've jumped through to keep all these balls up in the air. For the efforts I've made, the many times I've stayed patient, the many times I've found more to give inside when I thought I was empty.

I appreciate my husband. For the ways he has loved me, the fun we've had together, the humor and the companionship. For the times of support, understanding, and sympathy. For sweating and suffering too.

I feel thankful for the life I've already had, for the good parts of my childhood, for everything I've learned, for good friends and beautiful sights. For the roof over my head and the bread on my table, for being able to have a life that is healthier, longer and freer than most people have ever dreamed of. For this beautiful world, where each breath is a gift of air, each dawn a gift of light. For the hand that holds this book and the eye that reads this word.... For every good thing that was, that is, that ever will be.

---

[1] Adapted from Hanson, Rick, Jan Hanson, and Ricki Pollycove, *Mother Nurture: A Mother's Guide to Health in Body, Mind, and Intimate Relationships* (New York: 2002), 69. Learn more about this book, which should be in the library of every young mother, at www.NurtureMom.com.

WINNING SHABBAT

I AM WRITING A SHORT STORY about a Hasidic community in Jerusalem, and as part of my research for the story I have been spending a lot of time in the little-known neighborhood of Givat Moshe on the other side of Bar Ilan Street. During one of my visits, I noticed a flyer in a bus stop announcing a big charity event in the neighborhood, and I decided that this would be a great opportunity to gather more information about the local scene. So one night last week I showed up at the local Satmar yeshiva along with about a thousand other women, most of them recent arrivals from places like Monsey, Boro Park, and Williamsburg (as in Brooklyn, not Colonial).

The main event of the evening was a Chinese auction, which, I learned that night, means that you buy tickets, put those tickets into the box beside the prize you want to win, and hope that your ticket will be the one chosen. They had incredible prizes, but out of the thirty or so prizes on display to be raffled off – a year-membership at a gym, a Shabbat at a hotel in Netanya, a $500 gift certificate from a wigmaker – the Shabbat table drew the biggest crowd. The women were oohing and aahing at the beautiful set of china with gold rim for eight, the full set of silverware, lace tablecloth, and silver Shabbat doodads of all sorts – a matchbox cover, a napkin holder, a Kiddush cup. I looked at these prizes, thinking how nice they would look on our table instead of all the disposable stuff we use now, but I saw that the box near it was already filled to capacity with at least two hundred tickets, so I decided to lower my expectations and put all of my four tickets into the box beside the baby carriage. I thought of Nisa sucking her thumb and peering out at the world from a brand new carriage, also a big step up from the excuse for a carriage with the padding falling off its frame that I use now.

Before I go on, I need to explain that I have been working really hard over the past few weeks to make Shabbat the most holy, beautiful day of our week. Rebbetzin Yemima Mizrachi taught us a few weeks ago that for mystical reasons, Shabbat, the day that is supposed to be the most fun, most beautiful, idyllic day of our week, often ends up causing people, especially women, to wallow in bitterness and fester in resentment.[1]

Rebbetzin Yemima taught us that the most important step women can take to make Shabbat happier and holier is to make a mental switch about the work we do for Shabbat. We must decide that the work we do is a *teruma*, an offering that we give with joy to God, rather than a *temura*, something that we do for other people with the expectation that we are going to get something in return. When she said this, I realized the extent to which I prepare for Shabbat grumbling to myself about how I have a cold, and not even one guest offered to come before Shabbat to help me set the table. And how I'm making a special soup for the two vegetarians. What am I, A catering service? And how I worked so hard to make homemade challahs, and in the end got barely one compliment. And look who is left cleaning the kitchen all by herself after Shabbat!

A preferable model, Rebbetzin Yemima suggested, is to think of preparations for Shabbat as a *teruma*, to decide that all the work we do to make this holy day nice for our families and guests is, in fact, an offering to God. All the potato-kugel preparing, matza-ball rolling and dish scrubbing can be switched by a little change of attitude from weekly drudgery and extra work to a sacrifice offered with joy to our Creator. In honor of the holy Sabbath!

So, for the last few Shabbats, after hearing Yemima's class, I have been working really hard to keep my growling to a minimum and to think about my appetizer-clearing and apple-juice serving as my way of connecting with my Creator.

Maybe I am incredibly gullible, but this has totally transformed my experience of Shabbat. Before I even mentioned my new approach to my husband, he noticed that Friday night dinners were suddenly much more joyful, peaceful, and enjoyable than ever before.

So, back to the Chinese auction. The morning after the event, I was saying to myself, "I know I won, I know I won...." and then the phone

---

[1] *Likkutei Moharan* 119.

rang, and the volunteer at the other end said, "Hello, Mrs. Weisberg. I'm calling to tell you that you've won the Shabbos Table."

I have no idea how this bizarre mix-up happened. I put all my tickets in the box next to the baby carriage, and somehow my ticket got mixed up with the two hundred Shabbat table tickets on the other side of the room, and I won. When she told me this, my heart started racing. I was actually shaking. I could not believe this miracle. I felt like God was telling me that I had been working so hard to make Shabbat an offering to Him that He had decided to finish the job by giving me all these wonderful things to make my Shabbat table more beautiful. It was just like the volunteer said: "You've *won* the Shabbos table." Through changing my attitude and understanding that my work for Shabbat is a service for God rather than for my many guests, I won a Shabbat table. What was already true on a spiritual level, *Hashem* made true on a physical level.

It reminds me of how our Sages teach that Sarah was barren for many years because she had been born without a womb. And then, when she was ninety years old, after a life of praying and doing good deeds, God rewarded her with a pregnancy – without a womb! An incredible, impossible miracle. That was how I felt: that winning this prize was a wombless pregnancy, winning the lottery without even having bought a ticket. And it reminds me of another thing that Rebbetzin Yemima taught us: that if we manage to overcome our nature – our tendency towards jealousy, grouchiness, laziness, etc., then *Hashem* will reward us by performing acts that defy the rules of nature as well.

STEP THREE

FIGURING OUT WHAT WE NEED TO BE HAPPY

SEVERAL YEARS AGO, I attended a class that changed my life. The rabbi told a story about a mother of twelve children who ran her home very efficiently and was generally in a good mood. When this rabbi asked her how she managed to be in such high spirits considering all the responsibilities she had, she explained to him that many years before, she had decided that if she was a single mother, she would do what she needed to get everything done. And this switch in attitude, to deciding that she alone was responsible for her own home and happiness, changed her life. She sat down and decided what she needed to do in order to be effective as well as happy in her life as a mother, and she did it.

After I heard this story, I made a list of what I needed to be able to mother my children, manage my home, and still be a happy person. I wrote down that I needed a cleaning lady once a week, I needed to spend two hours at the library every Thursday reading the Torah portion, and I needed to stop making a cooked dinner on weekdays (what a relief to realize at the age of thirty that the nutritional content of food is not determined by its temperature).

While these requirements for happiness have evolved over the years, taking responsibility for my own home and emotional state have improved my experience of motherhood tremendously. On a smaller level, at stressful times like the day before school starts or the morning before Rosh ha-Shana, I find it helpful to take a minute to do a happiness check. Usually I realize that what I need to stop feeling like a martyr is simple: I need to take a fifteen-minute nap, I need to buy a honey cake for the holiday instead of making one, I need to put the baby in the carriage and go on a walk through the market to get some fresh air and buy a few green peppers.

We have all heard the prayer, "God grant me the serenity to accept the things I cannot change, the courage to change the things I can, and the wisdom to know the difference." While this prayer is especially popular among recovering alcoholics, it is also an extremely important prayer for mothers like you and me. There are aspects of motherhood that are undeniably tough and that we will have to learn to accept one way or another, but there are many other difficult, draining aspects of motherhood that we can change, but often fail to do so.

The greatest gift we can give our families (and ourselves) is a mother who is thriving physically, spiritually, and emotionally. The essays in this chapter describe hard times – being run down, depressed, exhausted and frustrated… and it also suggests ways to pull ourselves and our families out of the darkness.

Getting Our Priorities Straight

by Sarah Chana Radcliffe[1]

Self-knowledge is a prerequisite for successfully managing one's time and one's life. Decide which of the eleven major categories of time usage (including employment) are the most important to you. Order your five highest priorities with the numbers one through five:

Employment___   Recharging ___

Body care ___   Creating ___

Relationships ___   Running errands ___

Reflection ___   Housework___

Learning and growing ___   Child care ___[2]

Helping others ___

Now look at your "Number 1." Does the way you typically spend your day reflect the priority of that category? What about your numbers 2 and 3? Is their place in your daily schedule commensurate with their importance? If not, you may be spending your time as you think you must, but you are not living the life you want to live.

For example, take the theoretical case of a woman whose top priorities are relationships, housework, and growing/learning. We would expect her day to include a few hours of quality time with her children and husband (and perhaps friends and/or relatives), a few hours of housework, and at least an hour of learning (reading, listening to Torah classes on tape).

---

[1] Sarah Chana Radcliffe, *Akeres Habayis: Realizing Your Potential as a Jewish Homemaker* (New York: 1991), 38–39. A psychological associate in private practice, Sarah Chana Radcliffe is the author of several books. She has a marriage, parenting and individual counseling practice in the greater Toronto area (see www.SarahChanaRadcliffe.com).

[2] Child care refers to tending to children's physical needs: i.e., dressing, nursing, feeding, putting children to sleep.

However, if she actually spends most of every day doing errands, helping people in the community, and tending to her children, although these are all necessary and worthwhile activities, she might feel disappointed with her life because she is not doing the things she deems most important.

BURNT-OUT MOMMY IN A TREETOP

WEDDING INVITATIONS COVER the majority of our fridge at any given time. But Sharon and Dani's wedding last week was in a different league than most of the weddings we attend. It was at Maaleh ha-Hamisha, a beautiful kibbutz overlooking the Jerusalem hills, and when I got there the women were sitting on the grass singing around Sharon, who was stunning in her white dress, absolutely ethereal. Then the groom came to cover her face with the veil, and then there was the wedding ceremony, and all in all it took about two hours, but it felt like twenty minutes. It was incredibly romantic and even dreamlike.

And then, and then, I had a not-so-pleasant experience that I've been thinking about ever since. I introduced myself to an older American woman who was in her early fifties, a family friend who had traveled to Israel for the wedding. She was talking about this and that, and then she mentioned that she had always come to Israel for "sabbatical years." Then our conversation went something like this *(I have changed identifying details)*: "Oh, do you teach at a university?" "No, but my husband teaches Jewish Studies at Princeton." "What is your husband's name? Maybe I've heard of him?" "Why, what is *your* field?" (she is suddenly more interested in me). "Well, I'm a stay-at-home mother" (this earns me a patronizing smile). "Then how would you have heard of him?" (micro-awkward pause). "Well, I'm a well-read stay-home mother" (another patronizing smile).

Then the conversation drifted off to her work as a professor at the medical school of another Ivy League university. As I stood there, listening to her, I felt like I had been suddenly squished from my regular confident, I-am-mother-hear-me-roar self, to the size of an olive. A pitted olive, to be exact.

I made a quick getaway from that conversation, but still, breaking through the wonder of the wedding were unpleasant jolts of realization about what a hermetically sealed bubble I live in – in a community where nobody questions that dedicating one's whole self/life to childbearing and childrearing can be a profession, a calling, a meaningful and important way to spend one's life.

Yet worse than the encounter with this lady is the fact that over this past week I have started thinking heretical thoughts of my own. These thoughts have been sparked by my first-time-ever participation in a summer program for intensive Torah study. To put it mildly, I am having the time of my life, studying these incredible Torah stories and the nitty-gritty details of Jewish law. I am having such an amazing time because of what we are learning, and also because this is the first time I have been out of the house, away from my kids, for a serious chunk of time since I was pregnant with Dafna six years ago. At the beginning of that first pregnancy, I felt too sick to leave the house, and then stayed home more or less until I gave birth to her and nursed her for a year and a half, until I got pregnant with Tiferet, gave birth to her, and nursed her for a year and a half, until I got pregnant with Nisa, whom I have been nursing for a year and three months now.

So I am sitting in these classes every day from 9 AM to 3 PM, and my kids are being watched by a babysitter, and the first day I rushed home, feeling feverish from all the milk bursting to get out of me, and was amazed (and maybe a bit disappointed?) to open the door and find my kids really happy (in better moods than if I had been with them?). Nisa continued to play when I walked in, apparently just as satisfied by the bottle as from me. And I, to boot, was amazingly ungrouchy, energized, and inspired to have been learning such fascinating things the whole day. I will repeat, just in case you missed what I am confessing to you: I am finding myself really happy to not have to spend the whole day with my children.

In my classes, one thought has been clinging to my psyche like a barnacle. It is the fact that over the ten years since our college graduation, my college classmates, according to what they report to our alumni magazine, have been getting Ph.D.s in South Asian Studies, completing residencies in anesthesiology, setting up groundbreaking programs for Latino high school dropouts in Boston. And then, as I listen to a teacher who is equally accomplished and expert in her field, I ask myself: "And what have *you* been doing for the past six years? *What have you been doing, Chana?"* It is true that I have been raising children, shaping souls, but it has appeared over the last week that my kids could have turned out just as well spending their days with a babysitter, with a quality hour or two with mommy packed in during the late afternoon. And I could have been spending my time doing something exciting, out in the world, intellectually stimulating, easier – something else.

I am still in the midst of this mothering crisis, but yesterday I did hear something that made me feel a little bit better, giving a shadow of a justification for these past years. This came when I was speaking with a student in the summer program one day over lunch. When I asked her how she became interested in studying Judaism, she explained to me how, when she was a college student in California, she was a radical environmental activist. She and two hundred other activists constructed 150-foot-high platforms in redwood trees that the local logging company was planning to chop down, and lived in them. She loved her tree. It was over two thousand years old, and she told me, "It was a very wise being. Truly a rebbe."

One time, she spent a whole Shabbat in her tree meditating on her platform, watching a spider climb along a branch. She felt like she was at one with the heartbeat of the universe, entirely at peace. Then, a security guard hired by the logging company walked by her tree, and when he saw her up on her platform, he got absolutely furious, and yelled, "Hey, up there! You're nuts! Don't you know that the world is passing you by? Life keeps on going, things are happening in the world, and you are stuck up in this stupid tree!"

But she was totally unmoved by his words. She told me: "I knew that the people who drove by my tree on the logging road were the ones who were missing out. For them, the forest was gone before they could blink an eye. And I was right where I wanted to be, surrounded by the holiness of Shabbat, with the spider crawling by in this ancient forest. I was at one with life, and that was the moment that I started thinking for the first time in my life about the fact that there is a Creator in the world who made all of this life."

So that is what I am thinking about now. About the six years I have spent up in this tree, learning to be a mother, and being pregnant and nursing, and getting to know my children. What a blessing, what an incredible blessing these past six years have been. Those security guards have no idea how enlightening, how fascinating, how beautiful it can be to see the view from 150 feet up. The big question I have left, though, is about the security guard waving his huge flashlight around inside my own head. I'll have to get back to you on that one.

BLAH-BUSTER TIDBIT

A Jewish Mother's Highs and Lows

by Rebbetzin Feige Twerski[1]

Dear Rebbetzin Feige,

I am having a very difficult time right now. I feel almost as if I have hit some sort of spiritual plateau. I am an observant Jew who didn't grow up in a religious home. I spent a year learning at a seminary in Israel, came home and got married. And now I am the lucky mother of two. While I love my children more than anything, I can't help but wonder about my new role in life. I feel like I just don't know who I am anymore, or what I am supposed to do. I used to enjoy praying; now I struggle every morning just to recite the morning blessings. I feel very discouraged, and I feel like I am failing as a Jew. And I don't feel like I am all that successful at being a mother either. I do not understand how a busy mother can still have a close relationship with God. I know the woman has a special role in Judaism… but right now I am struggling greatly in understanding it. Please help.

Anonymous

Dear Anonymous,

One of the occupational hazards of the "seminary experience" or any extensive and intense learning endeavor is that it is often difficult to translate it into day-to-day living.

The transition from the halls of study, from the enchantment of dreams and aspirations, to the reality of never-ending mundane tasks and responsibilities is, as you describe it, a very rude awakening. It is a most daunting challenge to find coherence, congruence and cohesiveness between the lofty halls of spiritual learning and the pragmatic, less than inspired existence that a young mother finds herself struggling with daily.

[1] Reprinted with permission from Aish.com, a leading Judaism website. Rebbetzin Feige Twerski of Milwaukee, Wisconsin has devoted her life to Jewish education and outreach, giving lectures worldwide on a myriad of Judaic subjects. She is the mother of eleven children and many grandchildren whose number she refuses to divulge. She serves as the rebbetzin alongside her husband, Rabbi Michel Twerski, of Congregation Beth Jehudah of Milwaukee.

I cannot offer you a panacea, but I can tell you that what has to drive everything we do in life must respond to the simple question, "What does the Almighty want of me?"

Transitioning into the nurturing role of wife and mother, creating a home where the focus is on the thriving of others, requires a total paradigm shift – from the focus of "me" to "them." The adjustment can be quite traumatic and might feel as though one is losing herself and her identity in the process. Compared to the productive pre-family days, our mundane-oriented days may feel like a waste of time and, as some women report, like a softening of their brain power. Indeed, the legitimate question is, "What did our glorious education prepare us for? Diapers? Dishes? Vacuuming? Sitting home as our men walk off daily into their spiritual horizons and leave us behind?"

Establishing a happy home is the hardest job. It is a counterculture move in a narcissistic society. A contemporary thinker put it this way: "How do we access the nature of essential obligation in a society that sees only personal freedom?" Focusing on home and family requires a paradigm shift from the ideal to the practical, from the talk to the walk. It requires mobilizing all of the inner strength and resources available to consciously and deliberately, with unflinching determination, make every day a good day. When we succeed (and nobody is successful all of the time), in spite of the resistance of both the culture's alien values and the treachery of our inner ego, we will feel the exhilaration and the true joy that can only come of being in the right place and doing the right thing.

I suggest, my dear reader, that you consider the following:

1) "Grow where you are planted." Recognize that the life you have is not arbitrary, but orchestrated from above and hence is, at this moment, the context to which you must bring your finest efforts.

2) Make a list of the blessings in your life and post them where you can see them. They will help you gain perspective in your low moments.

3) Think in your mind's eye of how you would attend to your given role if you loved it and try to behave that way. Invoke the never failing principle that "internal feelings are shaped by external behavior."

4) Join a study group consisting of women like you and continue to learn. It will energize and invigorate you and provide the balance that we all need.

5) Long sessions of prayer may not be in the cards for this season of your life, but you can fill your abbreviated encounters with feeling and concentration. Be assured that [many] Torah authorities... state that the mother of young children fulfills her formal prayer obligation with the

recitation of the morning blessings.[2] Carrying on your own extemporaneous dialogue with the Almighty throughout the day is a wonderful means of connection. "Know Him in all your ways"[3] has been rendered to mean, "connect [with God] every step along the way – while dressing the baby, baking a cake, vacuuming the living room, shopping for clothes, food marketing, etc." Any and every moment is an opportunity to connect.

6) Take care of yourself physically. Eat well and set aside time for some form of exercise, a walk around the block, etc. Breathe fresh air. Align yourself with the beautiful world of nature around you. There is indisputably a mind, body, and spirit connection. If the body is tended to and healthy, the mind and spirit function is enhanced as well.

7) Credit yourself for all the victories, big and small. "The task of building eternity in the medium of fluid transience" is a mega-huge challenge. In order to maintain our perseverance, given all the stresses along the way, we must give ourselves credit for the daily victories even if they appear minuscule in our sight. Keep a list of all the times you are able to get a momentary clear glimpse of what will ultimately matter despite all the factors that work overtime to cloud your vision.

8) Take it from someone who's been around the block a few times: enjoy and make the most of these wonderful years. They go by so fast. Before you know it, you'll be revisiting this stage, these young formative years in your family's life in picture albums alone. Your heart will ache with nostalgia for the "good old days," days where you can be everything to your children, the smartest, the best, the most beautiful, etc. – times when "my mother says so" makes you an authority on everything. As you know, we can never turn the clock or the calendar back. Despite the demanding intensity of your current household, do your best to relish the moment. Keep a notebook handy to record the cute and often insightful remarks of your children. Share them with your husband, and take delight together.

9) I guarantee you that, with God's help, there will be seasons in the future that will allow you to do all that which attending to your first priority now does not allow for. Be careful not to squander the "now" of your life. It can never be replaced.

---

[2] The first prayers in the standard prayer book, reading from "*Modah Ani*" until the prayer that ends with the words, "*ha-gomel hasadim tovim le-amo Yisrael.*" As opinions on a mother's requirement for formal prayer vary, every woman should discuss her personal obligation to pray with a rabbi.
[3] Proverbs 3:6.

In conclusion, I'd like to leave you with two thoughts. A noted authority remarked that situational depression is a product of when "time is passing and the journey is not progressing, the soul feels the cold hand of death. Depression is no less than a minor experience of death itself. That's why it is so painful." Recognizing that you are making the right choices and engaging the appropriate journey is the only effective antidote.

Secondly, the Zohar, the classic Kabbalistic work, offers the following guiding insight. Commenting on the verse in Genesis, "and He called the light day," he suggests that all of us can choose to transform even darkness to "day" by the light that we infuse it with. The challenge for all of us is to bring the light of joy and positive affect to whatever season of life we find ourselves in. Let us try our utmost not to give darkness any claim to the precious moments of our life.

Gaping Black Hole[1]

By Denise Blumberg

My first struggle with postpartum depression occurred when I was still living in the United States with my husband and three kids. I was 33 years old, and had for the previous six years been working on my Ph.D. A mere two weeks after submitting the final draft of my thesis, I gave birth to a healthy, eight-pound baby girl. She was born at home, by choice, and I was surrounded by friends and care-givers.

The period immediately following her birth was exhilarating. My Ph.D. came through during Sukkot, which added to an already festive holiday. Life was normal and happy. I was busy with the kids, tending to my family's needs, the house, going back to aerobics classes – all the normal functions of daily living.

I was not prepared for the turmoil that awaited me some four months afterwards. I had not experienced any postpartum reaction with any of my three previous babies; I didn't recognize it when it began.

At first, I simply felt 'down.' The feelings of my after-birth exhilaration faded and left me hanging somewhere between birth and life. Then I began to lose enthusiasm for my usual interests and found myself milling around the house with the sense of having nothing to do.

As the weeks progressed, this intensified into a deep and terrifying feeling that I had nothing to do with my days, nothing to do with my life. A shroud of meaninglessness seemed to seep up from the depths of the earth and envelop my body. A gaping black hole began somewhere in my throat and ballooned when it reached my stomach. It made me physically nauseous. Although I lost my appetite and could barely taste the food, I ate a lot, trying to fill the ever-widening void within.

---

[1] Reprinted with permission from Aish.com, a leading Judaism website.

My brain was very detached from all of this. It was aware that my situation was growing worse. But for once, there was nothing my intellect could do to help me. Whatever was happening to me was not cognitive.

My ability to cope with the kids and the house deteriorated, which led to panic and despair. I feared that this was a form of insanity.

In normal circumstances, we take coping for granted and we don't realize the inner strength that goes into just coping. When postnatal depression descends like a black cloud, there's no such thing as coping. The word itself drops out of one's vocabulary as if it never existed.

The thought of shopping overwhelmed me with anxiety. The idea of juggling the demands of the kids threw me into a series of severe heart palpitations. I still had no idea what was happening to me. Had I not had a full-time nanny, I think I would have been out of my mind with fear.

The actual details of my life at that time are blurred. I remember more the feelings, the sensations and terrors. When I woke in the morning, the gnawing black hole inside almost devoured me. I could barely drag myself from the bed. Making a cup of coffee was unthinkable. Getting dressed was fraught with so many choices, I was torn apart by panic. Much better not to get dressed. Ever.

I was unable to perform the most minor tasks. Preparing a simple meal – toast and butter – was an enormous burden I could not undertake for anything in the world. An hour or so before the kids would come back from school I would feel a surge of panic in my throat, making breathing difficult. Something inside kept on screaming, "You can't cope with this! You'll never manage the demands!" And I didn't. Every time a child asked for something as minor as an apple, it felt like he was asking for a 747 jumbo jet.

The daily battles with the toddler about getting dressed made me feel as if I was in the middle of a war zone, as if I was about to be struck by a bomb. And indeed, I was far more terrified than I was during the security situation here in Israel. I found the terror within much more devastating than the terror without because I breathed it all the time – or, rather, it breathed me. I was its desperate slave. And those inner sensations threatened to consume me completely.

I just left everything to the nanny. [We then lived in the United States and were luckily able to afford one.] She fed the kids, she bathed them, she put them to bed when my husband wasn't at home. I don't remember who did the shopping – for sure, it wasn't me.

I still had no idea what was happening to me. I only knew that the worst thing in the world was to be conscious, because what I craved more than anything was the bliss of unconsciousness. I didn't want to know I was alive because I was where Hell was and Hell was where I was, and we were as deformed in our bonds as Siamese twins. If I wanted anyone at all in this purgatory, it was the baby, and the only thing I wanted to do was to coil myself around her in bed, go to sleep and never wake up.

The Turning Point

The turning point happened one morning. I was sitting on my bed, rocking backwards and forwards, hugging a cushion to my chest as if it was a life-support machine. My husband came into the room, and I remember bursting out, "What is the matter with me?!"

"You need to see a doctor."

My husband's reply was in itself a great blessing. Many husbands are utterly confused by this sudden change in their wives and the idea of her seeing a psychiatrist or taking pills only intensifies their fear.

My doctor was a highly sensitive woman who specialized in women's issues. She immediately diagnosed postpartum depression, and this gave me the light of hope. If there was a name to what I was experiencing, perhaps there was also a cure.

This light of hope enabled my husband to revolutionize. Before I was diagnosed, he felt completely helpless and unable to understand what I was experiencing. Once he knew that there was something clinically, medically the matter with me, he completely took over my role, cooking and dealing with the needs of the kids.

I was, again, very blessed. What might have happened had he been bitter or resentful? What if he'd been angry at suddenly finding himself the captain of a sinking ship?

My doctor advised me to see a psychiatrist who prescribed anti-depressant medication, which he said would take a few weeks to kick in. I was deathly afraid of pills, having no idea what this kind of drug would do to me. I was terrified of being out of control. But I was so terribly out of control, anyway, that I simply had no choice.

This medication was the difference between Heaven and Hell. I felt like an entirely new person.

Moving to Israel and More Kids

When my fifth child was born three years later, there was no recurrence whatsoever of post-natal depression, and I truly believed I was free forever of what I thought had been a one-time occurrence.

Almost two years after we moved to Israel, I gave birth to a perfectly healthy baby – but who weighed just over three pounds. Unlike the uneventful pregnancy of my previous postpartum baby, this pregnancy had been fraught with anxieties. There had been questions about the health of the baby from early on, and I didn't know what would be with her.

The birth was traumatic and she was separated from me. I was barely allowed to hold her, and I was certainly not allowed to nurse her. She was placed in an incubator for about two weeks in a hospital in the greater Tel Aviv area, and the daily trips to see her from Jerusalem involved a three-hour excursion.

During those weeks I was expressing milk at two hourly intervals, round the clock, in a desperate attempt to keep my milk and be able to nurse her. By the time we brought home this tiny little baby, I was completely exhausted, and utterly overwhelmed.

To my absolute horror, I began to experience those same old, terrible feelings. The same nausea, the same feelings of emptiness and panic, the gaping black hole, and the desperate imaginings of how I was ever going to cope.

But this time, there was no nanny. No one to take the kids, no one to make supper, no one to hold the baby – NO ONE.

My husband had professional commitments. He couldn't simply stay home and nurse me, which was exactly what I needed. This time, it didn't help him to know the name and condition of what I was going through. This time there was no nanny.

My husband's initial reaction expressed the stark difference between my postpartum depression in America and this new, Israeli experience. Fraught with anxiety, he told me that he never wanted to have more children because he couldn't cope with what I go through when I have a baby. And this from someone who always said he could manage with ten children. The sense of isolation and aloneness made him feel that now everything was on his shoulders and he felt completely overburdened and unable to face that task.

But this time there was NITZA, a non-profit support network for women experiencing postpartum depression,[2] which I had heard about through a friend who had been helped by them. I cannot over-emphasize the importance of quality support after birth. Hormones are in an uproar, sometimes causing extreme outbursts of anger or tears. Because a new baby brings so much excitement and joy, the fact that women may also be very vulnerable at this time is something often not understood. From the moment I heard Chana's voice on the phone, I knew that I wasn't alone. I was almost light-headed with relief knowing that she understood, that she had a network of support people in various roles pulling together to help me in the way that I needed help.

Because I had been through postnatal depression before, I was very aware of my needs. As per my request, Nitza organized natural medication through a homeopathic practitioner, which helped enormously to calm my

---

[2] NITZA, the Jerusalem Postpartum Support Network (www.nitza.org), was founded in 1997 to provide support to women and their families suffering from postpartum illness, including postpartum depression, psychosis, and mania. NITZA is currently the only organization in Israel that provides a full spectrum of services to meet the unique needs of those suffering postpartum illness. This privately run organization reaches out to women who would otherwise not seek help due to fear, shame, ignorance, and financial limitations. NITZA works closely with leading health-care professionals in order to provide the most comprehensive services and safety net possible.

anxiety. Meals were organized on an extended basis, to remove the pressure of taking care of my family. Young girls were brought in to look after the other children when I needed to rest, and others were recruited to hold the baby when I needed to spend time with the older kids. And eventually, Nitza found in-house help for as long as I needed it. They had taken care of my needs, preventing me from plunging again into the pit of postpartum depression.

If women experience trauma that is overwhelmingly intense, as I had in my first confrontation with this syndrome, conventional medication may well be a matter of life and death. The gentle effects of my homeopath's remedies may not be sufficiently aggressive to deal with a condition that is marriage-threatening, kids-threatening, and life-threatening.

In His great kindness, the Almighty brought Nitza to me, to my husband and to my children. I was amazed by the lengths to which these women were prepared to go just to help. With the personal emotional support and the practical help in the house that they organized, my spirits began to lift almost immediately, for I knew I was not alone and didn't have to cope on my own. Together, we had weathered a terrible storm.

BLAH-BUSTER TIDBITS

Tips for Coping with Postpartum Depression and Anxiety[1]

Recently, I was sitting on a park bench with a group of mothers when I noticed that one young mother, who is usually a vibrant and energetic person, looked sickly and pale. This mother starting telling us that since her birth to her second child two months before, she had felt like a "building gutted by fire." She had no energy, her days with her children seemed endless, and she didn't remember the last time she had felt happy.

An older mother responded, "When I was your age, I was home with five small children, and I was the happiest person on the planet! Your problem is simply that you haven't accepted your role as a mother!" I was amazed that nobody who heard this ignorant response came to my friend's defense.

Afterwards, I took my friend aside, and told her that I thought she might be suffering from postpartum depression. She had never even heard of postpartum disorders, even though they afflict a staggeringly large percentage of women – an estimated one in three first-time mothers.[2] If you are one of these women, the following is a list of suggestions on how to cope based on the book *This Isn't What I Expected: Overcoming Postpartum Depression*.

❖ **Set limits** – Accept that life cannot continue business as usual. Learn to say "No" if you are overwhelmed – for example to visitors, to Shabbat guests, to your boss.

❖ **Recognize and reduce your stressors** – Typical stressors for postpartum mothers include activities such as laundry, driving carpool, and preparing meals.

---

[1] Adapted from Kleiman, Karen, MSW, and Valerie Raskin, MD. *This Isn't What I Expected: Overcoming Pastpartum Depression.* New York: 1994.

[2] One in four first-time American mothers experiences postpartum depression or postpartum stress syndrome. Even more suffer from postpartum anxiety disorders, totaling one in three first-time mothers with postpartum disorders. Ibid, 2.

❖ **Discover postpartum stress reducers** – Figure out ways to reduce stress and stay relaxed. Sample stress reducers include taking a nap before older children come home, having a mother's helper come to take the baby on a walk or to help when kids come home from school, and taking a long walk on your own with the baby.

❖ **Passing time** – When agitated from postpartum disorders, every minute can feel like an hour. You can help yourself feel calmer by listening to a relaxation tape, taking a hot bath, or making a detailed list of what you will do in the coming hour in order to reduce anxiety.

❖ **Exercise** – Taking a brisk walk for half an hour produces endorphins that can, at times, lift your mood as effectively as anti-depressant medication. Also an excellent tool for combating anxiety.

❖ **Sleep** – Sleep while the baby sleeps. All of the books recommend this, but few new mothers follow their advice. The author of *This Isn't What I Expected,* Dr. Valerie Raskin, says that out of all of the suggestions on this list, this is the most important tool in fighting postpartum disorders!

❖ **Seek professional help** – There are many conventional and alternative practitioners who specialize in postpartum disorders who can help you to address the complicated factors that contribute to postpartum disorders. Seek out helpful medical personnel such as mental health professionals, naturopaths, homeopaths, and nutritionists.

❖ **Hospitalization** – If you are suicidal, your baby is in danger, or you can no longer cope, you should consult with a mental health professional about the possibility of hospitalization.

BLAH-BUSTER TIDBIT
The Nutritional Component of Happiness

After my fourth birth, I went to a dietician to find a diet that would help me to replenish my strength. This diet, which I've been on for the past two years, has had a dramatic effect on me. I feel calmer, postpartum mood-swings have become a thing of the past, and I have more energy than I've had in years.

Today, when I see a young mother who is looking run-down, I try, if possible, to tactfully suggest some simple nutritional tips that have helped me a great deal – eating more vegetables, cutting out sugar and white flour, eating three tablespoons a day of wheat germ and ground linseeds.[1] Within several weeks, the difference in these women I advise is so dramatic that I can see the difference in them from a block away. They look stronger and healthier, their skin glows, they are happier and calmer. My own experience and the experiences of other women I've advised have given me newfound fondness for dieticians (although I'm still working on liking the very thin ones).

Nutritionist Jan Hanson suggests that every day mothers of young children should try to eat[2]:

1. **Eight to twelve ounces of protein**. Because you lose protein during pregnancy and nursing, and your body uses more protein when it experiences a lot of stress, mothers need lots of protein.

   - Eat three to four ounces (about the size of a deck of cards) of proteins such as two eggs, a piece of lean chicken, or a handful of almonds at every meal.

---

[1] Ground linseeds contain high amounts of Omega 3, which has been linked in several studies with preventing depression. Other good sources of Omega 3 are salmon, trout, sardines, and walnuts. Wheat germ can help postpartum mothers to regain their strength because it contains more concentrated amounts of nutrients than any other grain or vegetable. Wheat germ contains more protein than most meats, and more iron and potassium than almost any other food. It is also a tremendous source of B vitamins and a significant source of Omega 3. If available, toasted wheat germ is delicious.

[2] Adapted from *Mother Nurture: A Mother's Guide to Health in Body, Mind, and Intimate Relationships*, 107–122.

2. **Five to seven servings of fresh vegetables and one to two fruits.** Vegetables are about the only thing that all nutritionists agree on, and they all agree that you should eat a lot of them. (A serving is a half a cup for most vegetables, and one cup for leafy greens.) If you find it hard to eat so many vegetables, using a juicer to make vegetable and fruit juices is a great solution.

3. **Unrefined oils and essential fatty acids.** Instead of refined or hydrogenated oils found in many processed foods, use small amounts of olive oil or butter instead of margarine.

    *   Omega-3 oils found in fish and flax can help prevent cardiovascular disease, rheumatoid arthritis, asthma, diabetes, and depression.

4. **Two to five servings of unrefined, varied whole grains.** Refining grains removes their fiber and nutrients (B vitamins, etc.). Grains such as brown rice, whole wheat, and barley definitely have a place in well-balanced nutrition.

5. **High-potency nutritional supplements.** You need more than the recommended daily values of nutrients. Growing and nursing a baby, as well as the hard work and stresses of raising a family, use up large quantities of nutrients.

6. **Zero or very little refined sugar.** Probably the most important ingredient in a mother's long-term health has been saved for last. Sure, when we're blue and want some comfort, most of us like to have something sweet to eat. But after your blood sugar surges, it quickly plummets. Suddenly you feel hungry, spacey, fatigued, jittery, shaky, short-tempered, or even panicky.[3]

---

[3] Sound impossible? Try not eating sugar for a few days and then treat yourself to a chocolate bar. There is a good chance that your emotional reaction will be so severe that you will have no trouble avoiding similar foods in the future.

PARENTING CLASS HAPPINESS

THIS PAST SUNDAY I woke up to a disappointment. It's probably not what you would call a major disappointment, but when you expect something and hope for it with all your heart, and then you find your hopes go ker-plop, two-year-old-got-into-the-fridge-and-dropped-the-egg-carton-on-the-kitchen-floor-style, it's so hard to maintain perspective.

So I knew that this was a Sunday morning that I definitely had to go to Rebbetzin Talia Helfer's parenting class for a serious pep talk. I've been going to Rebbetzin Talia's classes for about three years now, and every single week it is a huge struggle for me to give up a morning at the computer in order to go. There have been weeks and even months at a time that the sneaky voice that lives inside my head has convinced me that really I am doing just great as a mother, and that I'm certainly not in such bad shape that I need to give up a precious hour and a half of prime kidless writing time to go to a parenting class. But over the years I have learned to identify the voice's wily ways, and over and over I have learned the hard way what longtime classmate Yikrat Friedman expressed so succinctly: "If you don't go to Rebbetzin Talia's class, you gain the morning, but you lose the afternoon."

Years ago, Rebbetzin Talia told us that every mother has days when she is on top of the horse, a maternal Napoleon mothering her children with confidence, enthusiasm, and joy in her heart. And there are other days when she is on the ground, underneath the horse, feeling down, or low-energy, or lacking in self-esteem, and it is on those days that she is in serious danger of being trampled by that same horse. That is, if her children don't get to her first. I see over and over in my own life that staying on top of that horse is the greatest challenge I face in my life as a mother, and every week, when I manage to pull myself away from the computer for that hour and a half, I come home from Rebbetzin Talia safe in the saddle for a few more days.

I am especially in need of Rebbetzin Talia, and these frequent boosts back into the saddle, because I grew up believing that a dignified, impressive, intelligent woman was by definition a career woman: a lawyer, a clinical psychologist, the chair of a sociology department. And when I see Rebbetzin Talia, her very presence reminds me that today I live in a world where mothers are considered some of the most dignified, impressive, and intelligent women around – the future of the Torah and the next generation of the Jewish people in our hands. Every week that I go to Rebbetzin Talia, she picks me up firmly by the scruff of my neck, removes me from that old world, and plants me firmly in this new one. Through her eyes, she makes me see myself differently. When she looks at me I remember that I am not just a mother, I am a MOTHER.

By the end of each class, Rebbetzin Talia has gotten me so worked up that I rush home to pack up all my kiddies for a festive *Rosh Hodesh* trip to the science museum,[1] or to start a new sticker chart to encourage putting cereal bowls in the sink. Under Rebbetzin Talia's tutelage, my highest aspiration becomes making my children's lives into an ongoing theme party – with Torah and *mitzvot* replacing ballerinas in pink tutus and Ninja Turtles.

So, much in need of a pick-me-up, I spent this past Sunday morning learning from Rebbetzin Talia about the importance of instilling in our children a sense of *malkhut*, or kingship. First of all, she explained that a king never lacks anything. When he sits down to eat he is never without salt or a salad fork or his bottle of ketchup. He lives with a profound sense that he has everything he wants and needs. And this is how we need to live as well, and how we should raise our children – with the understanding that the lives we are living as Torah-observant Jews are the best lives on the planet, lives of abundance and fun and light.

She talked about bringing this kingship into our homes and the daily life of our children. She described the kitchen cabinets overflowing with food – even if that means stocking up during the sale on generic cornflakes and

---

[1] Rosh Hodesh, the first day of the Hebrew month, is a day of celebration, especially for women. Many mothers give their children special treats and take them on special outings in order to celebrate Rosh Hodesh.

vanilla wafers. She described the kitchen table set aesthetically for lunch with a tablecloth and silverware, grapes arranged above the peanut butter and jelly sandwich in a rainbow. And who cares if the dirty dishes from breakfast and last night's dinner are piled on the porch? She described telling the boy in his *tzitzit* [ritual fringes], and the girl with her shoes on the right feet that they are really looking the part of prince and princess to the greatest King.

Rebbetzin Talia told us that she used to live in a neighborhood where hers was by far the strictest family in terms of religious observance, to the extent that her children were socially isolated and very different from everybody else around. Her grown daughter, who today is already a mother of several children, told her recently that when she left her house each day and climbed the thirty-six steps leading up to the street, she would feel prouder and prouder with each step as she thought of the home she came from.

At that point, Rebbetzin Talia gave us a fierce, rousing look and told us that as Jews, we live lives full of "light and life!" That every day we must fulfill the verse "*yismehu be-malkhutekha*," "They will rejoice in Your kingship." All the people in the whole world live in the house of the King, but how many of them are actually aware of it as we are (or at least try to be, at least from time to time)? If we had to choose any life to live, this is the one we would choose.

What a difference this awareness could make for us and for our children as well! Imagine what it would be like to grow up in a house where the mother feels that she is raising princes and princesses in the house of the King, versus what it would be like to grow up in a house where the mother feels that she is surrounded by a bunch of runny-nosed pests in an overpriced three-room apartment with a nasty landlord?

It's like our Sages teach us – everything is from God except for the fear of God. God sends us our children, our financial situation, our spouses, our realities, our disappointments, and our joys – but it is totally up to us to see God in what happens or not. We can go around life feeling deprived and taken advantage of, but what we are supposed to do (and I am finding this very hard to do at this disappointing moment in my life) is to see God not only in the miracles and the amazing coincidences and the things that work out so amazingly at the last minute, but also to see God in the heartbreaks, in the things that discourage us to tears, and that make us feel totally and absolutely alone in the Universe.

I have learned over the years that perceiving God's role in my life, seeing that I am living in the house of the King, is one of the greatest challenges I face as a Jewish mother. I was thinking about this yesterday afternoon when Dafna and I went on our own to the Western Wall. Taking the children on outings one on one is one of my favorite things in the world, and yesterday afternoon I loved being able to listen undistracted to Dafna's running commentary on everything we saw, buying her an ice cream as tall as her forearm, and feeling her warm little hand tucked firmly inside mine as we walked down the steps to the Western Wall plaza.

At the security check, we ran into a group of about a hundred Americans in their early twenties, and I started talking with one young woman from New Jersey who told me this group had come with Birthright, the incredible program that has brought tens of thousands of young people to Israel for the first time on a free trip.

So I asked this young woman if she had ever seen the Wall, and she said, "No." And I was just so moved to be with her at that moment. A Jewish woman who had never even seen the Western Wall! But the fact of the matter is that she didn't seem especially excited, and in general few people have such moving, cathartic experiences at their first visit to the permanent residence of the Divine Presence. I remember going to the Old City for the first time twelve years ago and feeling like the Jewish Quarter was totally plastic, like it was an Epcot Center version of Jerusalem. It left me colder than cold. It left me frozen.

Other people remember being harassed by beggars their first time at the Wall, or being yelled at for wearing a halter top, or generally having absolutely no idea what the big deal was all about. And now, a decade later, I just approach the Wall, and my heart already melts. But it has taken a decade of learning and praying and motherhood in order for me to sense the holiness that resides among this pile of rocks that is overgrown with caper bushes and that, if you get too close, smells more like sweat than incense.

Rabbi Shlomo Carlebach used to tell a story about a man from a small village in Poland who moved to Jerusalem because a visiting Jerusalem rabbi had said that there were diamonds and rubies lining the streets here. After a few months, the man tracked down the same rabbi, and told him angrily that since he'd moved to Jerusalem he hadn't seen even one opal or emerald anywhere. And the rabbi just smiled and said, "Oh, but you will." And it was true: a few years later he also saw the diamonds and the rubies that the rabbi had told him of so many years before.

But at that moment, when life is just happening and moving by, it's so hard to see that we are living in the house of the King and raising His children, to see the jewels lining the streets. At the moment that I am microwaving veggie hotdogs, or that my wallet has just been stolen, or that I am on my way to buy a loaf of bread and breathing in car exhaust, I just don't see it (yes, even in the Holy City). Even though I know on a theoretical level that God is out there somewhere, I spend the vast majority of my life feeling like I am totally, absolutely on my own, on a solo mission to 120 with my husband and kids. On rare occasions, after the fact, sometimes I do figure it out. A few hours, or days, or years later I start to get it, I get a little dose of clarity, a glimpse of God's role in my life, before I fall back into a thick, swampy fog of existential solitude.

And, wow, is it hard to see and feel the Kingship all around us like Rebbetzin Talia shows us how to do! To see the diamonds and the rubies on the streets of our hometowns, in our homes, and in the eyes and the words of these children God sends us. And in the disappointments too, all the emeralds hidden inside the yolks of the eggs that go ker-plop on the kitchen floor.

STEP FOUR

LEARNING TO VALUE OUR SUPPORTING AND NURTURING ROLE

WE SERVE GOD by helping other people.

The world defines greatness in terms of possessions, power, position and prestige. We therefore idolize the CEO, movie star, and Superbowl-winning quarterback who have a chauffeur, a secretary, a maid, and an agent waiting to serve their every whim. In Western society's self-serving culture with its me-first mentality, devoting one's life to nurturing others is not a popular concept.

God, however, measures greatness by the amount of good deeds we do for those around us, not status. God determines your greatness by how many people you give to, not how many people give to you.

In the essays in this chapter, you will read essays on the joys and the challenges of supporting and nurturing our families.

Rebbetzin Talia Helfer's Parenting Principles

Recently I heard a parenting expert state that in our day and age, every mother should attend a parenting class for at least three years. I couldn't agree more. I wanted to share a little taste of the parenting tips that I've learned from my own three years spent in parenting classes with Rebbetzin Talia.

Bread in the basket. Different children need different things, and it is of great importance that a mother be sensitive to the special needs of each of her children. One child craves compliments, another wants his mother to dress him even though he is perfectly able to dress himself, and yet another must spend half an hour reading in bed and cuddling under the blankets when she comes home from school. By providing these basic needs, and thereby keeping "bread in the basket," we provide our children with something much deeper – the basic sense of security and unconditional love that they need to thrive. Example: Sara has only one skirt that she likes to wear, so her mother washes this skirt every other day so that it is always clean for her to wear to kindergarten. Sara loves the skirt, but more than the skirt, she loves the feeling that her mother supports her and takes care of her.

Minimize tensions. Try to say "Yes" to your children's requests as much as possible, unless this requires compromising on something that is important to you. If you must say "No," pick your battles wisely, so that your home will not be transformed into a battlefield of frequent and destructive power struggles. Remember, a home with a peaceful and happy atmosphere is better than a home run with strict discipline. Example: I let my daughter eat her Cheerios with a fork as she requests. I do not let her walk around barefoot in the playground like the other children, because this is an important rule to me.

Do not raise robots. Until the age of bar/bat mitzvah, our main goal as mothers is that our children should love the mitzvot, rather than simply perform them like robots, or out of fear of our disapproval. Example: [in dramatic voice] "Who is washing their hands before the meal? Mommy has a special surprise for whoever has washed hands!"

Don't be afraid of your children. At times when you must say "No" to your children, make sure that you feel absolutely certain of your decision, and don't be afraid of your children's reaction. State your ruling quietly, with total confidence, and without anger. If we are certain of our decisions and not afraid of our children's reaction, in almost all cases they will accept what we say. Example: Avigail's mother wants her to stay with the babysitter so that she can go on her own to a parenting class. Avigail cries a bit when her mother leaves, but sensing her mother's confidence in her decision, she soon stops and plays happily until her mother returns.

Mothers as gardeners. When a seed is under the ground, the gardener knows that in several months that seed will blossom into a beautiful flower. So too, when a child is young, it is the mother's responsibility to believe in her child's potential to grow into a good and responsible person, even when reality appears to be in direct conflict with the mother's faith. Example: Yedidya has been bullying his classmates. His mother works to address his behavioral problems at the same time that she has total faith in his potential to grow into a kind and generous person.

Don't put a stumbling block before the blind. Don't put your children into situations that you know they will not be able to handle. Example: Shoshy is tired and hungry when her mother leaves for the store. When her mother refuses to buy her a package of stickers, she has a tantrum. This is the mother's fault, since she put Shoshy into a situation that was too difficult for her to handle. David's mother takes him to the toy store to choose his own birthday present. David chooses five toys instead of one, and the outing ends in a tantrum. David's mother should have realized that taking a four-year-old to a toy store is the same as putting a stumbling block before the blind.

FIRST GRADE IN THE HOLY LAND

OVER THE PAST FEW MONTHS of decreased violence in Israel, I cannot tell you how much it has meant to me to see tourists walking around deciphering maps of Jerusalem once again, carrying big cameras around their necks, and wearing t-shirts with insignias from all over North America and the world. It makes me feel like I am seeing relatives that I had forgotten even existed during the past few scary years of Intifada, like we're having a big celebratory family reunion right here in Jerusalem.

But the happiness I feel when I see the tourists is nothing compared with the joy that I felt to see a flood of new immigrants arriving in Israel this past summer, and especially the three new young families who have made *aliya* to my neighborhood of Nahlaot. These families have arrived from Toronto, Philadelphia, and Brooklyn in order to live in our little corner of the Holy Land, despite all the challenges that Israeli life presents the new immigrant, or *oleh hadash* – the new ascendant.

I have never met anyone who has had a totally smooth time making *aliya*. In most cases, new immigrants fulfill, at least to a certain extent, the Talmudic statement that "The land of Israel is acquired through suffering."[1] For example, one of the three new families in our neighborhood, in addition to the hours that all new immigrants must spend in government offices and the stresses of finding employment, had $600 stolen when thieves broke into their apartment several weeks after their arrival. The following week, two police officers came to their door and said that they had located the thief's hideout in an abandoned house next door. They then informed the family that they would need to spend the rest of the day staked out in their apartment, along with the mother and her antsy young children who had not planned to spend one of the hottest days of the year cooped up at home. And, on top of this, the very pregnant mother twisted her ankle soon afterwards. I told her that she should write a book entitled *The Misadventures*

---

[1] Babylonian Talmud, *Berakhot* 5a.

of the New Oleh, which would provide much-needed validation and comic relief for a lot of new immigrants.

But for me personally, it has been eleven years since I went through my own *aliya* traumas – the struggles with rude bureaucrats who had no patience for my broken Hebrew and general confusion and the evil landlord who raised our rent in the middle of the year but wouldn't let us move out, and the dream job that I got fired from after only three months in a particularly traumatic and humiliating manner, and the terrible feeling that I would never ever feel totally at home in my adopted homeland. Eleven years ago, I cried many tears and suffered many palpitations, and wished that many people who had offended me would be hurt at least as terribly as they had hurt me.

But that was a long time ago. After putting in many years acquiring the land of Israel through suffering, today I know Hebrew well. I have learned when to let things slide and when to send my husband in for a battle. I know how to smile at the bank clerk and hold a baby on my lap so that she will be on my side, and that if I want to stay in a good mood, I should steer clear of the grumpy mushroom seller in the central market. When I pray, I thank God every single day for three things – for my husband, for my children, and for the fact that I live in Israel.

However, one thing that remains from those first years has never changed since I became a new immigrant. It is actually a positive thing. It is just how emotional I feel about being here. To this day, I cry every time I hear "Hatikva," I cry every time I see many Israelis gathered together – at the Western Wall on Shavuot, for example. Just like a new immigrant, my love for Israel is not tempered by a veneer of prickliness or toughness or cynicism that coats the love of even the most patriotic and idealistic Israelis.

But there is one thing that brings out my new-immigrant emotionality more than anything else. For years my husband has been teaching religious Israeli girls after national service, and when these girls come to my house, just seeing them makes me happy. Or actually, they make me want to cry, but the joy and tears are coming from the same place in my heart. They come from the same place that causes me to bawl every year when I walk alongside the tens of thousands of young religious kids who come from all over Israel to participate in the Jerusalem Day parade.

These religious young people make me so emotional because they represent for me my ultimate aspiration as a new immigrant, my Israeli equivalent of the American dream – that one day my kids will grow up to be like these kids. After years of careful observation of my husband's students, I have decided that these young women are as close as anyone can come to being a perfect human being. They are incredibly sincere, bright, creative, religious, full of life, modest, confident, graceful, giving, and beautiful. They also have wonderful personalities, and know the Bible and each and every corner of the land of Israel like I know the Pledge of Allegiance and my way around the peeling, pastel-painted alleyways of Nahlaot.

To be fair, I guess I should say that not all religious Israeli girls are like this, but looking back at the hundreds of young women that my husband and I have met over the years through his work, I am hard-pressed to think of even one who did not earn my affection and respect, who did not make me think, "If my daughters grow up to be like her, I will die a happy woman."

Which is why I am particularly excited to tell you about Dafna's first day of first grade last week. The beginning of the school year was the first experience that I've had in many years that reminded me of the confusion of my first years in Israel. It was also a very emotionally charged event – the first step of Dafna's initiation into honest-to-goodness Israeli girlhood after her years spent in the nursery school/kindergarten Little League.

The following are some of the misadventures of this past week.

Adventure #1 – The Minibus.

Over the summer, I had quite a few discussions with the neighborhood mothers about organizing the private minibus that would transport the nine neighborhood children who commute to Har Nof for school. This is especially difficult to arrange, since the children attend various schools that end at different times. But I heard several times the reassurance from mothers and school administrators alike that, "By the second week of school, everything will be running very smoothly."

From my years of experience with Israeli nursery schools, I have learned the hard way that important decisions (like who the teacher will be, where the nursery school will be located, or whether a nursery school will exist at all) are often made during the last week of summer vacation. And I have also learned the hard way that not getting too anxious about all this uncertainty is the best policy since, in my experience, things (almost) always work out for the best.

But it's a bit hard for me to be so relaxed now, since I am nervous anyway about sending my little girl to a school half an hour from home on her own. But, still, the whole summer I was trying to take it easy, to go with the flow, to be as relaxed as all the other mothers.

Then, the day before the first day of school, I got a phone call from the minibus driver that he would pick up Dafna the following morning. I felt relieved that things really were organized despite the appearance of confusion. "And will you also bring them home?" "Yes, of course. But please call tomorrow to find out at what time." OK, this must be the Israeli school way.

So I wanted to tell you about last Wednesday, my daughter's first morning in first grade.

10 AM: I call minibus company to find out when Dafna will be coming home. Answer: "Oh, there's no minibus back."

10:02: I call minibus coordinator. Answer: "No, Mrs. Weisberg, we don't want you to come to pick up your daughter. But don't worry, there will be a minibus home."

10:10: Call from minibus coordinator: "Please tell Dafna's school secretary to send a note to Dafna to find the minibus when classes end."

10:30: I call minibus coordinator: "By the way, when will Dafna be home?" "Around 1:45." "Why? School is over at 12 today." "What?! No one told me that!"

10:35: I call the minibus coordinator: "They're sending a special minibus for the kids from her school. She'll be home by a quarter to one."

12:00: Call from minibus coordinator: "Do you know where your daughter is? The minibus driver is there and can't find her."

12:01: I call the National Service volunteer sitting in school office: "Find my daughter!"

12:10: Call from Ronit, the most organized of the Nahlaot mothers: "My kids called me on my cellphone to tell me that Dafna is with them. Do you want them to take her home on the public bus?" I tell her that the minibus driver is looking for them. They find each other.

1:05 PM: Dafna arrives home with a big smile. She tells me of her first day adventures, how they played "Sea, Continent" during recess, and how she has homework, and how they study the whole day, not like in kindergarten (although today she told me that they don't study at all, just color the whole day like in kindergarten). Dafna looked a foot taller – suddenly such a big girl, so proud to go to school on her own. I didn't tell her that I'd had a busy morning as well.

Adventure #2 – Covering the Books

Then Dafna told me that her teacher said that they absolutely must cover their books with plastic by the following day. I vaguely remembered covering books when I went to school by cutting up paper shopping bags in some special way that I can't remember, but what did she mean by plastic? Would Saran Wrap do? I had already gotten through that morning's minibus problem, and I saw this as my next test. Just as Dafna would have to work hard to succeed in first grade, I too would have to do my best to succeed at covering these books with... plastic?

That afternoon, Dafna reminded me five times to wrap her books. I told her I would take care of it. Then I called Nisa's babysitter to ask what the teacher meant by this, but she said that her children were big and that they covered their own books, so she didn't know how to do it. Then I called Yikrat, who was born here, and she told me that I should go to an office supplies store to buy plastic on a roll, and then secure the corners in place with a little bit of tape. It sounded so easy when she described it. So, I searched around for fifteen minutes at the store nearby, not really sure what

I was looking for, and all the salespeople overwhelmed because of all the first day of school shoppers, and then I found it… something that looked like foggy thick Saran Wrap on a roll. I asked the lady at the register to confirm that this was the real thing, and yes! I'd found it.

So when I got back from shopping that evening, I sat down with Dafna's three books and some scissors and tape, and with a fair amount of excitement ("Now I am the mother of a real Israeli!"), I started. First, I tried to fold the plastic in different ways before taping it onto the book, but that made the plastic get all bunched up like a terribly botched up origami crane with a book underneath. Then I shortened the plastic wrap with scissors so that it was the same length as the book, although I didn't do it so evenly, so the very top and bottom of the book remained uncovered.

Perfection was never my strong point, so I decided that what I'd done was good enough and proudly put stickers with Dafna's name on the books, and placed them neatly in her backpack. Then I had a mommy-nightmare flash, that the teacher would tell Dafna that her mommy had to redo the covers. Or that the teacher would hold up another girl's books to point out how nicely her mother had covered them, as opposed to some other mothers (staring pointedly at my innocent daughter, the girl for whose mother perfection is not a strong point).

That night, we got a call from the minibus driver that Dafna would be coming home at 1:15 PM the following day, so I spent the next morning writing – answering and making not even one phone call – Dafna's covered (at least for the most part) books secure in her bag. And I felt and feel really excited, already a few days into this brand new stage of our lives in Israel – the parents of an Israeli schoolchild.

More Parenting Principles from Rebbetzin Talia

Discipline. Just as we cannot hammer a nail into the wall using only our right hand, we cannot raise children with only positive reinforcement and without discipline. When punishment is required, we should immediately deliver a quick punishment, and then return right away to using positive reinforcement. Example: Becky hits Jacob over the head with her new doll. Becky's mother takes the doll from her and states firmly, "If we hit with dolls, we cannot play with them." She then places Becky on her lap, and continues reading everybody a story.

❖ Four situations that require punishment:

- **Disrespect to sacred objects.** Shlomo grabs the prayer book out of his mother's hand and tears out a page.

- **Disrespect to parents.** Deborah bites her father.

- **Purposeful infliction of damage.** Matthew cuts a hole in his sister's skirt.

- **Uncontrollable tantrum endangering self or property.** Rebecca does not want to hold her mother's hand in the crosswalk and has a tantrum and collapses in the middle of the street. Eli has a tantrum in the grocery store and begins throwing cereal boxes off the shelf.

Special Note: These four cases require punishments only if there are not mediating circumstances. If the child is hungry, tired, or suffering because we have "put a stumbling block before the blind" (for example, taken Eli to the grocery store even though it is long past his bedtime) then a punishment is not in order. If a child is under two years old, a stern "No" will suffice.

❖ **Don't educate children in public.** If a child misbehaves, do not punish him in front of other people. Example: Yedidya hits a girl at the park. Instead of loudly rebuking him in front of the other mothers and children, depending on the situation, you can let the children work out the conflict between themselves, or alternatively, you can distract Yedidya from his foe by putting him on the swing. That evening, tell Yedidya a story about a child who hits another child in a park, and how this makes the other children feel towards him.

❖ **Do not compare children.** Avoid situations that cause you to have less confidence in your child. Example: Tehila is four years old and is still using a pacifier, which embarrasses her mother in front of her friends. Her mother decides to walk further to a park in a different neighborhood for the coming months so that she will feel more comfortable about weaning Tehila from her pacifier at her own pace.

❖ **You are in charge.** You are the commander of your house. Even if we forget all of Rebbetzin Talia's teachings, the one thing we must remember is to have confidence. Our confidence gives our children a sense of security to face the challenges that life dishes out. Example: I want Tiferet to put away her own toys. Before I request this, I take a few seconds to make certain that I am one hundred percent confident in my decision and prepared to enforce it.

At the same time, when we apply these principles we should bear in mind that we can do our best and still things may not work out according to plan. We must accept that not everything is in our hands. Our goal should be to remain upbeat and strong, continuing on the right path despite setbacks.

BLAH-BUSTER TIDBIT

The Art of Humming

by Ruchama King[1]

Years ago I taught creative writing to high school girls. I encouraged the girls to keep journals – daily records of their impressions. One student, whom I'll call Esther, wrote about her mother who had just gotten a call to bake a cake for a bris for someone in the neighborhood who had given birth. Esther watched as her mother began pulling out pans and mixing bowls and flour and sugar from the cupboards, humming under her breath as she flipped through a recipe card file. Esther thought her mother would've been annoyed or flustered at having to bake a cake on such short notice, but she seemed calm, unruffled, even happy to help out in this way....

We already know the obvious lesson here. The children are watching, listening, absorbing our every move and mood. This we understand. And we all try to live with the weighty knowledge (sometimes oppressive, sometimes ennobling) that we are being examined daily by our offspring, who have a finely-tuned radar for our inconsistencies, absurdities, and general foul-ups. Hopefully a radar for the good things we do, too, as Esther's comment would seem to indicate.

No, it was something else that struck me. Esther wrote that her mother was happy to perform the mitzvah. How did she know this? What made her intuit her mother's mood? Simple: her mother was humming as she worked. This led the daughter to conclude that her mother was happy.

This brought to mind something a rebbetzin once said, a woman noted for her talent in creating a serene, happy atmosphere in her home. She was asked how she conveyed a mood of joy to her children. She replied, "I hum."

Think of it. It's morning time on a school day. Socks need to be matched, lunches assembled, sniping comments smoothed over, breakfast eaten. Panic

---

[1] King, Ruchama Feuerman. "The Art of Humming." *Natural Jewish Parenting* 9. Ruchama King Feuerman lived for ten years in Israel, where she studied and taught Torah to women. Her short stories and articles have appeared in diverse places such as *The New York Times*, *Hamodia*, and *Midstream*. Her critically acclaimed novel, *Seven Blessings* (her first in the secular mainstream) is about matchmakers and match seekers in Jerusalem. She gives writing workshops in Passaic, New Jersey, where she lives with her husband and children.

hovers in the air. And there's Eema[2] hunched over the sink, trying to hold it all together, the hub in the center of the circle. I imagine that woman by the sink (all of us) as an energy source, both repository and a generator of all the multitude of feelings a child might experience during the day. How does she convey a calm cheerfulness in the midst of chaos? Through the simple power of niggun.[3] Humming lets the children know that despite whatever pandemonium might be reigning at the moment, everything is basically okay. Eema is taking it in stride, the world is a decent, cheerful place after all.

---

[2] Mom
[3] Music

INDEPENDENT CHILDREN

A FEW YEARS AGO, a friend who is a psychologist told me that from the moment a baby is born, parents are educating him or her towards independence. When I first heard this, I did not like it one bit. At the time, Nisa was only a few months old, and I thought of what bliss it was to listen to her breathing while she slept, or to nurse her and to feel such wonderful closeness with her, or even to change her diaper and see how effortlessly I gave to her – for the thousandth time, for the thousand and first time. I didn't like this talk about independence. It felt like she was taking a chainsaw to the bough balancing a rocking cradle on top.

But my friend's observation made me start thinking about the way I mother my older children. It made me think about how there is time for total nurture, and there is a time to let babies become children and children become adults. I started thinking about how I tend to think of the ideal mother as one who does for her children. This mother in my dreams spends her morning preparing a healthful lunch of schnitzel and peas for her kids, knitting them sweaters, and then, in the afternoon, takes them to the zoo to explain the difference between cold-blooded and warm-blooded animals.

And my friend's comment made me think of things a bit differently. A good mother is also one who lets her children spread their own peanut butter on their sandwiches, who teaches them to sew, who lets the eleven-year-old take the five-year-old to the zoo on her own – so that she will feel grown up and responsible. So that she will learn to become independent of her mother.

But this is an inner battle for me. As instinct defying as when I was studying to convert my American driver's license to an Israeli one, and the driving instructor told me that I must use the enlarged rear-view mirror rather than look over my shoulder to see my blind spot. I have three framed photographs above my computer, each one of me holding one of my children. There is one of me nursing Tiferet an hour after her birth in the hospital nursery, another of me holding Nisa and kissing her forehead at three months old during a trip to the Galilee, and another of a three-year-old Dafna squealing in my arms in Mitzpe Ramon. And this is how I like to imagine my kids, especially when I am at the computer and they are out in the mornings. I like to imagine them with me, safe, taken care of, as close and protected as a newborn baby.

Six weeks ago, my daughter, Dafna, started first grade. Dafna's beginning school has been an exciting as well as a trying and stressful experience for me. My husband and I were both miserable for a large part of our elementary educations – both of us were particularly unpopular and teased very cruelly by other children, and I, at least, was not such an academic success that I could console myself with stellar report cards or the attention of fawning teachers. Up until recently, just walking by a school yard full of children was enough to break my heart, since I knew that there was almost certainly one child in that crowd of children who was suffering as much as I had in my own schoolyard.

Things got better for me at a certain point, improving slightly in junior high school and then dramatically in high school and college. I figured things out socially and developed more self confidence, and I found academic subjects in which I did well.

But because of our elementary-school issues, when we were choosing a school for Dafna this past year, Josh and I went about it with great care. We consulted with many people, spent many hours engaged in emotional debates, and interviewed at several schools until we came to our final decision only in the middle of the summer, extending the deadline by several months by breaking the rules and registering at two schools. We wanted to ensure that Dafna would have a better experience than ours had been, that she would attend a school where she would fit in, where the other kids come from families similar to our own. Maybe a few kids from English-speaking families would be nice. In any case, Dafna is a wonderful, bright, confident kid, and in kindergarten she made friends fairly easily.

In the end, our decision finally behind us, school has started off well. Dafna loves her teacher. She has already made a bunch of friends. Dafna loves learning how to read, and she is picking it up quickly. Last night, when I walked by her room at night, I overheard Dafna reading quietly out of her workbook by the light from the closet, *"Hanna lavsha simla na'ah."* She loves gym, and art class, and learning *mishnayot* from *Pirke Avot* by heart.

And I am amazed by the change in her. She used to become grouchy easily, or act hyper, or pick on her sisters when she was bored. And now, school makes her feel grown up, and she acts it, almost like a junior mother. I cannot believe what a big girl she has become over the past six weeks.

But there have been rough spots as well. Once Dafna couldn't find the minibus that takes the children home to Nahlaot and she was left behind. Over the first weeks of school, Dafna came home several times in tears and told me that she did not have any friends, that everybody made fun of her, and that she did not want to go to school any more. After this happened a few times, I concluded that history was repeating itself, and my mind jumped full-speed ahead into crisis mode – I'll move her to another class, to another school, I'll home-school her, we'll move to America. But in the end, Josh had a long talk with Dafna's teacher, and we consulted with all sorts of people about what we should do. And after every hard day, Dafna went back to school the next day, and more recently, despite occasional tears and setbacks, she has been relatively happy. Things have been relatively smooth sailing.

But it's still hard for me to see Dafna having to learn to stand up for herself, to deal with mean children without me there to run to, to generally learn how to manage for herself in the big world, even if that big world is just first grade and the elementary school jungle.

A few weeks ago I had a really strange dream. I discovered that the Mossad had taken Dafna to live at a top-secret training center in Gilo, a distant neighborhood of Jerusalem. They had heard about her, and had decided to train her from a young age to work as a bodyguard, sort of like the Soviets used to take six-year-olds to train them to become Olympic gymnasts. When I finally tracked down Dafna, she was at this training center, sort of disoriented, but settling into the routine there. I was furious, yelling at somebody, "She is too young for you to take her like this from her family!" I woke up in the middle of the night upset, but relieved to realize that Dafna was sound asleep in her bed and would only be leaving for first grade that coming morning, and not for any top-secret installations of Israel's security services.

Yesterday I picked up Dafna after school with Tiferet, and Dafna asked if she could show Tiferet around. Dafna was so proud, and as we walked around, a bunch of kids I didn't recognize said, "Shalom, Dafna!" or "Dafna, did you do the art project today?" or "Dafna, how are you?" Dafna returned the greetings nonchalantly, eager to get past them in order to show her little sister the first grade classroom, but I was shocked to see my big girl with a life of her own, to see her so confident in this place where she is her own person, an independent little member of school society.

I thought about how Dafna is still largely under my care. I feed her, clothe her, listen hard to her when things are tough, and consult with mothers made smart by experience when I'm not sure how to help her out. But when I looked at Dafna yesterday, I saw how she is doing this pretty much on her own. She is growing up. And I thought about how it is a funny thing, how it ends up that the mother suffers from growing pains even more than the child.

BLAH-BUSTER TIDBIT

Expressing Unconditional Love

by Rachel Arbus[1]

It is easy to express our love for our children. Life provides countless opportunities through which we can express love in its truest form.… If you would just open your eyes, you could very easily transform many daily events into expressions of love.

When your child is leaving for school, you can say, "Wait for me. I want to walk with you today." When he comes home, it is enough to spread out your hands with joy and say, "I missed you very much!" Sentences like these convince our children more than anything else we can do that they are surrounded by love.

My neighbor tends to think about her children when she is preparing dinner. Occasionally, she cooks one of her children's favorite foods. When that child enters the kitchen, she says to him with joy, "Yaakov, today when I was making dinner, I thought especially of you. I imagined how happy you would be when you ate your hamburger." Our children don't need much more than this. A small candy that you give them because, "I love you, and I want to make you happy," will make their hearts race with emotion.…

I mention these examples in order to show you how simple it is to express love. If you will look, you will find many opportunities to light up your children's hearts. In many years, they will not remember how clean and tidy the house was. They will remember how you related to them, how you listened and paid attention to them. Let us enable them to experience many expressions of love such as these.

---

[1] (Translated from Hebrew) Rachel Arbus, *Korot Bateinu* (Jerusalem: 2004), 106–107. Rachel Arbus is one of the most prominent parenting experts in Israel today. For several decades she has been a popular lecturer as well as a facilitator of workshops in education, parenting, and self-awareness. She is the director of the Netivot be-Hinuch Yehudi Institute in Jerusalem.

SUPERMOM

IF YOU LIVE in a place like North America where it snows a lot, then you have never seen anything like the reaction of Israelis to a snowstorm. I spent my first two years in Israel studying at a yeshiva for English-speakers, so the annual day or two of snow in Jerusalem did not attract too much attention from the students. The snow came and was beautiful for a few hours, and, for me, brought back all sorts of cozy, wonderful childhood memories of waking up in the morning and hearing my mother announce the most fantastic words imaginable: "You can stay in bed, no school today." Snow days were spent in front of the TV sipping steaming hot chocolate with miniature marshmallows, and sliding down hills with my brother on the big orange slide that spent the rest of the year in the basement – our sled the first to leave a mark in the virgin snow.

So it was not until my third winter in Israel, when I was working in a government office, that I learned that Israelis have a whole different set of associations with snow that are not nearly as positive as my own. That winter, with the onset of the annual snow storm, the halls were filled with groups of workers conferring in tense, loud voices about the flakes accumulating on their windowsills. Those with cars locked up their offices and headed for the exit with quick steps as they pulled on their jackets, their car keys ready in hand to turn on the ignition. The rest of the workers lingered a bit longer, peering out the windows with pinched lips, making dire pronouncements like, "They say it's not going to stop for hours" and "I'm getting out of here before they stop the buses," and then calling out to no one in particular as they headed for the elevator, "Be careful, it's dangerous out there!"

And this winter, more than a decade since my first Israeli snowstorm, for the last few weeks there have been rumors flying all over the place that snow is on the way, but all of the promised dates passed like calculated predictions of the Apocalypse, with nothing more than some sweater-piercing wind or skirt-drenching rain. And then, this morning, my husband told me that he had heard on the radio that there was a very small chance that there might be some snow tonight. And out of the blue, as I was walking home from Tiferet's kindergarten in the pouring rain early this morning, I started thinking that the rain looked sort of like sleet. Or maybe very wet snow? And by the time I was halfway home, my heart started dancing when I realized that I was definitely in the middle of an honest-to-goodness blizzard. When I reached Bezalel, a four-lane street that is usually packed with traffic, I had a big smile on my face despite the fact that all the drivers were leaning heavily on their horns and mumbling under their breath on account of this white stuff that was making me so happy.

But the snow wasn't sticking. It melted into water as soon as it hit the ground that was wet from several days of heavy rain. So I walked the rest of the way home, said my prayers, and then, after a few minutes, I looked out of the window again and saw that the snow had started to accumulate on the railing of my neighbor's stairs.

My mind started racing. Dafna was at school, and if the snow continued, within a few hours the steep road leading to her school would be closed to traffic. So I put on a dry coat and tried to order a taxi, but none of the companies were even answering. All the taxis had already been taken by other nervous mothers. So I walked to the street and was fortunate enough to find a taxi that was letting someone off at that moment.

I got in, safe from the swirling blizzard in the overheated taxi with the radio playing at ear-numbing volume, and at that moment I was overwhelmed with the sweetest feeling in the world, maybe even happiness in its essential form. This was a bit strange, since a day or even a few hours of lost writing time usually leave me as grouchy and frustrated as those drivers out there cursing the snow.

But in that taxi, even at 9:45 AM on a weekday, I was infused with the glorious feeling that I was a mother coming to the rescue of my daughter. In the taxi, I imagined walking into Dafna's class, and how she would get a sheepish smile on her face as she put on her coat and packed up her colored pencils, so incredibly proud that her classmates would see that her mother had come for her – that her mother worried about her and loved her.

I had this same honey-sweet feeling a few months back when I realized one morning that I had forgotten to pack Dafna's lunch. After I left off Tiferet at nursery school, I got into a taxi, and brought Dafna a peanut butter and honey sandwich on whole wheat pita along with some apple slices. All in all, it took me an hour to get to her school and back, and it cost sixty shekels or fifteen dollars in taxi fares. When I told my husband what I had done, he laughed, and said, "That was a sixty-shekel sandwich! Couldn't Dafna have borrowed food from her friends?" But I shook my head and told him that he had no idea how much *nachas* I got out of that sandwich, that it was worth even more than sixty shekels to see Dafna's face when I walked into her classroom with that peanut butter and honey sandwich in my hand.

It's true that over the course of the day, I also do countless other unremarkable things for my kids to express my devotion to them. I wake up at dawn to get them ready for school, I fold their laundry in the evening after the long, tiring day, and I make sure that they are wearing turtlenecks underneath their sweaters so that they don't catch the flu that has been going around. And I talk to them, listen to their troubles, pray for them, and tell them that I love them. And I do love them. But those rare times when I can go that extra mile for them, when in times of trouble and distress I can swoop out of the sky and play Supermom – those are the highest, sweetest moments of my mothering life.

And the funny part about it is that I am not sure who gets more out of this giving – my children or me. Dafna, for example, doesn't understand the sacrifice involved in the shlepping, the financial cost, and the loss of my precious writing time involved in these rescue missions to Har Nof. But I know, even if she doesn't, that in these little sacrifices I am expressing that my love for her is infinite, that she is on my mind even when I am doing other things, that I would do anything for her. And I have discovered what a wonderful, almost unparalleled feeling it is to be able to give in this way.

Maybe this feeling I get is a hint of the great sweetness and satisfaction parents must feel when they can give their children a college education or a wedding or help them buy a house. Now that I am a mother, I understand this kind of giving very differently than when I was blessed enough to have found myself on the receiving end. I see now how it is almost a physical need to give in this way, to let out some of the infinite love we have in our hearts and express it in a limited, tangible form.

But it is also no coincidence that all of these Supermom stories I am telling are about my seven-year-old, Dafna. I think this is because now that Dafna is in first grade and comes home later than her younger sisters, she is simply not around as much as my other children to benefit from the rest of the routine giving I do. She is not there for the daily breakfasts spent joking around with her little sisters and divvying up spoonfuls of my tea into their cups, or for the long walk to nursery school when we discuss the names of trees and family plans for the upcoming holidays, or for the meltdowns and giggly reconciliations that often precede lunch. So while I got special satisfaction last week rushing to pick up Tiferet early from nursery school when she had a fever, when I can rush to help out Dafna, I feel especially happy. With these rescue missions I am saying that even though she is growing up, and spending more time with her new friends and new life in school, that she is still on my mind. That even though she is my big girl, she is still my baby.

So this morning in the taxi, when I saw the snow turn into rain, I willed it to turn back into snow again, but it didn't. And when the lady on the blasting radio said, "The municipality has announced that all the nervous parents should not come to pick up their children. The snow will all have melted within the hour," I told the taxi driver to turn around. And even though I felt disappointed to not be able to play Supermom that day, I didn't feel frustrated at all by my partially-wasted morning. Even if I hadn't managed to give a gift to my daughter that day, I had at least given a little one to myself.

STEP FIVE

LEARNING TO VALUE OUR ROLE IN THE HOME

HAVING CHILDREN means that we spend more time at home than ever before. For example, I used to be a person who spent ninety percent of her waking hours outside of the house working and studying, and now I spend ninety percent of my waking hours at home – taking care of my kids, writing, and doing housework.

The Jewish home is known as a "*mikdash me'at*," a miniature Temple, and people often compare the Jewish wife to the priests going about their various sanctified tasks. After I became a mother, though, this comparison made me cringe with resentment. What is the similarity between scrubbing sheep's blood off the altar and clearing bowls of soggy left-over cornflakes? Between preparing a sheep for a burnt offering and making meatloaf? Between preparing the priestly garments and putting in yet another load of dirty laundry?

And to this day, I still struggle with the tidying and dishwashing and chicken-soup serving that maintaining a Jewish home requires. But as the years pass, I have come to accept, at least in principle, that my home is not just a concrete structure filled with dusty furniture and strewn with toys and dirty socks. Today I know (once again, at least in principle) that as a homemaker I am working to create a truly holy place. This home I am cleaning is a place where I teach my daughters to thank God before they bite into those bananas, and that words can hurt every bit as much as sticks and stones. It is a place that absolutely glows once a week from the light of my Shabbat candles, and from the angelic entourage that follows my husband and guests home from shul on Friday night.

When it is hard for me to clean up the kitchen one more time, I find it helpful to remind myself of the tens of millions of Jewish homes that will never exist on account of Hitler's evil genocide and the silent tragedy of intermarriage. I remind myself what a privilege it is to be the creator of one of the remaining sanctuaries for the Torah's light to fill up the world, my own home serving as an unbroken link in the nearly severed chain between Mount Sinai and the end of history.

But that doesn't mean that it's always easy when I am faced with a playroom that looks like it's been hit by a hurricane.

This section addresses the often difficult transition from the focus on the outside world to the home, and coming to terms with our domestic role.

BLAH-BUSTER TIDBIT

Thinking of Bracha

by Sara Shapiro[1]

One night I called Bracha to get an idea for dinner. "Oh, I have a delicious recipe and it's easy as pie. Dice up some onions and peppers." (She might have also said tomatoes.) "Sauté it in a frying pan and then scramble it up with some eggs and mmmm! They'll love it."

I did as Bracha said, and it was much easier than pie. Not only that. They ate it.

It wasn't that I'd never made this dish before, but I think Bracha's confidence in its scrumptiousness must have affected the way I served it, and probably even the way I cooked it.

A lot of her confidence in the kitchen came from the fact that Bracha just loved cooking. Once, during one of Bracha's recovery periods following chemotherapy, she asked [a doctor] for advice about how to get her strength back. He said it was very important to do something she loved doing every day, and she said, "What I love most of all is cooking and keeping a house."

Another factor in the intense pleasure she took in cooking and housekeeping was the dignity and significance she accorded those activities.... One particular memory that keeps coming back to me about Bracha is how she called up one day a little after one o'clock and asked what I was doing. Feeling bored and depressed, I said I was just making lunch and waiting for the children to come home from school.

"How nice." She sighed fondly. "You're making lunch. And waiting for the children to come home from school. Isn't that nice."

How much pleasure Bracha took in having energy and mobility – the ability to do. As I go about my various life chores, I try to bear in mind how one woman treasured the privilege of standing before a stove, sweeping a floor, taking out the garbage, putting in a load of laundry, folding towels, serving a meal, cleaning up afterwards.

As she used to say, "Enjoy it, mammele, it doesn't last forever."

---

[1] Sarah Shapiro, *A Gift Passed Along: A Woman Looks at the World around Her* (New York: 2002), 98–99.

THE FLYLADY AND ME

TWO MONTHS AGO, I met Aviva for our weekly playdate at the park, and she told me about Flylady.org, the website that has hundreds of thousands of American women excited about making their beds, decluttering their medicine cabinets, and generally taking baby steps, baby steps towards full and total recovery from chronic CHAOS or Can't Have Anybody Over Syndrome.

Aviva told me about how the Flylady updates have gotten her really motivated about cleaning and have taught her an easy system for keeping her house orderly. Her husband is thrilled, she told me with a stunned look, and she is also proud of her newfound ability to keep her house tidy with such ease. As a person who has always hated cleaning and all sorts of domestic work, I wondered whether Flylady could help me too.

I was raised from an early age to see housework as the greatest drudgery imaginable. In my family, cleaning was always something that you paid other people to do for you or that I did on rare occasion, and even then with the minimum amount of effort possible accompanied by the maximum amount of complaining. For as long as I can remember, I was encouraged to spend all of my time studying and working and developing my mind and creativity and talents.

This was a wonderful way to grow up. It meant that I could invest all of my energies in learning new things, thinking about the world, and being a good student. And the truth is that if I hadn't been raised this way, there is a good chance that you wouldn't be reading this book today. However, on the downside, while this would have been the perfect upbringing for a career woman with a full-time maid, as a stay-at-home mother busy taking care of three kids ages four and under, being a mommy is the only profession that interests me at the moment, which means that there is a certain amount of housework I have to do in order to keep our home functioning and livable.

And my background leaves me absolutely stuck when it comes to the housewifely duties of the full-time mom, even with a helpful husband and a cleaning lady once a week. Since I married, I have seen every sinkful of dishes as a punishment, every stack of laundry to fold as an insult to my intelligence, every hour spent cleaning and cooking as a journey to misery and back, for myself as well as for my family.

At the same time, now that I have become a mother, I have seen over and over that there are many women out there who manage to maintain a fairly or even very positive attitude towards housekeeping. For example, we are close to a family with whom we have spent many Shabbats over the years. When we arrive there late on Friday afternoon, the mother is usually mopping the floors, ironing her kids' Shabbat outfits, or cleaning off the kitchen counters. She has spent the whole day on her feet, making two kinds of chicken for dinner, seven casseroles for lunch, five kinds of cakes for unexpected guests, and then cleaning the house with her older children. And this all comes at the end of a long, intense week working as a psychologist and taking care of her eight children.

But every time I see her on these late Friday afternoons, I am surprised anew to see that while she is tired, she is also in high spirits. I see that she derives a great sense of accomplishment from keeping her home clean, sweet satisfaction to know that there is no pile of gunk left in her kitchen sink, and real pride that each child is neatly dressed in an ironed white Shabbat shirt or dress to wear. When I see her, I realize the extent to which, as I was growing up, I learned about the wonderful satisfaction of studying for hours and scoring well on a test, or trying my hardest and finally turning in a term paper of which I was proud. But that I never ever learned how to feel happy about putting in an hour of hard work so that I could see the very bottom of my laundry basket – with nary an unmatched stocking or Lego piece blocking my view of the bottom's wicker spiral. Or about a morning spent in the kitchen creating a birthday cake in the shape of a butterfly that will bring a huge smile to Tiferet's face.

Seeing women like this mother has made me understand that I would be a happier person if I could learn to feel satisfied as well, at least a little bit, by my daily domestic accomplishments. While I could go around thinking for the rest of my life that every moment I spend on the physical aspects of maintaining a home and raising a family is a waste of my potential, this would also mean living a life that is too bitter and miserable to bear.

So the evening after Aviva told me about Flylady, I went to check it out. Right away, I could see what it is about the Flylady that speaks to so many women. She asks, "Do you feel overwhelmed, overextended, and overdrawn? Hopeless and you don't know where to start? Don't worry, friend, we've been there, too. Step through the door and follow Flylady as she weaves her way through housecleaning and organizing with a skip in her step and a smile on her lips."

The Flylady suggests, for example, that we dedicate a few days of every month to each one of the five zones of the house: the entrance area, the kitchen and dining room, the living room, the children's rooms, and the parents' bedroom, and each night cleaning intensely in that day's zone for fifteen minutes until our Flylady timers go off. Before you know it, she assures site visitors, you will have a clean house! She recommends, also, planning every morning what you will serve for dinner that night, so that you don't start worrying about this at 6 PM when you realize that all you have in your cupboards are two cans of sardines and a jar of applesauce with an expiration date from two weeks ago. But more than the actual, concrete suggestions of the Flylady, what I love most about her is her energy, her enthusiasm for cleaning, her sense of purpose, drive, mission even. Where do I sign up?

So that evening, I printed up my first Flylady assignment, and I was nervous with excitement as I waited for my kids to fall asleep and my husband to leave for his class so that I could fill both sinks with scalding water all the way to the rim, and put in a cup of Dr. Pepper-scented St. Moritz and let it sit for an hour. Then I let out the water, scrubbed with Ajax, and shined the sinks with window cleaner. And since then, for the past two weeks, my sinks have been as white as newly-purchased dentures.

But to clarify, it's not just that I don't mind cleaning since I started following the Flylady's rules. For the past two months, if a guest overstays her welcome, or if I am delayed at a less than riveting wedding, I get tense with expectation while counting the minutes until I can get home to clean.

Once on my own, I set my new timer to fifteen minutes, and I'm off. What a strange thing to suddenly look forward to something I so recently hated with such a passion.

Malka, my neighbor who is a Karliner Hasid and the mother of ten children, is my Flylady role model. Tiferet attends nursery school on the top floor of her house, so every morning I sneak a peek into her kitchen as I walk by to take Tiferet up the stairs. The kitchen is totally bare. There is nothing in sight except for three gray plastic containers on the counter for tea, coffee, and sugar, a *bencher*[1] on the tennis-ball green kitchen table, and a black-and-white picture of a rebbe that, Malka explained to me, is a *segula* [charm] to scare away the mice.

Malka and her Yiddish-speaking friends have never even seen the Internet, but even without the Flylady, they are the Flylady heavyweight champions of the world. They are out of my league, though. They are Olympic triathletes, and I am still trying to run around the whole track without stopping for a breather.

But still, I am making a lot of progress since I've started following the Flylady's directives. My kitchen counters are no longer scattered with crumpled drawings from nursery school, wrinkled tomato halves, and bowls of Cheerios attracting swarms of fruit flies. For the past two months, my kitchen has been as clean all week as it used to be for only about an hour a year on Passover Eve, after my husband covered the counters and sinks with extra-thick tinfoil, and before I made my annual triple batch of matzah muffins.

Like Aviva's husband, Josh is thrilled with the Flylady. He grew up in a spotless home and has always been the neat one in our marriage. While over the past six years I have managed to keep his expectations very low, when he came home the other night and saw me dusting the bookshelves in the living room in meditative silence, he stopped muttering about the fifteen flyminders a day clogging our inbox. Yesterday, he bought me a bouquet of yellow roses sprinkled with little purple flowers and said that they should take the Nobel Peace Prize away from Jimmy Carter and give it to the

---

[1] A booklet that contains the prayer recited after eating a meal.

Flylady for the domestic tranquility she's bringing to so many homes.

But to be honest, while I now love cleaning, I still have deeply mixed feelings about the kind of extreme cleanliness that the Flylady promotes. I feel like entering my kitchen nowadays is an almost eerie experience, like canoeing to the deepest depths of the Amazon basin in search of a rainforest, and finding only a desert whistling in the moonlight.

On the one hand, I love to have a clean house and to make Josh so happy, but on the other hand, I grew up in a house that was the polar opposite of Malka's. It was full of dusty Persian rugs, overstuffed, cat-hair-covered sofas, and copies of *Scientific American* and *National Geographic* that had been lying forgotten behind the sofa for a decade or more.

And the truth is that the cluttered coziness of my childhood home is part of what makes visiting my parents so wonderful. When I walk into their house, I see my childhood and the life of our family frozen in time like a dinosaur preserved whole in a tar pit. To walk into the living room and see the soft light seeping through the Venetian blinds onto the walls coated with books, and to find a letter I placed between two volumes of the Jewish Encyclopedia when I was a high-school sophomore, are some of the most satisfying and safest feelings in the world.

I love the neatness of Flylady, the sense of completion, of going through the playroom and ending up with a huge trash bag full of toys to give away, leaving that room clean and clear and orderly. But on the other hand, in the part of my heart where nostalgia lives, somewhere between my second and third ventricle, I crave the fertility and security of the Leaning Tower of Pisa of books and letters and newspapers on the kitchen table of my youth. I long for the dusty mahogany shelves crowded with decades worth of collected knickknacks – a house that contains bits and pieces of the family's life stashed away, just waiting to be discovered in every crevice and cranny.

Postscript

This Flylady mania, for better or worse, only lasted six months or so. Today, two years after I first shined my sink with window cleaner, I still have a more positive attitude to housework than I did pre-Flylady, but my relationship with cleaning is still very much a work in progress.

BLAH-BUSTER TIDBIT

Homebound Holiness[1]

Rabbi Shimshon Dovid Pinkus traveled around the world speaking about the power of sincere prayer. One of the most important topics to him was women's special gift to connect with Hashem naturally, through spontaneous prayer in their own words. He implored women to speak with Hashem for support like a second husband/mother/friend as we go about our days in our homes – comforting a child who is teething, peeling potatoes for kugel, or crying with frustration at a neighbor's thoughtless comment.

Rabbi Pinkus spoke often about his great-grandmother, a deeply religious woman who never learned how to read Hebrew because, he explained, she did not have any need to pray from a prayer book. He recalls how she prayed in Polish, crying out to God from the bottom of her heart as she went about her day. In her own words, he insists, she was able to express her needs, her love, and her dependence on Hashem better than if she read every word of Shaharit, Minha, and Maariv.

Rabbi Pinkus led the prayers for his community every year on Yom Kippur. He described how he would spend the whole day on his feet praying with great emotion and sincerity, and how his prayers would rise to Heaven, where they would stand behind a locked gate. At that point, one of the women in his community who was home taking care of her small children, "with a prayer book in one hand and a bottle in another," would start crying as she prayed for God to have mercy on her husband and children and the Jewish people. And it was, he explained, in the merit of that one young mother crying on her living room sofa that the prayers of the whole congregation would pass through the unlocked gate and make their way up to Hashem, just as the Talmud assures us that the gates of prayer are locked to everything except tears.[2]

Rabbi Pinkus also liked to tell the following story:

A husband says to his wife, "My dear wife, I feel so sorry for you that you don't wear tzitzit [ritual fringes]."

---

[1] Rabbi S. D. Pinkus, *Elul: Ani le-Dodi ve-Dodi Li*. Yad Shimshon, audio recording.

[2] Babylonian Talmud, Tractate *Berakhot* 32b.

She answers, "Don't feel sorry for me. I feel sorry for you. Why do men wear tzitzit? Because you must wear them in order to remember Hashem's Throne of Glory. But I always remember the Creator of the world because I spend my days in the house speaking with Hashem, and not distracted by everything I see in the streets like you."

"But, my dear wife, don't you feel badly that according to the Torah you are not commanded to hear the shofar?"

"Why would I need to hear the shofar? If any man would ever give birth, he would know why I don't need a shofar in order to awaken my heart to call out to Hashem."

"But, my poor, dear wife, you are not even commanded to dwell with the Divine Presence in the Succah."

"What do I need to dwell in the succah for? My house is a succah filled with the Divine Presence the whole year round. I sit in my home and my baby is crying, and I am together with the Creator of the World no less than you are when you study Torah in your Succah."

The Jewish woman in her home is always with the Creator of the World as she speaks with Hashem in her own words, in the language of her heart.

MOTHER MONARCHS AND THE MESSIAH

TONIGHT IS TISHA BE-AV, the anniversary of the destruction of the First and Second Temples. Last year around this time, I heard a famous rebbetzin speak about the destruction of the Temple, and right there, in front of an auditorium full of people, this woman started crying. This rebbetzin is someone I know fairly well, and she is not a person to start crying over nothing. In fact, I have never seen this rebbetzin lose her composure except for that time, and for weeks I was pretty bewildered by it. Her tears got me thinking about the destruction of the Temple, and in particular about why the thought of the events of Tisha be-Av did not make me as upset as they made her.

And then I realized something that had not occurred to me: that it was the destruction of the Temple that set us off on the past two-thousand-year journey to Hell and back again (at least almost) that the exile has been. Two thousand years that, despite pockets and centuries of relative quiet and peaceful coexistence with our non-Jewish rulers and neighbors, has been all too full of crusades, inquisitions, pogroms, one nearly successful attempt at genocide, as well as the Israeli wars and terror attacks of recent years. I realized that Tisha be-Av is the paradigm for all these tragedies that we have suffered as a people, as well as their starting point.

Which leads me (at least sort of) to tell you about this past Shabbat spent at Moshav Keshet in the Golan Heights and the two classes I taught there about my new book *Expecting Miracles* – one to a visiting group of American college students, and one to a group of Israeli mothers from the moshav where we were staying.

On Friday night after dinner, I spoke to the students, almost all of them single, new to observant Judaism, and trying to figure out what to do with their lives. Since *Expecting Miracles* came out two months ago, I have been giving classes to married women around the Jerusalem area pretty much nonstop, and the classes have been, I think and hope, very successful. In the classes, I have used stories from the book to show how Judaism provides women with the tools to overcome the challenges of pregnancy, birth, and motherhood. When we were preparing for the trip to the Golan, I didn't have a chance to make up a new source sheet for a special class for these students, so I decided to give the same class to these students that I had been giving to the married mothers.

So there I was, late on Friday night, telling these young women about Jewish motherhood and pregnancy. I told them a story about a powerhouse mother of fifteen kids, and another woman who screams out the names of childless women while she gives birth, and another mother who adopted a child after twenty years of infertility. I talked about the ways in which the Torah gives the women in the book the power to cope and triumph over challenges. Usually, when I say these things to mothers, I look around and see that everybody is with me. I see smiles and nods, and even a few tears if I'm really on.

But that night, I looked around me, and saw that I had totally lost them. I saw thirty pairs of blank, exhausted, and confused eyes. I tried to tell them that I was giving them a peek into what their lives would look like, with God's help, in a decade or two. I told them how nobody had ever spoken with me about the lives of religious mothers when I was their age, about their strength, and heroism, and spirituality, and wisdom, and that I wanted them to know that they were headed, God willing, for a future that would be very challenging and also incredibly rewarding.

But when I went home that night my heart was very low, since I felt that, with a few exceptions, I had not gotten through to them at all. I lay in bed for a while unable to sleep, and then, in an effort to cheer myself up, I got out of bed so I could watch my children as they slept, smiling at Dafna's propped-up knee sticking out of her blanket and Nisa's quiet snoring out of her open mouth. But even this did not help. As I sat at the foot of Dafna's bed, I realized that while it is inspiring to tell a thirty-year-old mother of three about a woman who screams out names during her births or a mother who raised fifteen children in two rooms, for most American twenty-year-olds, that is more scary and problematic than inspiring.

One nervous student came up to me the following day and said that she was going to law school, and how could she possibly balance being a lawyer with having so many kids? Another told me that she was worried that she would not be able to raise children and also find time to invest in her own spirituality. Instead of inspiring them, I had managed to scare them with all my talk of large families and fulfillment through motherhood. I even overheard one student saying, "As though Jewish women are nothing but baby factories!" Ouch.

I felt very down until I went the following afternoon to speak to the women from Moshav Keshet. A lot of young mothers live in Keshet, but to my surprise, the women who came to my talk were all over forty. Not that they were out of the swing of motherhood though. One mother nursed a newborn, and another one rocked her one-year-old in a baby carriage.

The night before, I had found myself in the role of the expert, the experienced mother who would tell these single women a thing or two about motherhood, and I had failed to a large extent. And I came to these women and I felt like the chairs had been switched. All of a sudden I was the new mother who needed to be encouraged, inspired, told that everything would be OK.

I felt right away that there was something very special about these women. After a few minutes, I realized that what struck me about them was the royalty of these women who, in most cases, had spent the last twenty years raising families of eight and more children, washing dishes, making roasted chicken for Shabbat, ironing their husbands' shirts, and working a bit on the side to make ends meet. But, instead of being worn-out, embittered dishrags, as I would have assumed before I became a mother, an intense regimen of motherhood had transformed them over the decades into women whose faces absolutely shine with kindness, holiness, and dignity.

As I sat with them, I felt so moved by these mothers that I had to hold myself back from crying. But I held myself back and I gave the class, and the women rewarded me with big smiles and nods of recognition and appreciation even though I felt ridiculous that I was the one teaching when I was certain that of all the women in the room, I had by far the least to teach.

So I went back to the guest house feeling on top of the world and telling myself: "You win some, you lose some." And I thought, if only I had kept my mouth shut the night before and had simply taken these visiting students to meet these mothers, then they would have understood what I was trying to tell them. They would have seen how a person can progress from being a confused single woman to an overwhelmed young mother to a mother monarch, absolutely confident of her place in the world and in God's eyes.

This week, Rebbetzin Yemima Mizrachi told us a great story. In Sephardic communities, it is a common tradition for women to start scrubbing and cleaning their houses during the afternoon of the Tisha be-Av fast. Just in case the Messiah arrives on that Tisha be-Av, they wouldn't want him to show up and see what a mess their kids had made while they were passed out on the sofa the whole day dying of thirst.

One year, many years ago, a rabbi in Morocco decided that this was a ridiculous tradition, and he announced in synagogue that the women should not clean their houses that Tisha be-Av. Later that week, that same rabbi was walking in the market, and he overheard the following discussion between two mothers:

"Did you hear what the rabbi said this past Shabbat?"

"No, I didn't hear."

"He told us that the Messiah is not coming this year!"

"What do you mean?!"

"He told us that we don't even have to clean our houses this year, since the Messiah's not coming anyway!"

In light of this story, Rabbi Ovadia Yosef, the leading rabbi of the Sephardic world, declared that women do not have to clean their houses on Tisha be-Av. However, if you know a woman who does this, it is forbidden to tell her that she should not do so, since it is only in the merit of the absolute "blind" faith of Jewish mothers that the Jewish people continues to exist at all. Over the past three millennia of Jewish nationhood, our men have found, on many occasions, all sorts of rationalizations and justifications to chase after the bright lights of the dominant non-Jewish culture. But Jewish women have tended to trust the feeling in their gut that tells them that the most important thing they can do in life is cling to the Torah and *Hashem* like a life preserver as they are tossed about within the vast ocean of Persian, Greek, Roman, Christian or Muslim or secular cultures.

So, on this eve of Tisha be-Av, I would like to draw our attention to the accomplishments of ordinary, everyday mothers in whose merit, our holy Rabbis teach us, the Messiah will finally come. The ones like the women I met in Keshet, who believe that by raising their children to be mensches who keep the Torah, that they are doing something of tremendous, everlasting importance. And the accomplishments of the mothers who still weep over the destruction of our holy Temple two millennia ago, and who continue to pray that this Tisha be-Av the Messiah will show up on their doorstep right before *minha*,[1] just in time for them to welcome him into their kitchen with the newly washed floor and offer him a cup of coffee and a piece of the chocolate cake that they had covered with plastic wrap and set aside in the fridge just for him.

---

[1] The afternoon prayer.

STEP SIX

CHOOSING TO GROW FROM HARDSHIP

SIX MONTHS AGO we hired a cleaning lady. She was a nice lady who fawned over my children, was easy to get along with, and did a great job. I recommended her to all of my friends, and before long this woman had so much work that she was turning away jobs. And then, yesterday, I discovered that this woman, in addition to all of her positive traits, was also a thief who stole hundreds and possibly thousands of dollars from my friends and me.

About a decade ago I read a book called *It's All a Gift*,[1] which teaches how to see the good hidden in terrible events, and this book improved my life immensely. Because of this book, this morning I was able to think about what happened, and instead of kicking myself for being such an idiot – for hiring this lady without recommendations, for leaving my wallet in an easy-to-find place, for recommending her to everyone I know – I was able to focus on the gift well-hidden within this irritating turn of events. This morning, instead, I can feel like an absolute idiot who has, as of today, learned to be a bit more careful and cautious about the housekeepers I welcome into my house and recommend to others. Today, I can feel like an idiot who was given an opportunity to thank God from the bottom of my heart that everything in my life that is truly important (or more exactly, everyone) is safe and sound. As of today, I can feel like an idiot who is, slowly but surely, becoming a bit less of one.

The essays in this chapter address difficult situations in the life of the Jewish mother: the tragic loss of a sick child, and about raising children in the frightening war zone that Jerusalem became during the most recent Intifada. They are about the difficult things we struggle with in life, and who we become in the process.

---

[1] Dr. Miriam Adahan, *It's All a Gift* (New York: 1992).

BLAH-BUSTER TIDBIT

It's All a Gift

by Dr. Miriam Adahan[1]

Rabbi Moshe Feinstein zt"l[2] once underwent a difficult medical procedure without anesthesia. When he did not cry out, his doctor asked him how this was possible. Rabbi Moshe replied that he was able to bear the pain because he was totally focused on how much more sensitive he now would be to the pain others might suffer who had to go through similar experiences. In other words, he concentrated on what he was getting in terms of his own expanded awareness, and not what he was feeling....

In the Ashrei prayer the word kol (all) appears seventeen times to remind us that our spiritual avodah [service of God] is to practice seeing everything [that happens to us in our lives] as a gift, to truly experience that whatever He does is necessary, wise and good. It is not an easy attitude to adopt.

We don't have much of a choice. Either we focus on the gifts, such as the revelations about man and God and the sensitivity and understanding which challenging situations bring us, or we become bitter and deadened to the Godliness in ourselves and in the world.

Example: "I have a very critical boss who makes life unpleasant for me. I used to stew in silent hostility the entire day until I began saying, 'She's a gift." Since I can't switch jobs, I use this as an opportunity to remind myself that my value comes from God, not people. For someone like me, who was always so crushed by people's opinions, I feel like a winner on a spiritual plane, even if my boss thinks I'm a loser. It's painful to face her day after day. In fact, I feel like my ego is being pulverized. But if that's what God wants me to deal with right now, then I can use her criticism to strengthen my sense of my inherent Godly value."

---

[1] Dr. Miriam Adahan, *It's All a Gift*. 12–13, 22–23.

[2] Rabbi Moshe Feinstein (1895–1986) was the *Rosh Yeshiva* (dean) of Mesivta Tiferes Yerushalayim, a *yeshiva* in New York. Rabbi Feinstein became the leading halakhic (religious law) authority of his time.

JERUSALEM MOTHER

WHEN A CAR BOMB exploded near the central market this past fall, the blast was so powerful that I ran out to the porch to see whether the building next door was still standing. My elderly neighbor was already on her porch conferring on the phone with her children who live outside of the city. She turned towards me, and it looked like her face was in shadow when she put her hand over the receiver and mouthed the words, "Shomron Street." We shook our heads slowly at one another, and as I went back inside and locked the porch door behind me, I felt my body start to shake.

Shomron Street, the next street over from my own, is one that I walk down several times day. Ever since the start of Israel's newest Intifada two months before that terrible November afternoon, when I was on my way home from shopping or errands, as soon as I reached Shomron Street, I would let myself relax again. I knew that if I'd gotten all the way to Shomron Street then I was safe; I had survived that outing. I was as good as home.

That afternoon, once back inside, I looked at myself closely in the bathroom mirror to make sure that my face bore no traces of what I had just heard, and then I opened the door to the girls' room and placed Dafna back on my lap to finish reading *The Very Hungry Caterpillar* before her afternoon nap while Tiferet tried, without success, to capture the clowns in her mobile. After the kids fell asleep, I called our families in America and Canada to tell them that we were OK, and then I turned on CNN.com to watch live video footage of the sheet-covered bodies and fire raging a block from our house.

After eight years of living in Jerusalem, I have more or less gotten used to being thrown back and forth by the waves of shock, mourning, and recovery that are part of living in this city whose name fills prayer books as well as newspaper headlines. But after the bombing on Shomron Street, things were different. That explosion, so close that I felt the impact of the blast in my body, pushed me into a state of shock that would not budge.

For weeks and months afterward, I looked pretty much like all the people around me who appeared to proceed through life business-as-usual despite the ongoing attacks: I took care of Dafna and Tiferet, I wrote in the mornings, I smiled at neighbors and shopkeepers. But despite the many responsibilities and distractions that make up my day, the only thing I could think about, no matter what I was doing, was how fast my heart was racing.

I knew, despite my terrible anxiety, that Jerusalem is the only place I want to be, the only city I have ever lived where I manage to wake up in the morning without an alarm clock. I love being in a place where Hebrew, a language I once associated only with Saturday morning boredom, is the language of songs from nursery school, morning *shaloms* on the street, and Jewish books full of ideas so true (and new, at least to me) that they leave me hungry for more. I love living in a country that is a common homeland to my French pediatrician, my Kurdish watch repairman, and my Hungarian neighbor, all of whom cluck their tongues at my crying baby with as much sympathy as a team of long-lost uncles. I love going to a synagogue where we sing so loud and dance so long that curious crowds gather by the windows. I also love that we sing louder when we get to the part about "*Yerushalayim.*"

For the eight years that I have lived here, I have never doubted that our life in Israel and the existence of a Jewish homeland after two thousand years of exile, is an absolute, outright miracle. But after the bombing on Shomron Street, the fear was not going away and my anxiety was becoming so intense, so unceasing, that thoughts of my American passport were the only ones that brought any relief.

When my mother-in-law came for a visit a few months later over Passover vacation, she suggested that we rent a car and drive to the north of the country. I was so terrified because of the security situation that even an outing to buy diapers at the pharmacy felt like a trip to a battlefront. And at the same time, I was so desperate to take a trip out into nature and to get out of the city that I had started daydreaming about lying down on the muddy patch of grass in my children' favorite park.

The fear that had been running my life for the past few months was yelling "No! It's too dangerous!" But I decided, for the first time in a long time, not to listen. Not to say that it was easy. That "No" woke me up several times the night before we set off on our journey, but once I got behind the wheel and saw the deep green hills on the outskirts of the city climbing all around us, it was so intensely beautiful that I almost felt my body rising up right along with my heart. My chest felt actually lighter, and I sensed the corners of my lips being lifted towards the sky that was so blue, so near.

As I drove, I remembered the weekly hikes in those same hills when I was falling in love with my husband, and envisioned adventures there in the years to come with our grown-up girls quoting verses about these hills in unaccented Hebrew from well-thumbed Bibles. That morning, I saw my dreams for my life in those hills so clearly, that the "No" floated away unnoticed, just as the smoke and debris from the bombing had already done several months before.

It is true that I am not a *sabra*, and my skin is not as thick and prickly as life in Israel requires at times. It is hard work for me to remember that Israel has been through difficult times before, and that, with God's help, we will move beyond these difficult times as well.

You will be surprised to hear that, unlike so many other American mothers with children in Israel at this time, my mother is often the one who helps me to maintain perspective. She reminds me during our weekly phone calls, "Even when you think life can't go on, life goes on." And this past week, she reminded me of something else I needed to hear: "Israel is a miracle," she said, "and at times, God gives us miracles that require a lot of hard work."

BLAH-BUSTER TIDBIT
My Wedding Ring

When my husband and I went shopping for my wedding ring at a small jewelry store in downtown Jerusalem, we eventually narrowed our choice down to two rings. When we went to ask the advice of the goldsmith who was working in the back of the store, he took one of the rings we had chosen and observed it from one side and then the other with obvious fondness.

This was, he informed us, the same ring that he had made for his wife a decade before. When he had made her ring, he explained, he had engraved their initials on the inside of the ring, and it had been perfectly smooth and untarnished. But because he had made it out of the purest gold, it was softer than regular rings. Over the years, he told us, their initials had gotten rubbed away, and the ring had become worn. It even looked a bit beaten up, every knock and bump and fall it had experienced over the last ten years had left the smallest mark on it. "But the most wonderful thing about this ring," he explained to us with a smile, "is that the more it goes through, and the more it gets knocked around, the more beautiful it becomes."

My husband and I agreed that that was the best sales pitch for a wedding ring that there ever was; what a tremendous lesson and blessing to bear upon my finger.

EVIL PEOPLE

MY FOUR-YEAR-OLD DAUGHTER has started talking a lot about *reshaim* – evil people. My husband and I are not sure where she picked up on this idea, maybe from all the Jewish holidays that star a *rasha* – Haman on Purim, Antiochus on Hanukkah, Pharaoh on Passover. Or maybe it is the influence of the weekly Torah portion – Noah's contemporaries, Ishmael, Esau. But, whatever the source may be, she has started talking about *reshaim* all the time, and she has started talking about how they are coming to Jerusalem to kill the Jews.

In another decade, in another country, maybe this would pass for a normal phase that children go through as part of their emotional development. But at this moment in Jewish history, her strange fixation makes me exceptionally nervous. I cannot help but wonder whether she is picking up on the feeling of siege shared by all of the residents of Jerusalem over the past two years of Intifada and bombings.

I wonder if I was wrong to tell her the truth when she asked what I was showing Josh on the Internet – a picture of a beautiful, curly-haired, red-lipsticked *reshait* who blew herself up along with an old Jewish man on Jaffa Street last week.

When my parents were visiting over Hanukkah, we saw a death notice next to Dafna's nursery school for a 19-year-old who was tragically murdered by a terrorist along with nine other teenage boys on the Ben Yehuda pedestrian mall late one Saturday night. I explained to my parents what the sign was, and Dafna started asking questions. Was this the Nir that she knew, one of her father's closest friends from his yeshiva days? No, this was another Nir. What happened? The *reshaim* hurt a boy, and he had to go to the hospital. Did he get better? My mother, the grandmother and child psychiatrist, jumped in, "Yes, he's feeling much better." "So we should pray to *Hashem* for him, right *Eema*?" "Right, beautiful, as soon as we get home."

Rebbetzin Talia Helfer was telling us last week that if there are tensions in the home that could cause the children stress, related to finances, health, personal issues, etc. then the mother must be like a sponge, soaking everything up so that the child senses none of it, and can grow up blissful and ignorant in a calm environment. Rabbi Shlomo Aviner also says that a major responsibility of mothers is to make sure that their children can stay children for as long as possible. They will learn about the evils and the tragedies of the world soon enough, and most likely too soon, without any assistance from us.

So last week I went up to Rebbetzin Talia after class and told her that my daughter has been asking about *reshaim*, and how I fear that she has started picking up on our hushed conversations about the daily terrorist attacks around the country. Rebbetzin Talia told me that I should do everything in my power to shield her from these events. And if Dafna still worries, I can calm her down by reading a chapter of Psalms together with her every day, and tell her that we are saying Psalms so that *Hashem* will have mercy on the Jewish people.

But the part that really got to me was when she shook her head after her advice and said, "*Haval she-asitem lah et zeh*" – it's too bad that you have done this to her. In the end, it was not the stories of a threatened Purim genocide that frightened my daughter, or stories of the destruction of the Temple – it was her nervous mother who has been unable to keep her own fear from trickling down to her children.

"It's too bad that you have done this to her," I think as I look down at my little girl intently focused on drawing a picture with her crayons, her tiny waist, her thin arms, her blond hair so wispy it floats as though it has been rubbed with a balloon. Why should she have to grow up frightened?

I decide that, from that moment onward, I am going to guard Dafna from the outside world so that she will be able to have a happy and carefree childhood. The next morning, on day number one of my attempt to shelter Dafna, I drop off Tiferet at her babysitter who is in the middle of making omelets for the children. She is clearly upset, as she gives me a report of all the tragedies of that early morning – a bomb found in an elementary school, four men killed by a bomb in a restaurant in Tel Aviv, a mother shot to death on the road from Gush Etzion. I think of pointing to Dafna, to hint that I do not want her tender ears to hear this kind of news, but how can I do this when Ruti so badly needs to talk? When we walk away, Dafna asks me what Ruti was telling me about. I tell her, "People fell down and hurt themselves."

I walk a bit farther and run into Batya, who also sends her daughter to Dafna's nursery school. We always speak in Hebrew, but she starts speaking with me conspiratorially and nervously in heavily-accented English, as though this is a language that Dafna will not understand. She tells me, "I could not sleep at all last night. Had a dream that the Arab workers from the construction site across the street came to kill me and my family. And today I wake up, and the workers are not here. Must be terror attack this morning, and they make a closure and don't let the Arabs come." I want to point to Dafna again, and tell Batya that I don't want her young ears to hear all this, but that might hurt Batya's feelings, she is so upset as it is. Everyone is so upset today.

At 1:30, I pick Dafna up and walk home with Tirtza, another American mother. Tirtza tells me how she wants to leave Jerusalem, how she is constantly worried that something will happen to her husband who is always walking around the city, to a yeshiva in another part of town, and then to another neighborhood for his work. Maybe they will move to the suburbs, possibly to Bet Shemesh? There, she explains, they will have everything they need – a home, a shul, a grocery store, as well as high-quality schools. They even have a car so that they will be able to drive into Jerusalem for shopping and errands.

She has just given birth, and I suggest that her nervousness might be part of a postpartum reaction, but she dismisses this explanation. And it occurs to me that maybe she is the sane one and I am the one who is acting crazy by trying to keep up a calm front despite the bombs going off day after day, followed inevitably by the sirens of the ambulances rushing by to treat the wounded and evacuate the dead from another bombing.

When I part ways with Tirtza, Dafna looks up at me. She says, "*Eema,* why is everyone falling down all the time?" I remind her that her little sister often falls down since she is just learning how to walk, and I try to distract and protect her by launching into a long and age-inappropriate explanation of the concept of balance.

BLAH-BUSTER TIDBIT

Life in God's Baby Carriage

by Rebbetzin Chava Sara Luban[1]

Rebbetzin Chava Sara Luban z"l was a young woman and newly married when she was diagnosed with a deadly disease that eventually took her life. Up to the week before her death, despite weakness and terrible pain, she taught a weekly class in Jerusalem's Shaarei Hesed neighborhood on prayer and maintaining trust in God through difficult times. On a day when I am grumbling about the half-hour I wasted in line at the bank or a computer virus that erased a week's worth of writing, nothing can help me to regain perspective like listening to the tapes of Chava Sara's last classes. I hear this young woman's voice, so full of kindness and wisdom and absolute faith that everything that is happening to her is Hashem's will, and my mood instantly switches gear from bitterness to gratitude and awe. Gratitude for Hashem's kindness, and awe for the faith of Chava Sara Luban.

The following is a quotation from one of the final classes preceding her death:

> Our relationship with Hashem is like being in a baby carriage, and we're in the baby carriage for the ride. There are a lot of things we have to do in that baby carriage; if we don't do anything in the baby carriage, then we are going to remain babies forever. So we should have that baby mindset of love and trust, knowing that at all times Hashem is pushing our baby carriage, at the same time that we need to develop our independence, our strengths, and exercise our free will.
>
> We need to develop this kind of reciprocal relationship with Hashem, loving Him and trusting Him, and knowing that we receive so much from him, at the same time that we must try to act in the world according to His will. Even when our baby carriage starts heading off down the mountain – Hashem is still holding that baby carriage. It may be bumpy, but that is Hashem's path for us in life.

---

[1] Rebbetzin Chava Sara Luban, *Tape 6: Modeh Ani*. Privately produced audio recording.

THE POWER OF BIRTH
AND THE POWER OF DEATH

A FEW MONTHS AGO somebody sent a question to my website, www.JewishPregnancy.org, asking whether pregnant women are allowed to attend funerals. As soon as I received this email in my inbox, I expected that Rabbi Sperling, the site rabbi, would not like this question so much, since he is against any traditions based on superstition rather than Jewish law. Over the years, I have learned that if any women write to me asking about the merits of red strings worn around wrists or about what kind of pearl to swallow in order to prevent miscarriage, that I should write a polite response saying that Rabbi Sperling is not the address for this question.

But I was not sure whether this question fell into the problematic category or not, and when I actually did ask Rabbi Sperling about pregnant women attending funerals, he was hesitant to give me a clear answer. On the one hand, he explained, there is no real basis in Jewish law for a pregnant woman not to attend a funeral. On the other hand, he explained, if a community has the tradition that pregnant women do not attend funerals, then there is probably some basis for this. And then he said something very strange: "It's something about mixing the power of birth and the power of death."

I did not think about this so much. It was the kind of cryptic statement that I knew was probably very deep, but that I did not have the time or attention span to focus on at that very moment. It is only now, on account of recent events here in Jerusalem, that I have had a chance to ponder Rabbi Sperling's statement once again and to think a bit about what he was getting at.

Last Wednesday, I took Nisa, my one-year-old, to the ATM down the block from our house, and then I took her to the grocery store like I do every week. Five hours later, when my husband and I were on our way to a wedding, that same cash machine was splattered with blood and glass in the latest bus bombing here, inhumanly killing sixteen Jews – depriving children of mothers, wives of husbands, parents of children, may God avenge their blood.

This past Shabbat, like most Shabbats, we had a lot of guests. It was a particularly magical Shabbat with lots of conversation, singing, and words of Torah. One guest, a recent medical school graduate, asked before we started the meal if he could hold Nisa for me. I wasn't sure what to say, since Nisa is going through a phase during which she does not like strangers to hold her, and I get the sense that she is particularly nervous around men she doesn't know. But I said, "Of course," and reluctantly handed over Nisa, expecting a squeal or a scream, requiring an awkward apology and explanation to save this young man's feelings. But Nisa just cuddled up against him, her head resting against his chest, as at ease as she is in my or my husband's arms.

The guest held her for a long time, until we served the chicken soup. I wondered if he had learned how to hold babies so well as part of his medical training, or whether maybe he was an uncle, but when I asked him he said that he had just learned how to hold babies on his own.

During the meal we went around the table so that the guests could introduce themselves, and the baby-holder explained that he would be returning to the United States soon to start his medical residency after he completed a year-long research project with the Ministry of Health. In his project he was researching the volunteers of ZAKA, a religious organization that sends its volunteers to the sites of terror attacks in order to administer first aid, often before the ambulances arrive, and to make sure that the dead bodies, or body fragments, are taken care of and collected with the tremendous respect dictated by Jewish law.

When the meal was over, at 1:30 in the morning, Josh and I walked all the guests out to the street, and when they had all gone, this young man stood with us for a few extra moments. He said that there was something he wanted to tell us that he had not wanted to say at the table – that as part of his research, he had gone to the site of the terror attack that past Wednesday with the ZAKA volunteers. He had seen people screaming in pain from their wounds, people dying whom he could not save despite his years of medical training, and afterwards, he had called his sister in America, and told her that more than anything he needed at that moment it was to hold a baby, to hold a new life in his hands. But he did not know where he would find a baby to hold until he came to our house that night.

In the times of the Temple, there were strict rules about maintaining ritual purity, and the supreme cause of impurity was contact with a dead body. And in the whole world there were only two places where a dead body did not cause impurity – in a ritual bath and in the womb. And the womb, the source of life, is still a place that death cannot touch.

This young man's story reminded me of Nisa's birth on Lag ba-Omer the year before. Lag ba-Omer is the anniversary of the death of Rabbi Shimon bar Yohai, who spent thirteen years hiding from the Romans and studying Torah in a cave with his son. Rabbi Shimon and his son would have certainly died from starvation if it had not been for a great miracle (*Nisa* in Aramaic), the appearance in the cave of a carob tree as well as a spring of water. And that was how Nisa got her name: from the miraculous, sustaining spring and carob tree that God made for Rabbi Shimon bar Yohai.

We chose Nisa's name because, as my husband explained at the kiddush in her honor, when a baby is born the parents cannot help but see what a miracle has just occurred, and that this new baby is a gift directly from *Hashem*. But he prayed that her name itself would remind us of this fact day after day, so that we would never forget the miracle of that Lag ba-Omer night even when our little Nisa was a year old, or eighteen years old, or forty-two years old. He prayed that we would always look into her face and know that we had merited to be the parents of a special soul and a great light sent by God into the world to banish the darkness, even when that darkness is as split-pea-soup thick as it has been in Jerusalem for these past few years.

BLAH-BUSTER TIDBIT

The Coffee Bean Blessing

I recently read a story about a girl named Estie who asked her grandmother how human beings can cope with all of the suffering that life sends our way. Her grandmother was cooking, and Estie thought that she was simply ignoring her as she tended to her pots – putting an egg in one, a carrot in another, and some ground coffee in the last.

After a few minutes, the grandmother removed the egg, the carrot, and the coffee from their pots, and asked the girl, "What do you see, my dear?" Estie said that she saw a hardened egg and a mushy carrot, and smelled the delicious coffee.

Her grandmother said, "In these foods, you see the answer to your question. People cope differently, even when facing the same difficulty. You saw how I placed each object in boiling water, but the difference between how each food reacted to the boiling water was very great.

"The carrot that used to be hard was placed in hot water, and became extremely soft, so that it will fall apart under the slightest pressure. The egg, which was liquid and so delicate under its thin shell, was placed in the hot water, and then became completely hardened. Only the coffee beans retained and expressed their true character in the boiling water. After being placed in hot water, they changed the water itself into something totally different, into something better.

"And which one will you be like, my dear granddaughter? When suffering comes to your door, how will you react? Are you like the carrot which looks so strong, but becomes weak and frightened when things get tough? Or are you like the egg, which continues to appear the same on the outside after experiencing loss or the death of a loved one, even when on the inside your heart has become hardened and jaded?

"And maybe you will imitate the coffee bean, whose role in life is to find the spark of goodness and potential inside the painful situation. People who are like coffee beans grow on account of a painful situation, becoming more sensitive to the pain of others, performing more acts of kindness, and growing closer to Hashem. As a result of their suffering, they take the boiling water of this world and cool it down a little bit for everyone."[1]

---

[1] Rieder-Reichman, Estie. "Editor's Note." *Mishpaha Tova* 43 (March 2004): 5.

GOODBYE, YOSEF CHAI

THIS PAST SHABBAT I ran into Rebbetzin Yemima walking down the street with Yosef Chai, her year-old son whom we have all been praying for so much over the past year. This Shabbat, Yemima, the person I know who is most likely to be mistaken for a movie star, looked pale and thin and worn by grief and worry. When I asked her how Yosef Chai was, she shot me her classic ironic smile and said, "Now, you know better than to ask a question like that on Shabbat."

And then, only two days later, when I was taking Tiferet to nursery school, I saw one of the smallest death notices I've ever seen. As I got closer and saw the name "Yosef Chai Mizrachi," I gasped. Tiferet asked me what happened, and I could not speak, my throat swollen with held-back tears.

Even though I only saw him a handful of times over the course of his thirteen-month life, I felt a real closeness with Yosef Chai. Looking back, I see that my connection with this holy little boy taught me a great deal. After months of praying for him day after day along with my own children, Dafna, Tiferet, Nisa… Yosef Chai, I would often long to see him, almost like a physical urge to see this beautiful little boy, so cute and cuddly that it took Yemima's pointing out to make me notice the blue feet, nose and fingertips that medical residents would make a special trip to see, in real life and not only in their textbooks, accompanied by an unpronounceable name.

For weeks, I had wanted to stop by to take a picture of Yosef Chai just so that I could keep a picture of him near my computer to make me smile, so that I wouldn't miss him so much. But, like a lot of things I think of doing, I never got around to it, and now the truth is that it is a bit of a relief. I just would not be able to see his face and know that I can no longer walk a few blocks and knock on Yemima's door and see him in her arms.

I can't exactly express what was so special about him. Maybe it was that Yosef Chai was a boy who seemed totally magical. A child who doctors said would never regain consciousness after a heart attack six months ago was laughing and playing with his adoring siblings at home a month later. Anyway, who ever heard of a child born with only two heart chambers who actually lived? And not only lived, but lived with such vigor and joy for life?

Yosef Chai never once ate a piece of solid food. He spent his life on a strict diet of mother's milk, sustained by liquid love. And this is how I remember him. Just as God rides on the praises of the Jewish people, so too was Yosef Chai sustained solely by Yemima's milk and the constant prayers of the hundreds of people who prayed every day for his well-being. I remember him glowing despite his blueness, a life that defied reason, medical realities, despair, a little boy who was the physical embodiment of faith and impossible hope.

A few months ago, this past spring, I went to visit Yemima, and she told me that she was taking Yosef Chai to the hospital to do the second operation in a series to repair his heart. Twice they had set a date for this operation, and both times Yemima and her husband had contacted everyone they knew and told them to pray, and then, right before the operation, there had been a disaster. Once, Yosef Chai even had a heart attack (isn't a heart attack something that you are supposed to have when you are seventy, and not seven months?) So, as I left that day, Yemima told me that because of the previous failed attempts, this time they had not told a soul that they were doing the operation, which was a dangerous one for Yosef Chai. She said, "You are the only person I am telling. When you light candles this Friday night, know that it's all on you." I assumed she was joking, but she repeated this phrase, "Only you," and I looked closely at her face, and saw she wasn't smiling when she said it.

I've prayed for sick people in the past, and I know just how terribly flaky I can be about it. What, as though my prayers actually make a difference? Why would God care one little bit about what I have to say? As though there aren't another thousand people also praying for him? But that Friday night, I stood for a whole twenty minutes by my candles, praying for Yosef Chai, crying and crying to *Hashem* to have mercy on him, to have pity on his holy mother and father and sisters and brothers who love him so much. And as I stood there, I imagined the impossible, that one day I would dance at

Yosef Chai's wedding and I would say to Yemima, "Who would have thought twenty years ago that we would be standing here today?" and she would wipe away a tear and nod as we remembered for one brief moment the despair that we had worked ourselves up into so foolishly so many years before.

After that Shabbat, I spoke with a few women, and it turned out that a bunch of us had actually known about the operation, and had prayed for Yosef Chai when we lit Shabbat candles. But what a lesson! I have never prayed like that in my whole life, really believing that everything depended on me, really believing that God (maybe, maybe) hears me. And ever since that Friday night, prayer feels different. It's not something so dramatic, so revolutionary. But I feel as though something clicked that night, like a dislocated elbow snapped back into place, or as though I'd been doing needlepoint for years wearing big bulky gloves, and then one day I took them off and realized that I could do the work better if I stripped my hands bare and got to work, even though it is a bit scarier that way. It's so much easier to get pricked by the needle and bleed that way.

And now I walk around Nahlaot, and I see the broken women remembering the hours they spent praying for Yosef Chai, or the women who spent days searching on the Internet for information to save him, or corresponding on Yemima's behalf with doctors in America and Germany, looking and looking for some sort of cure. And now, the end of hope, the train to salvation derailed. Since I heard of his passing, I still find myself thinking from time to time, "Maybe they could still do a heart transplant." And then I remember with a terrible jolt that we've passed over the line from very, very sick and dying to dead.

Yemima was supposed to take Yosef Chai to a diagnostic procedure to look inside his heart a week before he died. The specialist had told her that there was a good chance that Yosef Chai would not survive the procedure, which meant that she and her husband found themselves in an impossible situation – he couldn't survive without the procedure, and it was likely that he wouldn't survive with it either. So she told me that she had pushed off the appointment by a few weeks, and said, "I am supposed to take him tomorrow to this hospital where they are sure that he is going to die on the operating table, but I said to my husband, I don't agree! *Ani lo maskima!* If I can have one more day with him or one more month with him, then I choose a month!"

And Yemima was right. She and her family had exactly one more week with Yosef Chai, a week in which she held him, prayed for him, and knew more intensely than any other mother on the planet that the baby she held was a total gift from *Hashem*, a total miracle.

The last time I saw Yosef Chai was the day before he left this world. Yemima joked, "It used to be that people looked at me, and now all they look at are Yosef Chai's blue feet." Yosef Chai looked so adorable, so alive despite his encroaching blueness, that I couldn't imagine that the doctors were actually right, that just over twenty-four hours later his two-chambered heart would simply stop beating as his mother held him in the hospital ICU. In one moment he looked upwards towards the One who was calling him home, and his soul left his sick little body.

And isn't it supposed to be that when you believe in the eternity of the soul, death is not so sad? Right? But there is no way around the longing, the longing for Yosef Chai, the longing for a baby to nurse and push around in a baby carriage and hold and love.

May *Hashem* send comfort to this broken and mourning family, to our holy Rebbetzin Yemima and her husband Rabbi Chaim Mizrachi and to their whole family. May *Hashem* comfort them among all of the rest of the mourners of Zion and Jerusalem. Amen.

STEP SEVEN

DON'T WORRY, BE HOPEFUL

As A TEENAGER, I was certain that the world would soon be destroyed during a nuclear war with the Soviet Union. I believed that any of my classmates who thought that they would live to see our high school graduation were simply being irrational or were afraid to face the facts. And then, by my junior year of college, which I spent in Israel, I was the only student in my Hebrew ulpan who was not a new immigrant from the largely dismembered and declawed "former Soviet Union."

While I have changed in a multitude of ways since my high school years, one of the most fundamental changes has been my newfound willingness to have faith in a brighter future despite all of the indications to the contrary. I learned about the rationality of irrational hope when Marines found Saddam Hussein cowering in a pit (and I put five gas masks away into deep storage). When I danced at the wedding of the 47-year-old bachelor and his soulmate. When my neighbor gave birth to twins after twelve years of fertility treatments. When I boarded a Jerusalem bus for the first time in three years and my pulse remained steady and slow.

I learned this same lesson as well when last year I discovered I was pregnant again eight months after a traumatic miscarriage. I learned the lesson even more powerfully six months ago, when after a worry-ridden high-risk pregnancy I held my little Moriah for the first time in the delivery room, and planted a kiss on her forehead as my husband cried silently beside me.

BLAH-BUSTER TIDBIT

Sveta's Happiness

When Sveta started coming to our house for Shabbat meals several years ago, she was a recent immigrant from Russia who was in the process of converting to Judaism. While she was a kind and thoughtful person, she always struck me as very sad, even sullen. I supposed that she was lonely since her family was still in Russia, or that her studies at Hebrew University's cut-throat psychology department were getting her down.

A year ago she completed her conversion, and when she came to us for Shabbat the week following the conversion, she was transformed. She was smiling and radiant, looking like the name she had chosen for herself, "Gila," or joy. I asked her why she was so happy, and she just shrugged her shoulders and looked down.

The following week, when she arrived again with a big smile on her face, I asked her if she had a boyfriend, unable to think of anything else that could have caused this transformation in her. She shook her head, and kept on smiling. So I said, "So what happened? You seem so incredibly happy all of a sudden!"

She said, "I guess it's just that something changed with the conversion. I realized after I converted that I am not alone."

I nodded and said, "Right. Now you are a member of the Jewish people."

"No, not that," she said, "Now that I am a Jew, I have learned that God is always with me. And that makes me happy."

GRATITUDE AND MORNING SICKNESS

HANUKKAH IS PRETTY MUCH my favorite holiday. I love the candles in the middle of the dark, dreary winter, the long, restful evenings relaxing with my kids and husband, the daily outings with my kids during Hanukkah vacation – to the park, the museum, all over. I love it. But, as much as I love Hanukkah, I love the end of Hanukkah – seeing the kids go back to nursery school and kindergarten so that I can have my solitary mornings back. Every year Hanukkah reminds me how unfit I am for the homeschooling/kids-home-all-the-time model of motherhood. Never having a break from my kids ends up meaning that I am never really with them, my nerves wearing progressively thinner so that by day five I stare at a garden-variety "It's mine!" "No, it's mine!" fight like a deer caught in the headlights.

This year was even harder than usual, since I was exhausted from being in the first trimester of pregnancy. I was the kind of tired that I would wake up in the morning after eleven hours of sleep and still want to stay in bed the whole day. Author Jhumpa Lahiri described pregnancy exhaustion perfectly in her book *The Namesake*[1]: "Before her husband left for university he would leave a cup of tea by the side of the bed, where she lay listless and silent. Often, returning in the evenings, he would find her still lying there, the tea untouched." I was also terribly nauseous, throwing up pretty much everything I ate, so that I spent a good part of my time wondering whether the body receives any nutrients from thrown-up food and just how weak and falling over I need to feel before I'm supposed to proceed to my nearest emergency room.

Which all means that I've dedicated a lot of time over the last two months to considering why *Hashem* mixes our greatest happiness – finding out about a new pregnancy – with such terrible feelings of misery and illness. I experience this strange mixture of joy, thankfulness, and suffering especially strongly, since, as a nursing mother, nausea is always my first sign

---

[1] Lahiri, Jhumpha. *The Namesake*. New York, 2003.

of pregnancy. I still haven't come up with any convincing answers as to why one of motherhood's greatest joys is mixed with one of its greatest miseries, but these are a few of the ideas I've come up with:

I heard a new theory that morning sickness was a way for our ancestors, who lived many millennia before nutritional information had to be printed on food labels, to protect themselves and their little embryos from foods containing toxic ingredients. The researcher who developed this theory found that some of the things that make pregnant women nauseous could be, or at least used to be, harmful to babies *in utero*. But this theory doesn't work for me. When I'm not pregnant, I try to eat really healthy – whole-wheat bread, little sugar, lots of dairy, tons of fruit, and protein. And when I'm pregnant, I can only eat sliced challah. I throw up at the sight of glass of milk and haven't been able to keep down a piece of fresh fruit for over a month.

So my next idea was that maybe God gives us morning sickness so that we can't just ignore a new pregnancy and go on as usual. Morning sickness (which, everybody knows by now to be a sinister misnomer for something that makes you ill for the whole day and bellyache-awake for a chunk of the night as well) means that you have to stop, lie down, reschedule that early morning meeting and ask for an extension on an article due the following day. It forces you to recognize that pregnancy, and then motherhood, will require you to reorganize your life and put your new baby at the top of your list of priorities. That's semi-sort-of-quasi-convincing.

In the end, the only convincing answer I've heard came from Rebbetzin Yemima Mizrachi, who was talking not so long ago about how to deal with suffering. I heard her say this a few weeks ago and couldn't relate at all, but now that I can see the air clearing after two months of morning sickness as suffocating as a thick bayou fog, I thought again about what she said and realized it might be a helpful way to think about first trimester suffering in the future. She quoted the Maharal, who explained that the Hebrew word for troubles, *yisurim*, comes from the root *sur*, meaning "to go away." Our troubles will not linger forever. They will "*yasuru,*" go away, when *Hashem* decides that they have accomplished their purpose.

And a big part of the reason that our troubles stay around for as long as they do is because of complaining. The word *mitlonen* comes from the same root as *lina*, to spend the night.[2] In other words, if you complain, your problems will move into your guest room, or maybe, if you complain enough, they will even kick you out of your own bed, so that you have to get a sore back sleeping on the living room sofa. Morning sickness is something that you would think is difficult to complain about, since it's usually over by the time you could complain to anyone outside of your immediate family in your second trimester,[3] and how much complaining can your mother and husband take before they start looking at their watches and running out to dubious forgotten appointments?

But maybe it's not necessarily actual complaining we're talking about. Maybe it's more a state of mind, a general lack of thankfulness in life that suffering brings on. Rebbe Nachman of Breslov teaches that when someone can't pray, it's because his suffering is clogging up the pipes leading his prayers to God. He teaches that the highest state is when something happens to you and you wonder why, and then answer yourself, "*Kakha zeh*" – "That's the way it is!" "*Kakha*" is an acronym for "*Keter kol ha-ketarim*," the Crown of all Crowns. The way to open up the pipes of prayer, to make all of your suffering go away, is to accept the suffering in your life as a hidden gift from God, and to swallow another saltine and turn your heart to *Hashem*, and say "*Thank you* for this. I don't know why I have to be this miserable, but that's the way it is, and You, *Hashem*, certainly know better than I do."

After writing all of this, it all seems a bit silly, doesn't it? If I had to give up everything I own to have another baby, I would do it. If I had to stay in bed for nine months to have another wonderful little baby, it wouldn't even occur to me to say no. If I were required to go on a strict diet of stale pretzels and pickle juice until this coming July, I wouldn't flinch. I want this

---

[2] Maharal, *Netivot Olam*, "Netiv ha-yisurim."

[3] There is a Jewish tradition not to announce the pregnancy to people outside your immediate family until the second trimester. Of course, this does not include mentioning the pregnancy to doctors and rabbis whom you need to consult on various issues.

baby as much as I've ever wanted anything in my life, but it is so hard to focus on the big picture when you feel so downright rotten....

Rebbetzin Yemima teaches that the root of the word for women, *nashim,* means "forgetting,"[4] because women's ability to forget is a tremendous blessing. Forgetting enables us to sweep aside the difficulties of pregnancy, the pain of birth, the difficulties of motherhood (in other words, Eve's curse), so that we remember instead the hugeness, the miracle, the incomparable gift of being able to create a new life with God's help. May we be blessed that we should only remember the right things, the things that enable us to be strong and inspired mothers for our children.

Epilogue

The month after I wrote this essay, my fourth pregnancy ended in miscarriage. And the months that followed provided me with a whole new understanding of the meaning of suffering.

---

[4] See Genesis 41:51.

BLAH-BUSTER TIDBIT
Hoping Around in the Dark

Rabbi Yitzchak said, "Every person should be hopeful. Even if they are not otherwise worthy, their hopefulness, faith, and trust will be accounted to their credit.

"When people are suffering, let them remain hopeful. When they are sanctifying the name of God through their deaths, let them be hopeful." (*Midrash Rabbah*[1])

I am a person who tends to worry a great deal, as gifted as any spider in spinning what psychiatrist Edward Hallowell refers to as "the infinite web of the what-if."

But there are two beliefs that serve me well as mental broomsticks to clean away these webs of worry. I believe that redemption from our troubles can come in the blink of an eye, when we least expect it. And I also believe that Hashem is with us especially in the darkest moments of our lives, when redemption fails to come in the blink of an eye, or ever.

This is why I love this selection from the Midrash, which explains that we can pray and have absolute faith that our aunt's cancer will go into remission, that 9/11 will be the last major terrorist attack on American soil, that our pregnancy will result in a healthy baby in a few months' time. And we should also have faith when our prayers go unanswered, when the infinite web of the what-if turns into the terrible reality of the what-is. It is especially at those scary moments when, if we put out our hand, Hashem can grab hold of it, and lead us patiently through the labyrinths of darkness.

---

[1] Rabbi Shemuel Houminer, *Faith and Trust* (Israel: 1994), 27.

SEDER NIGHT HOPES

THE HASIDIC MASTERS taught that on Seder night, we can pray for anything we need. The gates of Heaven are wide open. And this past Seder night, I prayed so strongly to have a baby by the following Nissan[1] that I convinced myself that I *was* already pregnant. I was feeling a bit nauseous, which is always my first sign of pregnancy, and I felt as though I were on a spiritual high. Over and over I prayed, "By next Nissan, please, a healthy, whole baby."

The following night, right after the holiday ended, I washed a few dishes and then rushed to buy a pregnancy test at the pharmacy downtown. With shaking hands I opened the test, but afterwards, even though I waited and waited, no cross appeared in the second circle. I started sobbing, as broken as I had been after the original loss of my fourth pregnancy three months before.

For the next five months, at one point over the course of every month, I would start feeling nauseous, or moody, or tired, or I had a sudden burst of energy, and each time I convinced myself totally and absolutely that I was pregnant, that this was exactly how I'd felt at the beginning of all four of my pregnancies. But then I would do a pregnancy test, and the second circle was just a line, without even a shadow of a second line forming a cross, no matter how hard I squinted, or how many minutes I waited for it to appear.

My miscarriage this past January followed by these failed attempts to become pregnant again were without a doubt the saddest thing that I've ever been through, bringing on months and months of a low-grade fever of sadness underneath the mornings at the computer, the afternoons spent with children, the evenings cleaning up the kitchen. A film of sadness that coated everything – my heart, my ears, my eyes.

This past July, I computed that I would have to get pregnant that month in order to give birth by the coming Nissan, as I had been praying for every

---

[1] Nissan is the Hebrew month during which Passover is observed.

single day since Seder night. So, I convinced myself that I would get pregnant that month. Many things I pray for don't come true, but I remembered the high of Seder night, and how completely I believed that I would give birth by the following Nissan. And I believed that it was true.

And then, that month again, I did not get pregnant. My sadness and disappointment lasted for days.

I was worried that something had gone wrong with my uterus, that my body that had always gotten pregnant easily and then sustained healthy pregnancies to term, was now defective. Now I would be like all the women who are unable to get pregnant and then write to me to get their names added to my website's prayer list. I even thought of secretly adding my name to that list.

So, now we are in mid-August, and last Wednesday, I started feeling nauseous again. After the terrible disappointment of last month, I spoke with a rabbi who suggested that I needed to find a way to make each month of waiting to get pregnant less traumatic. I should assume, he proposed, that it could take another year to become pregnant again, and he told me that that was totally normal for women following a miscarriage. "Maybe you and Josh could go out to a restaurant each time you find out you are not pregnant so that you'll have something to look forward to?" he suggested. Actually celebrating these monthly disappointments sounded like more than I could handle, but the rabbi's words made me realize that waiting to get pregnant is normal, and that I needed to take steps to make this whole waiting period less difficult.

So, on the way to buy another pregnancy test last week, I focused on my three daughters, and how happy they make me, and how much I love being their mother. I thought of how, even though I would like more children, my girls are enough. Many mothers of three children consider that just plenty, my mother and mother-in-law, for example. I thought about how I would probably get pregnant eventually, and if I never did get pregnant again, then I would find a way to make my life feel full despite that. I did the test, and it was negative. And for the first time since the miscarriage, even though my heart sank for a moment, I didn't crash and burn emotionally.

And again, after Shabbat, I did another test. Negative. I was sad, but I had new hope. I would find a way to be happy with my reality, whatever it was.

And this past Monday, *Rosh Hodesh* Elul,[2] I felt like my stomach was all stuffed up with bread, like nothing was able to go down. My husband took our kids to the zoo on his own, since I was going to speak in the settlement of Tekoa that night about *Expecting Miracles*. And I went to the pharmacy to get another pregnancy test, sort of grumbling the whole way at the stupidity of all these dozen tests I've done that have turned out negative.

And then I got home, and did the test, and there it was – or at least maybe. It was the faintest blue line forming a cross in the second circle, but it was so light, as washed out as a line drawn by a blue magic marker that one of my girls left the cap off for a few days. So, I sat on the stairs, staring at it for ten whole minutes. At first my heart jumped with total, absolute joy, but then it fell again. I didn't let myself be happy, since maybe I was misreading the test. The second line was so light that it easily could have been all my staring and squinting and holding it up in different positions in the light that made me see something.

And then I looked at the instructions, and I convinced myself that this was the real thing. This was the pregnancy I had been waiting for. I stood up in my kitchen, and put my face in my hands and cried, and thanked God from the bottom of my heart.

Then I went to my computer to find a website that would enable me to compute my due date, and found out that I was due to give birth on Nisa's third English birthday, that in the Hebrew calendar had been Lag ba-Omer. I thought of how I would tell my husband, "Well, it looks like we're having another Lag ba-Omer baby" when I looked at the Hebrew calendar and saw that because of the extra month added this year because it is a *shana me'uberet*, literally a "pregnant year," I was in fact due to give birth on Seder night.[3] I

---

[2] The first day of the month of Elul.
[3] Once every several years, an extra month is added to the Hebrew calendar (just as an extra day is added to the civil calendar during leap years).

just stared at the screen as my heart raced and I put my head in my hands once again, unable to believe that this was really happening.

This week, Yemima was explaining that *Rosh Hodesh* Elul is a day that the whole reality of our year can change from one extreme to another. So, with my head in my hands once again, by the computer, I thought of what she had said and decided that this day, *Rosh Hodesh* Elul, was one of the best days of my entire life.

And then, that very night, I traveled an hour by bus to speak in Tekoa. I carried along ten very heavy books to sell, and after all that effort, only one woman bothered to show up. I've had small turnouts in the past – eight people, even four people, but one person? I tried to think about it in all sorts of positive ways – my first opportunity ever to come to Tekoa! Or maybe this one woman really needed to speak with me one on one? But despite all my "everything is for the best" efforts, it was still sort of irritating to shlep so far for nothing.

In the end, I had a sweet discussion with that one woman, and when I left I realized that I actually felt a little bit relieved. Too many good things had happened that day, and when things go too well I start to worry, as though all these good things are a tower of blocks that climbs higher and higher and is just asking for someone to stomp too hard or walk by without looking where they're going, and knock it down.

BLAH-BUSTER TIDBIT

Worry: Controlling It Wisely

by Dr. Edward M. Hallowell[1]

To keep faith, [you must] let go of control. The believer… [learns] that a grander scheme will take over if they can let it…. The people who worry the least usually have some sort of faith.

Medical literature and popular magazines are replete with studies of the formative, healing power of faith. A 1995 study at Dartmouth showed that patients who drew strength from religious faith survived open-heart surgery at three times the rate of those who did not. A review of 30 years of research on blood pressure shows that people who attend weekly religious services have lower blood pressure, by 5 mm/Hg, than people who do not. Many studies have found lower rates of depression and illnesses related to anxiety among those who have a belief in God. There have been studies that show that people who attend religious services regularly die from coronary-artery disease at half the rate of those who never attend, even taking into account smoking and socioeconomic factors.

We can learn from people who have strong faith. We can learn that belief itself… can stabilize the worried mind.

---

[1] Hallowell, Edward M. *Worry: Controlling It Wisely.* New York: 1997, 276–280.

MEETING THE *TZADDIK*[1]

RECENTLY I PAID a visit to Ruti, Tiferet's babysitter from a few years back, who told me about a rabbi whom her teenage daughters had visited the day before. She told me with a lot of enthusiasm about this rabbi, who is famous for the outreach work he does with Israeli young people, the smoking in the Central Bus Station, bleached-gelled-spiky hair crowd.

The next day, Ruti's daughter was babysitting for us, and when I walked her home, I grilled her to learn more about this rabbi. What was it like to talk with him? What was it like at the hall where he spoke? Usually a quiet, soft-spoken girl, she became almost animated as she described her meeting with the rabbi. She told me that he had seen right through her to what she was really feeling. He had spoken with her about the importance of dressing modestly and had given her a holy book that was "exactly what she had needed." This girl very sweetly offered to take time out of her busy teenage schedule to go with me to this rabbi, who received visitors at the deserted end of Jerusalem's industrial area. But we'd have to leave early, she explained, since there are always hundreds of people waiting there to see him. She'd had to wait six hours.

And while I thought I probably would not take her up on her offer to visit this particular rabbi, our discussion got me thinking about how I also wanted to get a blessing from a rabbi, something that I have never done before in my whole life. In the past, I have heard of people going to rabbis for blessings – of sick people, or women who can't get pregnant, or women who want a blessing for an easy birth. But I, personally, have never felt so exceptionally in need that I have tracked down a rabbi great enough to give a blessing. It sounded sort of intimidating, unfamiliar, and potentially awkward.

But recently, I have been thinking about how I am praying very hard that this coming year, starting with Rosh ha-Shana tomorrow night, will hold

---

[1] A righteous or holy person.

better tidings for my family than this past year. And I have been thinking that it couldn't hurt to have a great rabbi pray for me as well.

So, during Dafna and Tiferet's swimming lesson last week, I asked another mother about rabbis to go to for blessings. This mother spent twenty years trying to get pregnant before adopting her two young children, so she knows the Jerusalem blessings scene as well as anybody does. This mother thought about my question and then said, "You should go to Rabbi Avraham Dov Levin."

She was referring to the grandson of Rabbi Aryeh Levin, who was known as the "Rabbi of the Prisoners" because during the British occupation of the land of Israel, he was the only rabbi who was allowed to visit the prisoners from the Zionist resistance groups. He is one of the most beloved and respected figures in Israeli history, revered by religious and secular alike for his tremendous kindness, self-sacrifice, and unconditional love for all Jews.

I live around the corner from Reb Aryeh's house, and a few months ago I asked my next door neighbor, Miriam, if she remembered him. Miriam, who was born in the house next to mine, left Jerusalem in the 1940s at the age of fourteen to become a member of a *Ha-Shomer ha-Tza'ir* kibbutz. Until several years ago, this kibbutz did not allow rabbis of any kind onto the kibbutz grounds even to perform weddings, since the members were so ideologically opposed to traditional Judaism.

But, when I asked Miriam about Reb Aryeh, her face absolutely lit up, and she said "Of course I remember him." She recalled how she and her seven siblings enjoyed listening to the radio on Shabbat morning, and how one evening her mother received an unexpected visit from the great Reb Aryeh. Miriam imitated his bent-over posture, and his sweet high voice, and her mother's nervousness, and how he said to her mother, "Mrs. Yaffe, I understand that your children like to listen to the radio on Shabbat. But please... if they could keep it a bit quieter." How many people in the world do you think could give a rebuke in such a way that fifty years later, they are still remembered so fondly for the way in which they did it? Now that is a great man.

So even though I've lived around the corner from Reb Aryeh's house for almost a decade, I had never actually been inside until last week, when I took my girls out one long afternoon on a trip around the corner to the house of Reb Aryeh, where his grandson still studies and welcomes visitors every day between two and three PM.

My kids were very excited to hear that we were going to visit "the rabbi." And when we arrived at the house, first we knocked on the door, and then, at the encouragement of the neighbor, we knocked louder, and then even louder, all three girls and I together. But then, someone else told us that the rabbi usually arrived a little bit later. So we sat down, huddled together on a little step by the door. And then we saw a taxi arrive, and a little man in a long black coat and a big black hat got out and starting rushing down the alleyway towards us. As he approached us, breathless, the rabbi apologized profusely for keeping us waiting. Right away, I could see in his face the kindness and tremendous humility for which his grandfather was famous.

The rabbi unlocked the door, and we entered what looked like a mini shul, the size of half a hallway, and he gestured for us to sit down while he disappeared for about five minutes, explaining that, if we would please excuse him, he had to look for something. I thought that he was looking for a little charity box so that I could make a donation to his yeshiva in return for his time. But he came back, at long last, with a handful of toffees for my girls that he left in a pile on the table. Then he sat down across the table from me, and I noticed right away that I did not feel in the least uncomfortable being there. This was very surprising, considering that he is a rabbi of great stature, and also because men in black hats and long black coats have never been the kind of people to especially put me at ease.

At first, I told him that my girls were starting school the following day and that I would like to request a blessing for them to have a good year. With great care, he wrote down my children's names, which was not so easy, since my kids have the sort of creative names common in Nahlaot, but strange to ears more accustomed to names like Sara'le, Rivka'le, and Leah'le. He gave my girls a big smile, asking them where they were going to school. I was worried that he would be upset with me, that I am sending them to schools that he did not consider religious enough, but he did not seem concerned about this at all.

Then he prayed quietly, murmuring to himself for a few minutes, and then he read my girls' names out loud, along with the prayer that each of them should learn a lot, make a lot of friends, and have a very good year (or something like that, I can't remember exactly). Then he carefully placed a shekel down on the table, and told me that I should give it to charity. I told him that I had brought my own money to give to charity, but he said that this was the way he did things. He gave the shekels, not the person coming to get the blessing, which reminded me of how the Lubavitcher Rebbe used to give out dollars.

And then I told my kids that they would have to wait in the hall for a little bit. They really did not want to go, but I insisted, so they grumbled through their mouthfuls of toffees and left. And then I told the rabbi about what a difficult year I had had. I told him about the pregnancy I had lost this past January and the worries that haunted me about my current pregnancy. He furrowed his brow as though he were very concerned, and then he looked at me with a look of absolute kindness, acceptance, and understanding. It was a look that reminded me for the first time in a long time (for the first time since this past January?) that despite the hard times I had been through, God really does love me, at least as much as I love my own little girls.

And then, with a very serious look on his face, he launched into a detailed explanation about how a sick person may eat on Yom Kippur, eating small amounts every ten minutes. And he instructed me to speak with my doctor to see if she would allow me to fast. I nodded, but thought how I knew very well from years of experience that pregnant women are required to fast on Yom Kippur unless their pregnancies are high-risk. I had been to my doctor the day before and knew that this was not the case for me.

So I just listened. While I knew that Rabbi Levin is a very great rabbi, he exuded such innocence and simplicity, almost like a child, that I thought maybe he was explaining all of this to me because he had misunderstood me when I'd spoken, or, more likely, he was hard of hearing or found it hard to understand my American-accented Hebrew. Afterwards we spoke for a while longer. He was surprised that my husband and I had lived right around the corner for so many years, and yet had never met him. He wrote down my name and prayed for me in the same way that he had prayed for my girls. Then he gave me a shekel as well and promised to pray for me in the future. And he reminded me once again about how a sick person can eat on Yom Kippur, once again looking very concerned when he mentioned it.

So we headed back around the corner to our home. Tiferet declared that this rabbi was the "greatest rabbi in the whole world" and Dafna, the big sister, confirmed that Tiferet was correct. I thought of how small our world is, that my children really believe that they can walk fifty steps from their front door and come to the world's greatest rabbi. But I also felt very moved by this meeting with Rabbi Levin. I saw in him how years and years of learning Torah with great devotion can turn a person into an incredible mensch, into a person who absolutely glows with goodness, holiness, and God's lovingkindness.

A few days later, I went for a routine ultrasound and found out, to my amazement, that there were patches of bleeding in my uterus. My doctor confined me to bed rest and, of course, forbade me to fast this Yom Kippur.

Because this outgoing year has been a difficult one for me and so many other mothers I know, it has provided an opportunity to develop a deep appreciation for what rabbis do – for the hours they dedicate to the down and out, and to helping people who are coping with terrible sadness and need a blessing or a pep talk or both. So I would like to take a moment to express my gratitude to our rabbis, who deserve to receive from the Jewish people far more appreciation for all their efforts on our behalf and far less grief.

BLAH-BUSTER TIDBIT

Morning Song

by Varda Branfman[1]

Hang up the wet to dry
but don't sew on a button
one thing will lead to another
and you'll find yourself mending
everything in the house

Assuage your thirst
but ignore the hunger pains till later
watch the clock
and wake the children
pour the water for their hands[2]

Do what you can to ease
arms into sweaters
sandwiches into side pouches
soft, wet eyes
into clear openings

Make little of the lost bus card
the lonely shoe
the phantom notebook
but find them
by whispering segulahs[3]
and dropping coins in the pushkes[4]

---

[1] Varda Branfman, *I Remembered in the Night Your Name* (Jerusalem: 2003), 74.
Varda Branfman, a former director of the Maine State Poetry in the Schools Program, is a former homesteader on the Maine Coast during her first lifetime. During her current lifetime, she lives and writes in Jerusalem with her husband, children, and grandchildren. Her book, which spans Maine and Jerusalem, is available on her website, www.carobspring.com.
[2] Reference to the ritual washing of the hands performed upon waking.
[3] Auspicious verses.

Arouse hope
kiss away shadows
turn the cheek
to their heartfelt revenges
watch the storm subside

Give them real food
and don't panic at the last minute
if the sky suddenly erupts
in clouds
embrace the unexpected

Allow yourself to look each one
straight in the eye
when you say "goodbye"
believe, yourself, that help will come
from Heaven

Then sit, do nothing
drink silence

---

[4] Some people place money in a charity box *[pushka]* when they wish to find a lost object.

PRIVACY, PLEASE

RECENTLY, IT HAS BEEN pretty jarring to look around the Internet and find myself popping up in all sorts of unexpected places – articles about *Expecting Miracles* appearing in the Jewish newspapers of Cleveland, San Francisco, Chicago, Baltimore, New York City. Tens of thousands of people I have never and will never meet have read articles about why I wrote this book, and then have glanced up at the picture of me smiling in an armchair with a borrowed wig perched on top of my head.

It is pretty funny to me that while my picture has been making its way across living rooms all over the continental US, in real life I have been as secluded and unadventurous in recent weeks as a medieval monk spending his days in a cave overlooking the Dead Sea. Pregnancy has slowed me down tremendously and the recent bed-rest orders from my doctor have slowed me down even more, so that I now have almost totally ceased movement, like molecules frozen at -273.16 degrees centigrade. And today, even the most minor outing to the post office across the street to mail a letter or to the corner store for two bags of milk is a substantial event, an honest-to-goodness daily outing. I come home with my bags of milk in hand, satisfied that I have ventured into the great big world outside of my front door that day, and then head straight for the sofa for another half-hour to recoup.

As much as my life has become a totally isolated one, there is one aspect of my life that is even more private than the rest – the precious secret guarded under lock and key in the safe deposit box in my lower abdomen. The thought of this delicious secret, this pregnancy growing within me, is incredibly satisfying. It makes me smile a big smile to myself, a decadent, glorious, unbelievable surprise that nobody knows about except Josh and me. All the metaphors I can think of are pretty far fetched, but it is as though we hired a babysitter and went out to the fanciest restaurant in Tel Aviv in a ball gown and tuxedo, ordered the most expensive thing on the menu, licked our lips, came home, and did not tell a soul. An amazing treat that I do not have to share, a special secret just for me to sneak a smile to my husband and God about when no one's looking.

And I am planning on keeping it this way. With my last pregnancy, it was not long after I started telling people about my pregnancy at the beginning of the second trimester that I found myself playing the leading role in a real-life nightmare. And so, I have decided that this time around, I am never going to announce this pregnancy, until, with God's help, Josh sends out an email seven months from now at three in the morning saying that I was pregnant, but am overjoyed to not be any longer.

The Talmud teaches, "Blessing only comes to things that are hidden from the eye."[1] Most happy events we cannot and do not hide. We don't hide engagements, weddings, newborn babies, or new homes, even though we pray with all of our hearts that God will bless them with only good things. As far as I can figure out, pregnancy is the only thing that we actually do hide in this way, probably since it's the event with the greatest potential in the whole world and the greatest risk of disappointment as well. Pregnancy is not a new baby yet, it is only life in potential. We don't say *mazal tov* about a pregnancy since in our wombs the fetus still exists in a no man's land between this world and the next, the twilight zone between life and absence of life. Not yet *mazal tov* but merely *be-sha'ah tovah*.[2] May this become a *mazal tov* at the right time.

But still, every week there are a few people to whom I must reveal my buried treasure for one reason or another. And every time a new person hears about my secret, it is a bit jarring for me. First there was my gynecologist, who didn't flinch. Then the lady at the lab where I went for blood tests, who asked me so publicly, so nonchalantly in front of everybody in the line, what week I was in. No one else seemed to care. Another religious woman in another one of her dozens of pregnancies, what's the big deal? But I was reeling from that minor act of exhibitionism all the way to the elevator. Then the young security guard at the entrance to the pharmacy

---

[1] Babylonian Talmud, *Bava Metzia* 42a.
[2] Literally, "In a good hour." In this traditional blessing for a pregnant woman, we bless her that she should give birth at an auspicious time.

started moving his handheld metal detector in the direction of my body, and I quickly moved my hands out to guard myself as though he was about to punch me in the stomach. "No, I'm pregnant." "Oh, OK," he said, a bit embarrassed.

But despite my desires for absolute privacy and secrecy, there was one person that I felt terrible about not telling. I have always told my mother right away when I know I'm pregnant, right after Josh and right before he takes the phone from me to call my mother-in-law. So I kept it a secret from my mother for five long weeks, and I felt OK with it, even though at times I felt absolutely duplicitous during our weekly phone calls. But I egged myself on with thoughts of precious treasures and blessings for hidden things. But then, with the new declaration of bed rest, I realized during our last phone conversation that I had to tell her. It felt wrong to keep the details of this exciting and also worrisome pregnancy from her.

So I said, "Mom, I have big news." "You're pregnant," she said. It turned out that she had known for weeks, ever since I told her that I was calling a sudden halt to my speaking tour about *Expecting Miracles* – that I was bored with it, that I wanted to stay home to "work on a new book."

And then my mom said, *"Mazal tov!"* and I felt relieved to have told her. And anyway, how could I, in good conscience, deprive her of this most basic privilege, the right to worry about and be happy for her own daughter? How would I feel if, one day, one of my daughters dared to keep this kind of secret from me?

BLAH-BUSTER TIDBIT

Living and Birthing

The book *Baby Catcher – Chronicles of a Modern Midwife*[1] by Berkeley midwife Peggy Vincent presents 322 pages of amazing birth stories that I found hard to put down for my 11 PM lights off. But the birth in the book that really sticks in my mind was Vincent's first birth at the age of nineteen, when she was a student nurse in North Carolina. At this birth, a twenty-two-year-old African-American woman named Zelda runs up and down her hospital bed streaming with sweat during her birth with her third child. She tells Peggy, who is pretty horrified at what she is seeing, about her last two births at her grandmother's house, how she would "walk and sing and dance the pains away." During contractions, Zelda screams out an ecstatic "Ooooh, my dear Lord, guide me and bring me out of these troubled waters, up and into Your arms. Ahhhhh, yeoooow, oh, oh Loooordy! Yes, yes, yes, yes… and I thank you."

And this year, at Rosh ha-Shana services, I was thinking quite a lot about Zelda. I thought about how this has been a scary year in a lot of ways – a year of young widows and car crashes and Arab armies sniffing at every border. Not to mention the routine scary events faced by mothers: what with one-year-olds falling down stairs, five-year-olds getting stitches on their heads, and even three-year-olds getting cavities filled under sedation. Life is scary, and motherhood is especially scary because we have so many people we love so much to worry about.

But, despite all the scary things that can happen, on Rosh ha-Shana, we are required to believe, to have faith that whatever happens this coming year is from Hashem, and that no matter what happens, Hashem loves us and will help us to make it through. But the fact of the matter is that I feel like crying all of Rosh ha-Shana. I feel so overwhelmed by the thought that my family and I are being judged for the coming year that I would prefer to spend Rosh ha-Shana curled up in fetal position, thinking existential, mournful thoughts. But I can't. I am required to have festive meals and to be happy on Rosh ha-Shana.

And birth is the same way, which is why I was thinking so much about Zelda this Rosh ha-Shana. I was thinking about how scary birth is, the pain,

---

[1] Vincent, Peggy. *Baby Catcher: Chronicles of a Modern Midwife.* New York: 2000.

the terrible vulnerability to the unknown. But, as Peggy Vincent writes, after participating in thousands of births, she has learned that positive experiences of birth are guaranteed less by any objective preexisting factors than by the laboring woman's ability to maintain a good sense of humor throughout the laboring process.

During birth, our natural reaction is to be miserable from all the pain, to yell at the nurse putting in our IV, to throw the tennis balls that are supposed to be used for counter-pressure at our poor, panicking husbands. But the Jewish way is to see past the pain, to see that God is there and that He is waiting for us to turn to Him for help. The Jewish way is to say, "God, I have been waiting my whole life to meet this baby. I can't do this on my own. You've got to help me out!" In the way we live our lives, we need to learn from birth, and vice versa. We're supposed to do it Zelda's way, not to be afraid, to keep on smiling, to dance up and down on our beds until it's over, and to believe. Oh, Loooordy.

YOM KIPPUR SOUP

LAST THURSDAY, I went to do a follow up ultrasound for the patches of bleeding in my uterus, and the ultrasound technician on duty was the same one who had picked up that something was wrong last January. This technician is a wonderful combination of professional as well as very sweet and empathetic. She didn't remember me right away, and then when I reminded her of the events of this past January, she was so happy to see that I was pregnant again.

The truth is that you can see very little in an ultrasound at nine weeks, but she kept on saying things to make sure I wouldn't worry: "Look, he's moving around! He has a pulse! He's developing exactly in accordance with his age! His limbs are about to start to form!" And as far as the uterine bleeding that had put me on partial bed rest for the previous two weeks, she said that it was almost entirely gone. Although, of course, my doctor would have to decide what the little patch of bleeding still left really meant. Once she said this, I was already thinking about getting back to my regular life – going on my long daily walks to pick up Tiferet from nursery school, going shopping, cooking a whole lot of casseroles and some healthy things for my kids to eat. Maybe I would even be allowed to fast when Yom Kippur started the following night?

I left the ultrasound report for my doctor who was working that afternoon, and she finally called me the following morning to tell me that while I don't have to be flat on my back, I still needed to be on partial bed rest. And no, I was not allowed to fast on Yom Kippur.

This is the seventh Yom Kippur in a row that I've been nursing or pregnant or both, and every year I've called our rabbi in hopes that I could somehow get out of keeping the fast. I try to convince him, "But my milk will dry up if I don't drink or eat," or "But I have morning sickness and I will throw up if my stomach is empty." But he just tells me, "Then you should pump milk beforehand. And if you throw up, you will be performing the mitzvah of self-affliction on Yom Kippur extra well...."

Every year, he explains to me the danger signs that will require me to drink a mouthful of juice or eat a matchbox full of food every ten minutes, and each time that I've fasted during early pregnancy, I've thrown up once in the evening, which means I am allowed to eat two or three matchboxes full of bread at ten-minute intervals, and then I lie in bed for the next twenty hours, and I do pretty much OK. I dread the fasts of Tisha be-Av and Yom Kippur almost to the extent that I dread giving birth, and keeping them are the most difficult *mitzvot* that I perform all year. And afterwards, I'm always amazed by myself that I really did it, and am thankful that there's a whole nine months between the months of Tishrei and Av.[1]

Which is why it was surprising that this year I found myself calling the rabbi for the opposite reason. I told him that my doctor had told me that I was not allowed to fast, but that the ultrasound technician said that I'm pretty much healed. Maybe I could try to fast, and see if I could do it? It's funny, that after all those years of hoping so hard that I would get out of the fast, the first year of my life that I couldn't fast, I was half hoping to be able to do it. I think that this is on account of a few factors, and primarily the fact that this was a hard year. It's a year that I want to move beyond, that I want to wipe off my board with an eraser and then go over with a wet rag. I want to start off this new year on the right foot – with more blessing, with fewer problems, with more health and happiness than the past year. And not fasting on Yom Kippur feels like starting the year off the wrong way.

So I presented my argument, and the rabbi said, "Well, I'm very sorry, but you are not fasting this year. This a case of *safek pikuah nefesh,* that a life is possibly at stake. You are going to make a soup, and put it in a blender, and then eat very small amounts of it every ten minutes. And this is a very serious business. Just like it's a *mitzvah* for other people to fast, it's a *mitzvah* for you to eat this soup. You may fast in the evening, and you may take a

---

[1] Rosh ha-Shana falls at the beginning of the month of Tishrei, and Tisha be-Av is nine months later during the month of Av. While there are other minor fasts, these are the only two fasts that pregnant and nursing women must observe.

nap, and you may go to shul for an hour if you feel strong, but other than that you must sit the whole day drinking your soup every ten minutes."

So, Yom Kippur was a very different experience this year from the years I fasted, and even from the years before I became religious when I ate on Yom Kippur. In her class before Yom Kippur this year, Rebbetzin Yemima quoted Rabbi Kook's *Orot ha-Teshuva*, in which he says that a major barrier for people to do *teshuva* or become closer to God is on account of physical weakness resulting, in large part, from not eating well. We have become a physically weak people, he explains. We want to prepare for Shabbat in a good mood, but we're collapsing from nursing and cleaning and the all-around demandingness of our lives. We want to light Shabbat candles, and pray afterwards for our children and our husbands, but we're exhausted from being sleep-deprived as well as on a diet, so we mutter the blessing quickly and collapse on the sofa. And eating correctly, healthily, and in abundance at the meal before the Yom Kippur fast, Rabbi Kook suggests, will give us the strength for the rest of the year to break out of this cycle of being hungry and tired and falling short on a spiritual level.

And this is what I was thinking of this Yom Kippur, as I sat drinking my half shot-glass of blended squash and carrot soup every ten minutes. I thought of this being a day to eat in order to get strong again and start anew, to wash away the sadness that I dwelt in for a large part of this past year. I went to shul for *Kol Nidre*[2] on the other side of my courtyard, where the women can barely hear the prayer leader, since they pray behind a thick concrete wall with a small window in it. And despite this, I was absolutely beaming, a great big smile spread across my lips. Most years I mostly feel like crying on Yom Kippur. The sealing of God's judgment terrifies me. But this Yom Kippur I was on a high, thinking of this as a day to start clean, to start on the right foot, to move on.

The whole next day I lay in bed, sitting once every ten minutes to swallow my soup, and I imagined it giving strength to the baby inside of me. I would drink some, and think of how that swallow would go to making its brain, and I would drink some more and think how that swallow would go

---

[2] The opening service of Yom Kippur.

toward helping its spine form. Over the course of the day, sip by sip, I prayed for my baby's whole body. Most of the time, I eat such large amounts relative to those mouthfuls of soup, but it never occurs to me to think of their purpose. To think of what I want and pray will be accomplished by consuming all this food.

I have a friend who had a sick daughter, and she used to pray out loud with every pill she gave her daughter, "May it be Your will that this treatment for Batya bat Rivka will bring her a full recovery, because you are the ultimate Healer."[3] I thought this was a wonderful idea. Usually we think that we make our physical efforts in this world – we eat well, and we go to the doctor, and we take our vitamins. And, on the other hand, we make our spiritual efforts – we pray, we give charity, we get blessings from rabbis. What an incredible thing to combine the two, to wrap the spiritual around our physical efforts, a blessed burrito.

Ironically, I felt much better this Yom Kippur than I did on Rosh ha-Shana. Despite the shot glasses of squash and carrot soup, or maybe because of them, I started to feel the first signs of hope awakening within my heart. Like the very first patch of red and yellow blossoms by the road leading through the Jerusalem forest at the end of February.

---

[3] Babylonian Talmud, *Berakhot* 60a.

BLAH-BUSTER TIDBIT

Make Yourself a Shore

by Varda Branfman[1]

Hear the boom
Of ordinary sounds
Revive
In the smell of laundry
Feel blessed
By the taste
Of buttered toast

Be aroused constantly
Awakened not once
But many times
Out of the billowing blankets

The light of day
Makes everything shine
Like a shelf full of new pots

Put yourself out to the edge
Make yourself a shore
And the sea
Will touch your full length

Holding nothing back
Even the black perspective
Everywhere you look
Even the black certainty
When black sheep waits

---

[1] Varda Branfman, *I Remembered in the Night Your Name,* 153.

Lift your hands
And feel the door
Smack in front of you
Clasp the handle
And push out
To the streaming broad daylight

Then whole black days and nights
Black years
Are swallowed by that sea of light

You will always find the door
You will always be the shore
That waters kiss

THE REDISCOVERY OF HOPE

LAST NIGHT, we officially finished up the High Holiday season with the end of Sukkot. Eight days of serving and clearing meals, putting fancy dresses on little girls and then throwing them into the overflowing laundry basket once they got just too covered with dirt and melted popsicle for public display. To be honest, though, this list of action verbs is not a realistic reflection of my own activities over this past week. While Josh gallivanted around with our girls to Sacher Park and the science museum and the Old City, I spent this Sukkot lying in bed reading novels, as sick as a dog in its first trimester, as worn-out and bleary-eyed from frequent throwing up as a hundred-year-old woman suffering from heat exhaustion.

We tend to think that holidays are fun for everyone. Who wouldn't mind a bit of quality family time and good food? But when you are suffering from morning sickness, more good food is absolutely not more of a good thing. Every meal is a culinary minefield that the nauseous woman navigates with more quease than ease.

This year, Yom Kippur fell on Shabbat, and I was actually relieved that there would be one less Shabbat to face this trimester. One Shabbat for which I would not have to feel sick to my stomach while making the shopping list, or while making the unappetizing dishes that pass for food when I feel this way (white rice mixed with cheddar cheese and boiled chard etc.), and above all else, not having to sit at the meals with all sorts of foods that make my stomach lurch into my esophagus, and then send me running to the bathroom if I get too adventurous. Shabbat as a gastrointestinal Russian roulette.

And then, over Sukkot, in the midst of my ongoing malaise coupled with the medically-enforced lethargy that is bed rest, we got some incredibly good news. I went for an ultrasound with a specialist, and he assured me that all of the bleeding in my uterus had disappeared. He said that I no longer have to be on bed rest, and that from then on my pregnancy was officially low-risk.

If I'd received this diagnosis a year ago, I would have shrugged my shoulders, sort of like I still react now to my blood test results for glucose and hematocrit.

But now, after what we've been through, it was such a weird feeling when the doctor told us that everything was fine, as though it was all too easy to be true. When the doctor said "goodbye," I felt a great need to stay longer with him, to tell him that we are veterans of the nightmare that takes place when he tells a couple that everything is far from all right. But we didn't.

So we left the clinic and I felt profoundly disoriented, as though someone had spun me around for five minutes and then let go. I had been totally prepared for disaster, and was unable to accept, to digest, so much good news all at once. As though I had ceased to believe that I am a person to whom inexplicably good things also happen upon occasion.

Josh and I left the building, not sure what to do with ourselves.

We decided to walk downtown for lunch, and by the time we reached the restaurant, Josh was more relaxed and happy than I'd seen him in weeks. But I still couldn't believe it – a healthy pregnancy, a healthy pregnancy. I realized to what an extent I had spent the past few weeks preparing myself for all possibilities except the most likely one.

The rest of Succoth was easier, lighter. I was free to walk and shop and go wherever I wanted for the first time in a month. The afternoon after the ultrasound, I took Dafna and Tiferet to their swimming lesson, finding that I was suddenly not nearly as tired as I had been only a few hours before as I walked with my girls past the hundreds of barbecuing picnickers in Sacher Park. At one point, I looked down at Tiferet, and she was staring up at me with her mouth gaping open. She said, "*Eema*, you are so beautiful," and then looked down at her feet with a silly, bashful smile as though she was swooning with love.

Today I received an email from Babyzone.com officially welcoming me to my second trimester. It said, "These weeks, weeks 13-24, are a time when the pregnant woman has the chance and peace of mind to really learn about having a baby. A woman has become somewhat accustomed to the strain on her physiology, her physical complaints usually decline and the visits to her doctor are mainly to make sure that she's still happy, alive, and pregnant.... It's amazing how quickly this makes a difference."

And it's true. This morning I woke up and felt no need to chew on some cookies before I got out of bed. Also, since last Tuesday's ultrasound, I have started thinking that this is a pregnancy that is going to make it. With God's help, it will stick like the snow I used to see through my window as a child when the radiator by my bed was so hot that it scorched my knees through my quilt. In a few months, maybe, we will even be able to tell our kids that their dream has come true – that there is once again a baby in mommy's belly, and this one will be coming home and not doing a U-turn back to the Garden of Eden. This time around, Tiferet will not run outside to stand with her arms extended by the front steps, just in case the baby should fall back to the ground from Heaven and there is no one around to catch it.

I have started thinking about the birth, about going to buy some maternity clothing, and when I rest I imagine how delicious and wonderful it will be to nurse and to hold a little baby. I can almost smell the sweet-sour milky smell of newborn as I type these words.

BLAH-BUSTER TIDBIT

Mothers in the Gold Mine

by Rachel Arbus[1]

Think of a miner in a gold mine. He works in the darkest depths of the earth, exposed to countless dangers. He could die from landslides, floods, poison gases, and even possibly from hard labor.... What motivates him to continue working and endangering himself? What inner strength enables him to forge ahead despite so many difficult challenges? Faith. His unwavering faith that in the depths of the earth he will discover gold.

We should relate to our work as parents and educators in the exact same way. The work of the educator is similar to the work of a miner. It is difficult, demanding, and at times even drives us into despair. But we as educators are fixed on our goal. We know the value and the power of the Jewish soul. Like every member of the Jewish people, our child received a great soul.... It is possible that his soul is hidden under a layer of conflicting impulses, stubbornness, and rebelliousness. And it is possible that his soul is in need of long years of polishing, but the Divine spark within him is alive and well. In every single child there is buried "good." This treasure exists even when the child and parents are still not aware of its existence. The constant faith in our hearts that within our children is buried a Divine spark will help our child to reveal it during the years of his or her education. This faith will also give us, their educators, the strength to overcome difficulties, to rise again after stumbling, and to continue to educate our children.

[1] Rachel Arbus, *Korot Bateinu*, 26–27.

WANDERLUST LOST

WHEN MY PARENTS come to visit us, they spend most of their time in our living room and at nearby playgrounds with the kids, so before every trip to Israel they spend a few days in a place where they can just be tourists. So a few months back my parents asked if I would like to join them on one of these pre-Jerusalem trips – to Barcelona, Cyprus, or Eilat, or some other exotic location. For years, I've turned down their invitations. I was always nursing, or taking care of a baby, and the idea of taking along an infant on a big trip was totally unappealing.

It *is* possible to travel with children, I suppose. I once heard of a rabbi who traveled with his wife and five children around the Indian subcontinent for six months, equipped only with two backpacks – one for kosher food and the other for diapers and clothing. But I'm not like that; I hate shlepping to places with a baby. I literally lose sleep over the thought of folding up the stroller with one hand and holding the baby in the other in order to get into a taxi that will take me to the Western Wall.

But whether these travel restrictions are self-imposed or not, the fact is that over the past seven years of nearly uninterrupted nursing and pregnancy, one of the only regrets I've had about my life is this inability to really travel. I still see young not-yet-marrieds I know heading off for India, China, or South America, and while I don't envy their years of tortuous searching for a soul mate or the existential and religious crises that seem to often go hand-in-hand with prolonged independence and solitude, there are definitely moments and hours in my mothering life that I find myself envious of the total freedom single people enjoy. The ability to pick up for six months and travel to Australia's outback, sending an email off every now and then to mom and the buddies back home to brag about their exploits.

So, when my parents invited me to join them on a trip this month to Cyprus, I really thought I couldn't turn down this opportunity. This would be my chance to stop coveting and to start doing, a chance to see a new place, to leave Israel for the first time in two years, to get a breather from my life and responsibilities for a few days – before I give birth in four months and breathers become a thing of the past. I envisioned coming home refreshed and invigorated from the trip, excited to have seen a bit of the world outside of Israel, and with new energy for motherhood and home.

But I made a serious miscalculation, and I should have known better. I could have figured out that something was going on when two weeks ago I attended a seminar from 9:30 AM until 6:30 PM, and this day away from my home had a traumatic effect on my system. I got a terrible headache, and felt down and frustrated and even resentful (even though I was the one who had signed up and paid a lot of money for the seminar of my own free will). That whole day, I craved my home like a nursing baby longs for its mother's familiar smell, like I would crave my bed after a few hours spent trying to sleep mattress-less on frozen asphalt.

But I didn't pick up on the signs to diagnose myself with a very early and severe case of nesting instinct. So, this past Wednesday, I left for Cyprus with Tiferet and my parents, and from the moment I got into the taxi to the airport, I missed my two-year-old, my sink full of dirty dishes, my husband, these essays in need of urgent editing, my six-year-old, my home – with such intensity that it was as though I was, from that first moment in the taxi, in mourning for my life.

The flight to Cyprus took less than an hour, and when we arrived at the hotel, Tiferet went right to the pool, and swam all around in her fluorescent pink bathing suit, having the greatest time. But as I sat watching her, and read a book, I did not feel happy, rejoicing in the luxury of sitting next to a pool and reading on a sunny, blue-skied Wednesday morning. Tiferet frolicked and my heart was in my knees. My heart was in Jerusalem.

And for the next five days, I shopped and toured around and watched the clouds pass by my window while I yearned for home. I was as miserable, as homesick, as when I was ten years old and attended a special summer camp for gymnastics in rural Pennsylvania. Back then, I dreamed of one day becoming an Olympic gymnast, the next Mary Lou Retton, but in reality, I couldn't even do a back handspring, and all the kids in my cabin thought I was the world's biggest reject, and I felt more lonely and miserable than I had ever felt in my whole life.

Recently, in an old trunk, I found some letters that I had sent home over the course of that summer, written with a silver pen on forest green stationery. I wrote in one letter: "Dear Mom and Dad, I am a bit worried since I have been hydroventilating (*sic*) a lot, and the nurse here says there is nothing she can do." And I hoped beyond hope that my parents would think that I was in the midst of a medical emergency necessitating a rescue mission ASAP. I spent countless hours watching the cars driving up the rural highway (I am not kidding) praying that my parents would understand my subtle plea for help and that they were coming to save me from my misery, but to no avail.

And that, ridiculously enough, was the level of yearning for home that I felt during this dream trip to Cyprus, that my parents had so generously invited me on in order to provide me with a bit of adventure as well as rest and relaxation before the baby comes. We stayed in really nice hotels, and every day my father planned a different outing to some sort of fascinating place, and every Cypriot we met was incredibly friendly, and Tiferet was a total sweety (the deal was, every site/museum we see, she gets a chocolate bar). And I tried so hard to have a good attitude, to take pleasure in this trip that I should have enjoyed immensely – the release from 6:30 wakeups and the mountain of laundry to put away and the wet sheets to change when I am too tired to brush my teeth before bed. Not to mention this exciting journey to this island nation with a different culture, language, political situation… everything.

But my efforts to get myself psyched up didn't work. I spent our whole time in Cyprus in a blue funk.

It did not help any that Dafna, my first-grader, was also feeling ambivalent about my trip to Cyprus. On the first day of the trip, Dafna's teacher placed an emergency call to Josh at work to tell him that Dafna was crying at school because her *eema* had abandoned her. Dafna had seemed totally nonchalant about my going before I left, and she had been amazingly understanding when I explained to her that I was taking her younger sister and not her since we did not want her to miss so many days of school. But once I left, Dafna missed me terribly.

It seemed a bit strange that Dafna missed me with such intensity, even during school hours when I usually do not see her. But I realized that for Dafna, and for all of our children, the fact that I am at home, to send them off to school with a multivitamin and a blessing, and to give them a big smile and a "It's great to see you!" when they come home, provides them with a feeling of stability and confidence, no matter where they are. The fact that I am at home enables them to go about their independent lives with a bit of home and security in their hearts – a scaled-down, mothering version of Divine Providence.

And just as much as Dafna felt abandoned to suddenly not have me around, I missed not being around. I realized in Cyprus that over the past seven years I have become a person who thrives on being in the heart of the playing and yelling and falling and laughing and crying that is my family. Deprived of all the hullabaloo that I'm accustomed to, I felt lonely and bored to the point of depression.

Yesterday, on the morning of our last day in Cyprus, I felt as though I would still never see the end of it. I felt as though the fourteen hours until our 10 PM flight would never end; it was a day that was as long as a week.

That whole last day, I walked with Tiferet all around Nicosia while my parents visited the famous Cyprus Museum, and wherever we walked the Cypriots we saw would give Tiferet this huge smile as she passed, as though she was the cutest child they had ever seen. Their Greek Orthodox love of large families combined with their modern European low birthrate drew them longingly to my daughter, patting/scratching her on the head like a cat, and all the storeowners gave her little gifts.

And over and over I thought to myself how these people had no idea. They thought I was so lucky to have a wonderful daughter like this, and they had no idea that I have two more treasures like this at home.

While I think that I am a person who manages to maintain a relatively high level of awareness of the blessings of my life, and I do wish that I had been spared the misery of this trip, at times maybe it is good for mothers to get away, if only to open our eyes to what we have waiting for us at home. I thank God every day for all that I have, but a few minutes past midnight when I walked through my front door after that trip, I felt God's blessing of my life with the intensity of a physical sensation. My gratitude and love for my husband, my children, our home, experienced as a tightening of the heart, a wetness in the eyes, hands reaching out for someone to hold on to – to give to.

BLAH-BUSTER TIDBIT

Jewish Women and Hope

Rabbi Shlomo Aviner teaches that the name Miriam comes from the word for rebellion (*meri*), since, according to Rabbi Aviner, she was the leader of a grassroots movement among all of the Jewish women in Egypt – a massive underground uprising to battle Pharaoh's decrees, which sought to prevent the survival of the Jewish people.[1]

Rabbi Aviner explains that Miriam's first revolutionary act took place when Pharaoh decreed that all Jewish boys should be killed at birth. The Midrash teaches that the Jewish men threw up their hands and decided to divorce their wives because they did not want to have babies just to have them be killed. All would have been lost – self-inflicted genocide without even one sword drawn – if six-year-old Miriam hadn't challenged her father, telling him: "What you are doing is worse than what Pharaoh is doing! He has only made a decree against the boys, and you are decreeing also against the girls who could still be born!" The Midrash teaches that Miriam saw, through prophecy, that her parents would give birth to the redeemer of the Jewish people, and as a result of Miriam's holy hutzpah her parents remarried, as did all of the Israelite couples in Egypt, and Moses was conceived.

Once again, when Pharaoh's plot to kill all the Israelite boys failed, the Midrash teaches us that he decided to put an end to the Jewish people by moving the men to the rural areas and the women to the cities. But under Miriam's leadership, the women were undeterred. After a day of backbreaking slave labor, the husbands just wanted to sleep. But their wives were determined to bring more Jewish babies into the world and ensure that the Jewish people continue. So they would travel hours to where their men were working, bringing fish stew to nourish their exhausted and abused husbands, and then they would lie down next to them underneath the apple trees in the fields. They would use their mirrors in flirtatious games in order to arouse and seduce their husbands so that they could become pregnant. The men had long given up hope that they would ever be free, but their wives would assure them night after night: "We will not always be slaves. God is going to save us!"

---

[1] *Perush al Haggada shel Pesah* by Harav Shlomo Aviner. Jerusalem: 2001.

After the Exodus, when the Israelites were building the Tabernacle, all the women went as a group to the entrance of the Tabernacle in order to donate those same mirrors to make the sacred vessels. Moses became angry with the women, telling them that he had no need for such disgraceful tools of vanity, but God corrected Moses. He told him: "These mirrors are more beloved to Me than any of the many gifts brought to build the Tabernacle, because it was through them that the women succeeded in establishing a huge Jewish nation in Egypt."[2]

All of this is not just ancient history. Rabbi Ezriel Tauber tells the following story about his parents' survival of the Holocaust in Hungary and Auschwitz. At one point, Rabbi Tauber's mother was the only woman in her whole town who continued to go to the mikve,[3] giving birth to four sons between 1940 and 1944. The other Jewish husbands in the town rebuked Rabbi Tauber's father, saying, "What? In times like these to continue building a family? It is absolute insanity to keep on having children when one doesn't know what will be tomorrow."

But the rabbi's mother, who survived Auschwitz along with her husband and all but one of her children, explained after the war, "I never thought for a minute that we were better than any of the millions who sanctified Hashem's Name with their deaths. But we believe in the resurrection of the dead! When one bears a child it is eternal! I did my task, I kept on having children in accordance with Hashem's commandments. We didn't make calculations." Today, this mother lives in Israel with her nine children, over a hundred grandchildren, and more than twenty great-grandchildren. She tells them all frequently, "Be happy that you are alive! Appreciate the gift of life with faith and whole-heartedness!"[4]

The name of the woman in Jewish mysticism is "I will be (*Ehyeh*)," meaning that in her essence a woman is focused on the future. She has the unique potential to not be bound by the limitations, the fears, the threats of the present. Or, as Rabbi Aviner explains, the women were responsible for the redemption from Egypt because of their ability "to overcome the law of gravity, uplifted in the air, freed from the ground and limitations of the

---

[2] *Midrash Tanhuma*, Exodus 38:9.

[3] Since sexual contact between husband and wife is dependent on a woman's purification in the ritual bath following menstruation.

[4] Goldstein, Sarah. *Special Delivery: Jewish Birth Stories of Faith and Inspiration*. Jerusalem: 2004.

physical reality." We have the ability to maintain hope in the darkest moments of Jewish history – hoping that God will part another sea for us, bring down another one of our enemies, even revive the dead – bringing redemption from a place we could have never imagined.

SUFFERING AND SONG

THERE IS A RULE of nature that I have found to hold true over the years, right along with Heisenberg's Uncertainty Principle and the Law of Inertia, that while pregnancy, childbirth, and motherhood can be wonderful, fulfilling, and all the rest, there is still always a certain amount of suffering involved in bringing a new baby into the world. If you look around and it appears that there are other women for whom childbearing is an absolutely easy, painless process, then this is most likely an illusion. If you take a closer look you will notice that the cousin who passes through the first trimester without the slightest hint of nausea will get debilitating varicose veins in her second. The friend who gives birth as painlessly as a goldfish lays eggs will suffer from postpartum depression that puts her in bed for six months. And the sister who bakes the pastries for her son's bris will get so many breast infections that she will have to give up nursing at four weeks. Every single woman, no matter how athletic, young, or spiritual she is, will experience difficulty when bringing a new child into the world. That's the way things are.

Even though I've known this for years, I was pretty quiet about it, since I knew that this sweeping conclusion was based solely on extremely unscientific research conducted while speaking with mothers at the shul kiddush, in the obstetrician's waiting room, and while reading the heartbreaking letters I receive at my website. And then, this past week, my husband told me something that made me really happy: that two thousand years before I was even born, the authors of the Midrash came to this very same conclusion.

Josh and I have a wonderful arrangement this year. Most mornings, before he heads off to prepare his classes and study at a yeshiva, he sits down to drink a coffee at the French café across from Tiferet's nursery school. So, after spending an hour fishing lost shoes out from underneath the sofa, placing cream cheese and tuna sandwiches in backpacks, debating the virtues of ponytails vs. braids, and transporting Dafna, Nisa and Tiferet to day care, nursery school, and school, I breathe a sigh of relief at this major daily accomplishment and reward myself with a visit to the café to talk with my husband for ten minutes or so. What an incredible luxury! A mini-date at the beginning of almost every day.

Last week at the café, Josh read me a midrash on the book of Exodus which asks why *shira*, the Hebrew word for song or praise, is feminine. And the Midrash answers that this is because we women, across the board, know more about praising God than our brothers and husbands and fathers and sons. The Midrash explains that this is because true praise and song can come only from a person who has suffered in the past, which is the case for every single woman who is also a mother.[1]

The Midrash is not only talking about the fact that if someone is bonking you over the head with a wrench then you will be exceptionally jubilant when he finally puts his wrench into his pocket and goes off to find another victim (although that's definitely part of it). It's talking mostly about a way of seeing the world with which mothers are blessed. Mothers learn over the course of their lives that suffering is not a permanent state, that things get worse before they get better. We are privy to this knowledge because of our biological reality. A woman throws up day and night and feels exhausted and terrible, and she knows that in nine months she will beam like the sun when she holds a new baby in her arms. The same woman who, at the birth, swears that she is leaving her husband, eventually forgets and recovers and falls in love with her baby and forgives her husband for getting her into this whole mess in the first place, and finds herself, a year or two or three later, crying at diaper commercials and desperate to take another spin on the fertility merry-go-round.

And it is not only pregnancy that teaches women this lesson; raising children teaches women this same thing. For me, one of the biggest surprises of motherhood has been to see how quickly children can change from one extreme to another. I have witnessed with my own eyes how the biting, bullying, impossible three-year-old who earned me a year of dirty looks from

---

[1] *Midrash Tanhuma:* Vayera, siman 20.

all the mothers in the park became the teacher's favorite by the age of four. I have also seen how a five-year-old can have a tantrum, throwing furniture and spewing venom, and then ten minutes later she can be quietly sitting on the sofa, singing to herself as she helps her three-year-old sister zip up her coat. Over the years, I have learned that optimism and faith that my children will grow out of difficult stages is not an irrational leap of faith, but rather the most logical conclusion I can come to based on years of accumulated mothering experience.

And this is a powerful lesson for life, the reason why the Hebrew word for mother is based on the word for faith (*em/emuna*). Because suffering is not an inherent aspect of men's lives, they can easily experience difficulty and believe that things will never change, that things are bad and are only going to get worse. But women, when faced with difficulty, know based on their own biological and mothering reality that it is exactly when life looks absolutely hopeless that things are most likely to change for the better. And the fact that women have this strong faith has made a major contribution to the morale of the Jewish people throughout the wars and trials and objectively impossible situations that make up Jewish history.

Last year, I heard a talk by Rabbi Yona Goodman[2] called "In the Eye of the Storm" about how mothers can help their children to cope during times of frequent terror attacks. He spoke about the importance of maintaining hope and conveying that hope to our children. And he told us that he has seen over and over how mothers are often the family members most capable of maintaining an atmosphere of optimism even in the most difficult times.

Rabbi Goodman recalled a visit he made several months before to one of the settlements in the Gaza Strip where hundreds of mortars fall every month – destroying homes and at times injuring and killing residents. The parents there must be constantly on alert, waiting for the sirens warning that a mortar is about to fall, and then rushing their children to the bomb shelters.

---

[2] Presented at Binyan Shalem, July 2004. Rabbi Goodman is the director of advanced studies at Michlelet Orot.

The speaker confessed that he had been horrified by this way of life. He could not understand how parents manage to live and raise children in an environment so conducive to fear and despair. But when he asked the mother of the family that was hosting him how she managed to maintain an atmosphere of calm and normality in her family despite the attacks, she dismissed his question. She said, "It's really not so bad. We just have to be very organized. For example, I keep a backpack by the door at all times in which I keep snacks and toys so that we will always be ready to run to the bomb shelter with the kids when the siren goes off."

But the speaker did not like this answer. The backpack constantly at the ready reminded him of the constant state of fear and danger his own parents and grandparents had experienced while fleeing the Nazis during the Holocaust. He said, "A backpack always ready so you can flee from the mortars? It sounds so terrible!" But the mother just laughed, and said, "No, really it's not as bad as you make it sound. This bag is no different from the hospital bag I keep ready by the door during the weeks before I give birth."

Because of the realities of motherhood, women like this mother learn that suffering is simply a stage of life; suffering is what must come before redemption does.

And this is a lesson that I was forced to learn this past year. A year ago this week, I was coping with the death of a fetus whom I had believed with complete certainty would grow up to become one of my children – to read stories to, to love, to feed, to talk with in the quiet dark of my bedroom at the end of the long day. And exactly a year ago tonight, I was at the hospital, waiting to meet with the doctor who would perform the surgery to remove the fetus. I had sent Josh home to put the girls to bed, and as I sat next to the other women on the bench outside of the doctor's office, I felt like I had an encyclopedia sitting on my chest; I was terrified that I was going to hyperventilate and suffocate. When the doctor poked his head out to call in another patient, I asked him if I still had a few minutes to run to my room to get something.

He nodded, and I dashed down a floor to my room to get a small book of Psalms that I had borrowed from the hospital synagogue. I should explain that I almost never read Psalms since the Hebrew in them is just too hard for me to make heads or tails of. On most days, saying Psalms for me is less like prayer and more like a punishment, like having to write "I will not throw spitballs" one hundred times on the blackboard.

But that evening, alone after dark in that huge, creepy hospital, just a few steps away from the delivery room where I had felt such tremendous joy after giving birth to Dafna and Tiferet, I needed that book of Psalms as badly as I needed my husband's hand to hold. I opened it right to the famous Psalm that we sing every Shabbat, "A Song of David, God is my shepherd, I shall not want...." And I read until the line, "Though I walk through the Valley of the Shadow of Death, I will fear no evil, because You are with me." I read it over and over, and cried as I felt God's presence. I was amazed by how precisely King David described what I was feeling. I was for the first time in my life in the Valley of the Shadow of Death, that was the most exact possible description of where I was. And the only comfort I had was that God was with me, that He would stand by me as He had the many other people who had opened that very same book of Psalms when they were wandering around in the impenetrable darkness of death's shadow in those hospital corridors.

But what I really wanted to tell you is that a year ago, sitting outside of that doctor's office, I was unable to imagine that only a year later my reality would switch so drastically from one extreme to another. Please note that the Midrash does not claim that faith is linked to the X chromosome. It is simply a kind of wisdom that a woman's life gives her. And a year ago I believed, at least on a certain level, that the sadness of the loss of that pregnancy would stay with me for the rest of my life. Or, more exactly, I did not believe. I had no idea that that old sadness would disappear so completely, evaporated somewhere within the happiness, the expanding belly, of this blessed pregnancy.

And even more surprising for me is the extent to which I am not alone. Almost all the women who suffered losses a year ago are now pregnant. Last month, Yemima pointed to my growing belly, and whispered, "Me, too! I am due on Yosef Chai's first yahrzeit! Pray for me!" My friend Anna, who also miscarried last January, now shares my due date. So does Elana, a friend who was unable to conceive for four intensely difficult and sad years. All of these long-awaited babies are due to join the world this coming Nissan, the month that the Israelite women fled from Egyptian slavery with drums in their bags, ready for a celebration despite the fact that the whole Egyptian army would soon be in hot pursuit. Because the holy women of that generation, of whom we are the reincarnation, knew that the way of the world is that things get worse before they get better – that if morning sickness passes, and labor pains pass, and the terrible twos pass, then this too will pass. And they were right.

Monday, May 9, 2005/ 29 Nissan 5765

12:31 AM

Shalom!

Chana gave birth to a healthy (hefty at 4.1 kg/9 lb.) baby girl at 8:35 tonight after a long wait and a short labor. Like one of her sisters, it took this baby a while to decide when to make her entrance, but when she was ready, was she ready.

Thank God.

Joshua

SEVEN SECRETS FROM
SEVEN MOTHERS

THROUGHOUT THIS BOOK, you have read a lot about my experiences as a mother. But I feel that this book would not be complete without including the stories of other mothers who, like me, have been helped to overcome hardships by seven secrets of Jewish motherhood.

But there is another reason I want you to read the stories of the women in this coming section, and in order to explain why, I would like to tell you about a mother from my neighborhood. I pass this woman in her plaid housecoat almost every morning as she waits with her four small boys for the van that takes them to *heder*.[1] At least several hundred times she has greeted me with a Yiddish-accented "Shalom," and commented with a shy smile on the weather, or the progress of Passover cleaning, or the questionable nutritional content of the pretzels her children are eating for breakfast.

This mother, whose name is Sara, is a simple woman. She married before she finished seminary, and spends her days cooking and cleaning and caring for her children as well as one or two other small children from the neighborhood. Twice, while returning home late at night, I have seen her strolling with her husband on the sidewalk by her house when he returns from yeshiva after 10 PM, her shy smile replaced by a glowing one as she looks up at him.

Last night, as I walked by Sara's home at around 8:30, I heard her comforting one of her children who was crying out in pain. I thought of how hard it must be for her to care for this crying child after her long day on her own taking care of her children. And I thought of all the similar acts of kindness and self-sacrifice that she must perform throughout the day, without fanfare, behind the closed door of her two-room apartment.

---

[1] Yeshiva for young boys.

I thought about how no journalist will ever write an article about this woman, and how no street will ever be named after her. I thought about how in the eyes of the world, this woman is absolutely insignificant, utterly forgettable. But I, for one, am fascinated by her, and even in awe of her. If someone offered me the choice of a morning spent interviewing Condoleezza Rice or this young mother, in a second I would choose a discussion with Sara about recovering from her recent C-section over a chat with Condoleezza about her new vision for the Middle East.

This final section of this book is a collection of inspirational excerpts and honest interviews with mothers about what we think and feel and struggle with behind closed doors. It's about overcoming and knowing that you are not the only one.

BLAH-BUSTER TIDBIT

Nechama Greisman's Survival Tips for Mothers[1]

Rebbetzin Nechama Greisman was a popular teacher as well as a devoted mother of a large family. I never merited to meet Nechama Greisman in her short lifetime, but through her down-to-earth and inspirational books on Jewish motherhood, she has influenced me as much as any teacher I have ever had.

❖ You, as a mother, should work on being confident about who you are and what you want. Know that YOU are a living example and that YOU are the most important person and role model in your children's world. You are the one whom they look up to and imitate and follow.

❖ When a mother is happy, everyone is happy.

❖ Look for small opportunities to spend time alone with each child, even if only for a few minutes. This makes children feel very special.

❖ Before your child goes to sleep at night tell him that you love him, and that you are the richest person in the world because you have a child like him. Watch his eyes light up....

❖ NEVER, EVER compare yourself with others. You don't know someone else's energy level, financial situation, stresses, health, etc. Do the best YOU can.

❖ Let your children know how precious, special, loved, and important they are. Tell them that as soon as they were born, you added an extra Shabbos candle, and thus the world became a brighter place because of them....

---

[1] Adapted from Rabbi Moshe Miller, ed. *The Nechama Greisman Anthology: Wisdom from the Heart.* Jerusalem: 2000, 170–171.

AYALA'S STORY*

LEARNING TO VALUE OUR MOTHERING
ACCOMPLISHMENTS

AYALA IS A THIRTY-SEVEN-YEAR-OLD mother of five children who grew up in a Modern Orthodox home in South Africa and moved to Israel fifteen years ago. She teaches Bible in a junior-high school, and lives in the Givat Mordechai neighborhood. She and her husband are today Haredi Leumi, (or National Ultra-Orthodox), believing that the State of Israel is the first step in the establishment of the Messianic era. At the same time, they value Torah learning over secular education and are more strictly observant of Jewish law than her parents.

Ayala spoke with humor and insight about her life as a mother. She discusses her evolving attitude to motherhood over the past decade, changing from being a person who felt that she had to be a teacher in addition to being a mother in order to maintain a sense of self-worth and individual identity, to becoming at peace, in recent years, with having motherhood at the center of her life. It is interesting to note that despite this change in outlook, Ayala is still a committed and successful teacher. Her change in attitude has been expressed more in coming to terms with her life, accepting the limitations that being a mother puts on Torah study and synagogue attendance, for example, as well as opening her eyes more and more to the blessings of raising religious children.

---

* In this and all of the interviews in this section, I have changed names as well as identifying details.

BEGINNINGS

I was always a quiet person, but if it means anything, I was an official in the school government. I wasn't necessarily a leader, but I guess people always respected me and I think that's why I was elected to this position.

I grew up in a Modern Orthodox home. My father is the principal of a Jewish day school, and my mother was a teacher in the same school, so we definitely grew up in a very *frum* [Orthodox] home. The fact that my parents work in Jewish education meant that it was a home where we were always discussing Jewish ideas, and where Jewish as well as secular learning were always encouraged.

MARRIAGE

I was twenty-two when I got married. I met my husband because he was becoming a *baal teshuva* [newly religious], and he enrolled at my father's school, even though his parents weren't so happy about it, and he was also his class's representative in the school student council.

He was one of my father's favorite students, and when we were in high school together he became like a member of our family. So we got to know each other over the course of years, from the time I was about fourteen. I mean, it was a natural friendship that developed, so it was a very nice way to meet somebody, and because of that we really knew each other well before we got married. We were actually going out for maybe two of those years, but I used to go places with him and people would think he was my brother, and they'd say to him, "How's your father?" meaning my father. So, it was just really natural when we decided to get married.

We got married right after I completed university, and right away we came to live in Israel. From one day to the next, my life changed drastically in a lot of ways – because we left South Africa and came here and started a new life, and also because being married was really, really wonderful. It was a totally different life from living as a single woman in my parents' home. I had always been a very quiet person and I became much more outgoing and confident in social situations because my husband made me feel so good about myself. Marriage was very good for me in a lot of ways.

MOVING TO ISRAEL

Making *aliya* [immigration to Israel] was also wonderful. You know, we came as newlyweds and everything was exciting. We moved to a settlement called Bet Haggai near Hevron, which was at that time a really small settlement with eighteen families. We felt like we wanted to be pioneers, like we wanted to build up the Land. So we *davka* [purposely] chose this settlement that was small and unknown, and it was a really big mistake. It was horrible. Let me rephrase that. It was awful for me. It's a very nice settlement, but I really didn't like it. It was just such a different way of living.

When we got to Bet Haggai there was not even a paved road within the settlement. There were no telephone lines. It was freezing. There was almost no heating inside the houses. We would sit there, and snow would come in under the doors. I mean, it was really pioneering, and I don't think I was prepared for it. Socially, there was only one other English-speaking couple. We had chosen this settlement because we wanted to be in an Israeli environment, but I realized very quickly that you can't pretend to be an Israeli just because you've made *aliya*. You can't pretend that you're not an English speaker coming from a different culture. Even though our Hebrew was already good, that wasn't the problem. It was just that everybody was Israeli and had grown up differently from us in so many ways.

Also, it was during the first Intifada, and we used to travel to Jerusalem every day and we'd get stones thrown at us, and it was dangerous. We had to drive through Hevron as well as Bethlehem, and it was a scary time, so it got to the point where our parents called and said, "Look, we want you to move out of there. We'll pay for you to buy a place in Jerusalem." And I was relieved that they said that because besides the Intifada, I just wasn't happy there.

We were there for a year, and then we moved to Jerusalem, straight to Givat Mordechai, and we bought this apartment and have been here ever since.

PREGNANCY

Another problem with settlement life was that it was centered on the family and children, and we were married for two years before I fell pregnant. Living in Bet Haggai put even more pressure on us and made my inability to become pregnant even more painful.

When we were engaged, Asher was studying in yeshiva while I was finishing up university, and several months before the wedding I said to him, "Look into all the books you can, and look for a *heter* [permission] to use birth control because I don't want to have a child straight away." And after looking into the matter, he came back to me and said, "I've tried my best, but my rabbis won't give us a *heter.*" I was really upset. I thought this isn't any good, that it would destroy our marriage if we didn't have time to consolidate as a couple without children. Anyway, I was really upset.

But I said, OK, what can I do? I'm going to have to have a child straight away. So then, as soon as we got married, I mean really from day one, I was dying to fall pregnant. My whole thinking completely changed. I thought, "Why did I not want to have children?" I don't know if you can say such things, but I really thought that *Hashem* was sort of paying me back *midah ke-neged midah* (measure for measure), because in the end I couldn't get pregnant for two years and it was really very traumatic for me. That's how *Hashem* organized it.

We started minor fertility treatments, and soon after, when we'd been married for two years, I became pregnant with our oldest daughter, Rivki. It's interesting that since then I've always become pregnant without any difficulty or medical intervention.

So the whole fact of becoming pregnant was like this big miracle. I started out with this attitude that *Hashem* had given us this tremendous gift, and that I was not going to pay any attention to the stories people had told me about how hard pregnancy is and how sick you feel. I decided that this was going to be a great pregnancy and a great birth and this was going to be a great child. And I was right on all accounts. It was a wonderful pregnancy. No medical problems. And the birth was also really wonderful. It was very much my attitude to it.

If we were to speak objectively about how the birth was, in somebody else's eyes it would have been considered long. It was very long. I was having hard contractions for two days, and it ended with a vacuum delivery, but I was just so excited about having the baby, that although it was uncomfortable, I didn't feel pain. And I just felt so focused on meeting this baby that I had been waiting for for so long that I felt like it was a really wonderful experience. I was controlled. I just felt like I was going to do it, and *Hashem* was going to help me, and it was going to be great.

CHALLENGES OF EARLY MOTHERHOOD

Becoming a mother was obviously something that changed my life. Completely. And in the first few days and the first few weeks I felt like everything I did was going to have an impact on this baby for the rest of her life. You know, if I didn't change her diaper for an hour, I thought it was going to ruin her in some way. I loved having a baby even though I was nervous about everything I did. I also really liked the experience of breastfeeding, once I got used to it.

I was a student at the time, and I went back to study when she was two months old, but it was only a few hours a few times a week. I left her with my upstairs neighbor and I used to express milk for her and it was fine. Then I started teaching when she was about six months old, and that was hard but it was manageable.

With my first few children, I enjoyed having babies but I was also always itching to get back out there, to go back to school and then to go to work. I couldn't see myself taking care of a baby twenty-four hours a day, just being home and looking at them and smiling at them all day. I was still fighting against losing my independence, and I found it incredibly challenging, for example, not being able to go to shul on Rosh ha-Shana and Yom Kippur, and having to just stay home watching the kids and doing mundane things. I felt very confined.

Because of all this, my third pregnancy was difficult. On the one hand I wanted to be pregnant, and on the other hand I just didn't know how I was going to cope with having three kids and still have a life for myself. So I was tense and nervous the whole pregnancy. And also the birth was very difficult.

COMING TO PEACE WITH MOTHERHOOD

I think by the time I had our fourth child, I'd made peace with it, and I knew that I was a mother and that's who I was. So, all those concerns about career and having my own independent identity stopped bothering me so much, and I stopped fighting it. I really don't know how this happened, but when number four came along I felt like I had come to peace with being a mother, and that it was good to have another child.

With number five, my most recent baby, I wasn't working and I stayed home with her until she was ten months old, and I enjoyed that. I felt by then that I was so busy with so many other children that I just needed to be home, and I wasn't bored in the least. I felt completely satisfied with just being at home with my kids.

At a certain point, I just became more relaxed about being a mother. Motherhood had always been a bit difficult for me, because I perceived myself as a person who is not just a mother. Well, I shouldn't say "just a mother," but you know… I just didn't know who I was. I was trying to find myself really. And I think when number four came along I was just really content – that that's who I am. I'm a mother. And I shouldn't be ashamed about being a mother or upset about being a mother or trying to be something else at the same time as being a mother. It was OK to just be a mother. Accepting this took a huge weight off my shoulders.

I did still go to work after my baby was born. But I felt like my work had taken a back seat, like it wasn't so important anymore. I didn't feel like I needed that fulfillment from the outside so much anymore.

A SICK CHILD

The most difficult experience I've had as a mother was when my youngest child was in the hospital. That was pretty scary. She was seven months old, and she was just sleeping all the time, and I thought that there was something wrong. If I had been a first-time mother, I don't know if I would have picked up on this, but I just felt like this is not the way a seven-month-old should be acting. She had no energy, and her weight wasn't going up. So I took her to the doctor regularly and he said that as long as she's not going down in weight, there's nothing to worry about. So for several months she was maintaining the same weight.

And then the last time I took her to the doctor, she had dropped almost a kilo, and I hadn't even noticed. And she looked really thin and gaunt, and the doctor said straight away, "Take her to the hospital," and it turned out that she was malnourished. It was difficult emotionally to feel that what's wrong with your child is that you didn't feed her well. It's a very big issue. Or that because I was only breastfeeding her, she wasn't getting what she needed to get. She just refused to eat solids.

But this is something that I'm still grappling with: what type of responsibility did I have in this? How could I do that to my child? How could I not know what was going on? It's all this self-blame which I know is very negative and not very helpful, but it's hard to just distance myself from the thought that it was my fault. Nobody else was involved here. It was only me.

She was on her way to recovery once we got to the hospital, and they started feeding her through a tube down into her stomach. But it was traumatic. It was traumatic for the actual time we were in the hospital because we had to have someone take care of the other kids. But you know, there was a lot of lingering trauma that I've been dealing with since we got back from the hospital. I used to be totally into breastfeeding and thought it was the best thing for a child. And now I just feel like I would never breastfeed again.

The doctors were focused on treating the problem and not apportioning any blame or even figuring out why it happened or how it happened. They just wanted to make her better. But there were certain hints they dropped. They would say things among themselves like, "His mother is exclusively breastfeeding her and has never started her on solids." But they really didn't say much, which was good because I wouldn't have been able to stand it if they'd said anything against me.

Actually, one of the nurses was extremely nice. They were giving her bottles and she said, "Now we're giving her bottles, but you can breastfeed at the same time. Why don't you try and do that?" I said to her, "I don't want to. I want to stop this breastfeeding. It's no good and I don't want to have anything to do with it." It's not something you get over that easily.

And when this happened I thought I'd done the worst possible thing for her. And I thought that I was a really bad mother. And I thought, not only am I a bad mother for her, but I was also probably a bad mother for the other kids when I was breastfeeding them, which was a totally ridiculous thought because they were fine and healthy. It was rather challenging.

RELIGIOUS OUTLOOK

I'm a person who used to really like going to shul every Shabbos, so for me it's really difficult not being able to go to shul on Yom Kippur or Shabbos because I'm home with the kids. So I've had to find a way to deal with the fact that I have to *daven* [pray] by myself and grab a moment to *daven* while someone's pulling at my skirt as opposed to spending the whole of Shabbos *davening* and connecting with *Hashem*.

My husband used to say to me, "You have such a great opportunity when you're breastfeeding a child to just sit and learn Torah!" And I did that for a short while, but then I realized that it wasn't so realistic. Now, most of my religious feeling is connected with passing on religion to my children. I feel a responsibility as a religious mother not only to make sure my children are good people, but to see to it as well that they will devote themselves to being holy people who are close to God.

The best moments of motherhood are when you see the years you've spent educating and mothering the children pay off. When the kids do something or say something that is totally unexpected, and it's so beautiful and you wonder where did this child come from? How did I get such a wonderful kid? Like when my four-year-old said, "*Eema* [Mom], when I grow up, I want to be a rabbi and learn a lot of Torah." I was amazed that he came to think that and say that. Or when the baby started speaking and one of the first things she learned to say was "*Baruch atah.*" It's just these beautiful moments when I feel that my children are so cute that make me feel such gratitude that I have these children, and that they're growing up with really good values. That they're growing up religious and *Hashem* and Torah are a big part of their lives.

VIEW OF OWN MOTHER

I saw my own mother being a mother and going to work, so I assumed I would do that too. But I think she did a better job of it than I do. That's probably because I'm actually doing it now, and I can't get into her head and see how she felt when she was the one bringing us up. But she always had these beautiful dinners for us every night, even though she was working and had five kids, and I just can't manage to make dinner during the week. I find it's just overwhelming, and I don't have time.

The truth is that I don't know how it was for her, since she was the one doing it and she didn't tell me how it was. She just did it. Now I realize a lot of things about my mother that I never realized as a child. You know, I realize how hard she worked when she was raising us. Now that I have children, I have more respect for her, and I have more understanding of what her life was like.

HOPES FOR DAUGHTERS

I hope that my daughters will first of all live religious lives, stay in Israel, build good families, be good people. Whatever they decide to do, whether they decide to work or to stay at home with their kids or to be a different level of religiosity than we are, I just want them to be good people. You know, to also be doing what they believe is true.

BLAH-BUSTER TIDBIT

Coping with Mothering Frustration

by Miriam Levi[1]

Our anger at our children usually stems from Low Frustration Tolerance, a belief that we cannot tolerate pain, discomfort, or frustration. Children do, however, cause us no end of inconvenience and frustration as they grow up. They deprive us of sleep; they tie us down to the house; they cause us extra work; they are a financial burden; and, because they have minds of their own, they do not always act exactly as we want. Even though we might sometimes wish things to be different, we can nevertheless continue to be reasonably happy, so long as we learn to accept these inconveniences and frustrations with equanimity. Annoyance or inconvenience in themselves cannot make us angry unless we tell ourselves, "I shouldn't be inconvenienced in this dreadful way!"

The next time your children fight, don't become enraged by telling yourself, "They shouldn't be acting this way; they shouldn't cause me so much aggravation!" Tell yourself, rather, "It's a shame that they're acting like this, but let me see what I can do about the situation as it is."

When we get angry over frustrating or annoying circumstances, our anger is frequently increased by the feeling that there is nothing we can do about them. We tell ourselves, "I can't stand being so helpless. It's awful to be so powerless to change anything!" Observe that it is not our helplessness, but rather our evaluation that the helplessness is awful, which intensifies our anger. Some things are not up to us to change. We had best learn to tolerate such conditions, and stop upsetting ourselves over our inability to change them.

Frequently, however, trying circumstances can be effectively dealt with. In such situations we can prevent anger by looking for steps to take to minimize our inconvenience or irritation. For example, if a child's tantrum is

---

[1] Miriam Levi, *Coping with Anger*, 262–264. The author, a mother of three grown sons, is a consultant and instructor in special education. She conducts parenting workshops in Israel and abroad and has written many books on issues related to parenting. Mrs. Levi received her B.A. in early childhood education from Hunter College and did graduate work in special education at Teacher's Institute of Columbia University. She has lived in Jerusalem since 1970.

wearing us down, we can put him in his room. We can even listen to some music, turning up the volume to drown out the noise. The unfortunate child is not helped by our listening to his screams, and meanwhile, we can get some badly needed respite. We can check up on him, from time to time, to make sure he is all right.

Parenting expert Rachel Arbus: "Don't say, 'Why is this happening to me?' and 'When will this ever end?' Say to yourself, 'What should I do now?'"

GITTEL'S STORY

LEARNING TO LET GOD HELP YOU OUT

GITTEL IS A 45-YEAR OLD stay-at-home mother of ten children ranging between the ages of five and twenty-three who lives in Jerusalem's Maalot Dafna neighborhood. She grew up in Baltimore in a minimally traditional family, became observant as a teenager, and now identifies as Haredi, drawing from the Lithuanian and Hasidic traditions as well as her "own stuff," which she defines as trying to "connect to God every minute, and knowing that He's in control." Her "own stuff" turned out to be a major theme in Gittel's story of her life as a mother; her transformation over the years from being a controlling and stressed-out parent into a more accepting person who allows her children more space while reminding herself that God, not she, is the one in charge.

GROWING UP

My parents grew up in kosher, *shomer Shabbos* [Sabbath observant] homes. Growing up, we went to an Orthodox shul, but nobody, including my family, really kept the *mitzvos*, except the rabbi maybe. My father was a dentist and my mother ran the office.

I started becoming religious when I was in Sunday school in seventh grade and I started thinking about existential issues. I got involved in NCSY[1] and after that I went to Neve Yerushalayim[2] for half a year and then went back to the States for college.

---

[1] The National Council of Synagogue Youth is a youth movement that engages in Jewish outreach among American students.

[2] A women's yeshiva in Jerusalem's Har Nof neighborhood. Affiliated with the Haredi world, it attracts mostly students from non-observant homes.

MARRIAGE

When I came back to go to college in Boston I got connected to a religious congregation that a lot of young singles attended. My husband was there also, but we didn't meet for a number of years. We saw each other at Shabbos tables because back then families would still invite single men and women to the same Shabbos meals. And then he asked me out, and we got engaged about three months later.

One major problem when I got married was that I was bored. We moved to Cleveland so my husband could start law school, so I lost all my friends, and he was never home. I started school again and I worked a very little bit, but basically I was bored. And then I got pregnant pretty soon after, so that kept me busy, and my daughter was born right after our first anniversary.

PREGNANCY

Pregnancy was horrible. I'm very sensitive to my body and every single change so I noticed every single thing that was going on. I was always complaining about this, that, or the other thing, and I suffered a lot with headaches. It was pretty miserable. It wasn't that way every time. After we moved to Israel I got involved in alternative medicine so I learned that there are a lot of herbs that you can take to strengthen and balance the body so that pregnancy becomes a lot easier.

It was also a horrible birth, a 25-hour labor. The truth is, I wasn't going to have any more kids after that. And I made that very clear to my husband after I hit him in the face with my IV and told him that I was running away. I'm laughing now, but it was not funny at all at the time. It was an unusual birth. My mother had called wondering where I was and when she didn't find me home she called the hospital and they stupidly told her I was there. She took a plane and still made it in plenty of time for the birth. She heard all my screaming.

My doctor was on vacation, and I had this young resident who didn't know how to operate the new hospital beds. He couldn't even stitch me up properly, and it caused me a lot of problems until I had corrective surgery 12 years later. I couldn't sit down for months. I couldn't nurse. It was the worst experience of my whole life. It was absolutely horrendous.

After the birth I was feeling horrible in all of my body. The baby would cry a lot because I wasn't nursing right and she was allergic to the formula I was giving her. My husband was up almost every night with her because I just couldn't handle it anymore. Those were very difficult times.

My oldest daughter is still difficult. I think the first child is just always a first child and that's the end of that. She was very allergic and I didn't know and we were always preoccupied with what to do with her. When I got to Israel four years later, alternative medicine helped. But you know, by then there were other children, and I never really had time to focus on her and her needs because there were so many overwhelming needs and situations that I couldn't deal with everything. My husband wasn't around either because he was always working, so I forced that daughter to do whatever I wanted her to do and to fill in the role of substitute parent. At a young age she had to take on a lot of responsibility, which she has a lot to say about. You should interview her.

LETTING GO

When I was first starting out as a mother my big, big line was "I want to raise my children so they won't have to go to a psychologist like all the kids in America. I want to avoid all the pitfalls." But, forget about it! As much as you do, and you can be aware and you can try your best, but from left and right field, your kids are going to have challenges that you didn't count on. No matter what you want, *Hashem* has His plan. That's one major lesson I have learned. There's no such thing as raising perfect kids. Things are going to happen that are out of your control, that you never wanted to know about in your entire life.

One of the things that happened to my kids was when my daughter was seven years old. We were living in Betar, and I sent her next door with her sister who was four years older. Very simple. But on the way, there was this weirdo who was going around and she walked by his car and she had a very bad experience. He did not touch her, but she saw things I never wanted her to see. Things happen that are totally out of our control. But we *daven* [pray] and we do our best and *Hashem* does whatever He wants.

Another child of mine went to a neighbor's house, and it turned out that the father was doing stuff to girls. Not to my daughter, but almost. I went into shock, I can't even tell you for how long. It was a very wonderful family, and I knew them well. Did I ask for this? Did I order this? Did I want this?

That's why a mother has to always *daven*. *Davening* doesn't mean from a *siddur*. We need to be talking to *Hashem* during the day, we need to let out a primal-scream type of thing to express a part of us that's not expressed in words. When I was younger, there must have been three years or more that I didn't even manage to say *Shema*. My *davening* was just, "I want to go to the bathroom by myself without nursing a crying baby on my lap!" Or when you light candles and everyone's screaming around you and you can't even remember to say "good Shabbos" to your kids after you've finished lighting because you're so angry at them for not leaving you alone for long enough to say a blessing, let alone talk to *Hashem* at this moment when you know you're supposed to. You just want to break down and cry and go to your room until tomorrow. So you crawl into bed and you cry under your blanket and you talk to *Hashem,* and that's real *davening.* That's the kind of real *davening* that motherhood has taught me about.

I've become much less controlling over the years. My first set of kids grew up in a more ordered house, but I was very strict and unyielding with them. I told them what to do, and that they had to do it right away, or else. They would just wear me out completely. I was totally frantic and screaming a lot, and I was out of control. They have a lot to say about the way I was, and they will tell you how spoiled my younger kids are now, that I let them get away with murder. It's true, my little ones get away with not listening to me a lot more.

My older kids say, "Why don't you do something, *Eema?*" when things get out of control or when things happen. But I try to explain to my older kids that I'm using a different way of educating my younger kids. Now, instead of trying to do what I used to do, like screaming and tearing down egos, I try to remain calm and use problem solving techniques I've learned. If nothing works, I just say, "There's nothing I can do." I let go, and let *Hashem* take care of things more. The environment my younger kids are growing up in is so different. Life is different now. I'm a different mother and my husband is a different father. Each child has a different set of parents because life isn't static. This second set of kids has their father around a lot more, which makes a tremendous difference because a lot of what was going on in the house was because the children really needed their second parent, and back then my husband was working all the time and never home. So now it's a two-parent family instead of a single-parent family, so that makes a big difference as well.

Also, my little kids have more space between them than my first ones and that makes a difference, because now I'm not pregnant all the time, having all kinds of physical problems and not getting my needs met. So I have more time and more patience now. My little ones could be my grandkids. I can enjoy them more. So I ask, "Why does *Hashem* make us have kids when we're young, when we know so much more, and can be such better parents when we're older?" The answer is that it's a mystery, it's all part of His plan.

When you get older, also, you can finally see the hopefully positive results of what you've done, because the true rewards of motherhood come quite late and you have to wait, you know, fifteen, eighteen, twenty years to see what happens. So when you get older and you see that you've actually done all right, then you look at life differently, and you look at your kids differently. When you're young, there's so much going on that you can only see short-term, and you can't see the whole picture. You just can't. A forty-year-old can enjoy her children more, and appreciate them more, and appreciate the differences between them. Today I can look at my younger kids and laugh at them instead of crying and getting upset about all the stuff that's going on.

Now with the children I focus on my priorities such as educating them in *derech eretz* [good behavior] and self-control, and I let the other things go more or less. By self-control I mean that children need to learn that they're responsible for their choices. I want them to be able to tell me, "He hit me, and I chose to hit him back" rather than "He hit me, and I had to hit him back." I want them to know that *Hashem* sends us everything, and it's our duty to choose what to do with it and how we're going to react to the challenges sent our way.

THE STAGES OF MOTHERHOOD

I think all the stages of motherhood have their own big challenge, if you really want to know the truth. Each stage at the time seemed overwhelming, but maybe that's just my personality. Becoming a mother for the first time was challenging because it required me to give up my own schedule and just have the baby's schedule. That was really difficult because when I was younger, I had always thought that I would be a career woman, either a lawyer or a professional of some sort, and having children wasn't even on my list. So, this whole transition to becoming a stay-at-home mother and housewife was very traumatic for me.

And then, after that there was having a lot of little kids and not knowing what to do first and whom to take care of first while still trying to meet my own needs, let alone my husband's. It was very challenging not having any extended family and minimal finances and really not having much help with the babies.

And teenagers are a whole other thing. *Hashem* gives us children to make us do our *tikkun* [spiritual fixing], and teenagers will tell you exactly where you need to do it. Recently my teenagers have been criticizing my Torah practices. They tell me I'm interrupting my *davening* in places I'm not allowed to. I did the same thing to my mother, criticizing how she kept kosher, when now I see that she knew better than I did. So a mother has to have self-esteem like a coat of armor that nothing can pierce, because teenagers know you better than you ever knew yourself. Not everything they say is true, so that's why you have to learn not to take everything too seriously, and to always know that God loves you, and that you're unique, and that you and God are a team. That's what you need to know to get through adolescence with your kids. If you never knew that you were in this world to do a *tikkun,* then you think, "My kid has a big problem," but if a mother keeps in mind that her children are also *shelihim* [messengers] from *Hashem* to teach her what she needs to learn and that *Hashem* is in control, then they're not going to be able to hurt her feelings.

TIPS FOR MOTHERHOOD

The most important thing a mother needs to do is work on herself and on her connection with *Ha-Kadosh Baruch Hu* [the Holy One, Blessed be He]. You need to realize that *Ha-Kadosh Baruch Hu* runs the world and that no matter what's happening around you and in your house at the time, you can just stop at that second and say *"En od mi-levado"* [there is nothing beside Him]. At that moment you say, "*Hashem,* You gave me this situation. I don't feel like I'm coping, but this is what You want to happen right now because it *is* happening, so please help me."

And I've found that about a hundred percent of the time, *Hashem* does something at that point when you give it all over to Him, when you relinquish control to Him. And that's what He wants us to do. This is very important. It covers all the issues of helping us to reduce stress and anger and frustration, which are the main ways to destroy motherhood. You say to *Hashem,* "This kid is having this problem, and if you want me to help him, please help me find the tools." So, all of a sudden, your friend will give you a book, or you'll hear about a class. You know? This is what *Hashem* wants, He wants you to ask and to start looking for a solution so He can guide you.

Another important thing for mothers to remember is that what you do is much more important than preaching and telling your kids what to do over and over. For example, I've been working on saying *asher yatzar*[3] for about eight years now off and on. So, now I decided that each time I step out of the bathroom I'm going to read the prayer off the sign we posted on the wall. And now, all of a sudden I see all the kids coming out of the bathroom

---

[3] The blessing after using the bathroom.

standing and reading the blessing from the sign. And I think "Hey, that's pretty good."

Also, a woman needs to learn how to cook good food that her kids will like. Even if you fail in the other areas of mothering, at least your kids will want to come home for *Shabbos* for the food. This is very important to kids. When they grow up, they won't remember if the laundry was done on time, what the house looked like, but they remember that they liked your cooking, and it affects them in a very big way, especially boys. They'll want to come home, they'll want to bring friends, and this is extremely important because you want to try to keep your kids at home as much as you can. The home should be the center of their life, and not somebody else's home, or the street.

The last thing I would tell every young mother is to go to a *gemach* [lending society] or to your parents or wherever and get down on your hands and knees, if necessary, in order to have help in the house, for two hours a day or two hours three times a week. The Rabbis have said over and over that the most important thing a young mother needs is help in the house – help with cleaning, help with children, because sanity's really important.

HOPES FOR DAUGHTERS

My oldest daughter got married three years ago, and it was hard for the rest of the kids. For me it was a little bit of a relief because I felt she really needed her own space that I was never able to give her. *Baruch Hashem,* she has a wonderful, wonderful husband, really a good *shidduch* [match]. She's grateful every day that she's married and that she has a good husband.

I don't have any specific dreams for her. I mean, I hope she'll have children, which hasn't happened yet, but that's up to *Hashem.* I really don't have expectations from her. Expectations from my children are another thing I've learned to do away with. My only hope is that *Hashem* should bless all my children, that they should be *yirei shamayim* [God-fearing], that they should get married with *mazal* [luck] and at a good time, and that they should have healthy children.

My list of what I hope for went out the window a few years ago when I learned one of the most profound lessons of my whole life at the grave of the Baba Sali[4] in Netivot. I saw one old Sephardic lady screaming at the top of her lungs over and over, *"Bri'ut u-shelom bayit!"* [Health and marital harmony.] What a lesson. I was glad my kids were with me to see this. Can you think of anything else you need? If you have health and you and your husband are getting along well then *Hashem*'s blessing will come down. The *shefa* [Divine abundance] comes down. Period. This lady, who knows if she could even read, but she had the pure, simple heart of a Jewish woman. Amazing.

---

[4] Rabbi Yisrael Abuhatzera (1890–1984) was from a distinguished Moroccan rabbinical dynasty and was a great scholar of Talmud, Jewish law, and Jewish mysticism. His grave in southern Israel is a major pilgrimage site for Sephardic Jews.

BLAH-BUSTER TIDBIT

Nechama Greisman's Survival Tips for Mothers[1]

❖ Decide what NOT to do when you tend to overdo!

❖ Tape this saying to your fridge: "THIS TOO WILL PASS...."

❖ Don't let your children become "emotional orphans." It is possible to be home a lot and not really be there. Children won't remember how clean the floor was, but they will remember the quality time that you spent with them.

❖ So much of our time is spent on housework, that it is a means of expressing our attitudes about life in general. If we hate it and complain, our children will feel rejected. But if we take care of our homes with happiness, then all those around us will feel loved.

❖ A home is a home, not a museum.

❖ Staying up very late usually results in an unproductive next day. One can't burn a candle at both ends.

❖ Reduce time spent on food preparations by doubling or tripling recipes, and storing for future use in your freezer.

❖ When you're not feeling well, cancel any extra heavy activities for the day.

❖ Ask for help when help is needed. People will respect you more for doing so. Don't be ashamed.

❖ Bored and depressed? Get involved and get out! Do acts of kindness and find things that bring you JOY!

---

[1] Adapted from *The Nechama Greisman Anthology: Wisdom from the Heart,* 170–171.

ADI'S STORY

FIGURING OUT WHAT WE NEED TO BE HAPPY

ADI IS AN ISRAELI-BORN 28-year-old mother of four children who grew up in the small settlement of Enav in Samaria, and today lives in the settlement of Kokhav ha-Shahar. Like the family in which she grew up, she identifies today with the National Religious community.[1]

As you read in the first section of the book, Adi is the kind of woman that I have a tendency to idealize, a religious sabra and mother who lives in a settlement. When I see Adi and women like her, my heart flutters as I see my dream for my own Israeli-born daughters.

Adi is by nature an upbeat and optimistic person. Because of this, as well as because of my idealization of women like her, I was surprised that Adi's interview focuses on the difficulties she has faced over the years. She discusses, for example, the problems caused by marrying young and having children right away, as well as her and her husband's painful decision during the recent Intifada to leave the settlement where she and her husband grew up. She also discusses how difficult it has been for her to choose to take off a year from her work as a teacher in order to stay home with her children, because of the assumption among her friends and family that a woman who does not work outside of the home is wasting her potential. I was amazed to hear that until she moved to her new settlement, she had never in her whole

---

[1] The National Religious camp is more or less the Israeli equivalent of modern/centrist Orthodoxy. Like those who identify with modern/centrist Orthodoxy, National Religious Jews are also interested in finding ways to bridge the gap between the modern world and traditional Judaism, but the term "National Religious," unlike Modern Orthodox, also implies a right-wing political orientation and adherence to the belief that the modern State of Israel is the first step in the establishment of a Messianic Age.

life met a woman who stayed home with her children by choice, except when her high school brought in a stay-at-home mother as part of their annual Career Day.

In this interview, she describes with excitement her struggle over the past year to figure out, for the first time ever, what she wants from her life, as opposed to what others expect from her, or what is required of her based on necessity.

[Translated from Hebrew.]

GROWING UP

I grew up in a very, very Zionistic home. My parents were founding members of the settlement where I grew up. It was just a regular family, totally regular. My father works in a government office, and my mother is teacher. There were little rebellions, but only little ones.

When I was in elementary school I was like what I learned from home. I was a good girl, a casebook example of a second child. I was the oldest daughter – always giving in, never getting in trouble, never fighting with my parents, mommy's best friend. I have a brother who is two years younger than me, and then my younger sister was not born until I was seven, so I really was like a mother to her. I was the free babysitter.

In junior high school, I went to a school for girls from all the local settlements. When other girls from my class went off to boarding schools like Kfar Pines for high school, it was clear to me that I would go to the local girls' high school. I would stay on the standard path, and not wander off to strange fields. You could tell by looking at me what I would be in the future – that I would get married, and that I would be a teacher.

MARRIAGE

Itamar and I got married when I was very young, nineteen and a half. I did National Service for a year working at a school in Bet Shean, and then after I got married I went to study to be a math teacher. My husband also grew up in Enav, and we were counselors together in Bnei Akiva,[2] so it was just a natural thing that we got together. We went out for two years because we were waiting for Itamar to finish the army before we got married.

Itamar and I have been talking a lot recently about how we got married so young, since my sister is also getting married now to a boy from our settlement, and they are the same ages we were when we got married. We have been talking about how getting married early has its drawbacks. I, for example, went to study education without thinking so much what I really wanted to do. We knew that my husband would study in *kollel*,[3] so I needed to find a way to start making money, but there was not time really for self-fulfillment. I had to jump right into life without taking the time to think.

Now, because of that, today I find myself at a point of crisis, at a juncture in my life, because I realize now that I do not have any desire to go back to teaching. All of this comes from the fact that I married young, and had children quickly, and now, for the first time in my life, I am starting to think a little bit about myself. Who am I? What's good for me? The marriage relationship when you marry so young is childish, sort of unripe. It is like a half marrying another half rather than a whole marrying a whole. I'm exaggerating, but a couple that marries after they have studied, and traveled, if they want, and who have done more things on their own in their own private world, can get married and build a world together right away, without having to wait for each person to fulfill his or her own needs.

My husband knows how to build his own world within the framework of marriage and family. Having children limits him a little bit, he can't do everything he wants. But he knows how to satisfy his own needs in addition to the needs of the family. I think that for men this is much easier to do. He had many years to be in the army and to study in yeshiva, and then engineering school. He had time to connect with what he really wanted from life, and figure out that he wanted to become an electrical engineer. I studied at the university, but I never had the opportunity to take the time for myself

---

[2] The largest religious Zionist youth movement.
[3] Yeshiva for married men.

in order to figure out what I really wanted. I think that for men it is much easier, since they are home far less.

I feel that because I did not have this time to myself, I am a very dependent person. I always learned to be dependent on others – on my parents, on my husband, and even on my children. But it is really important for people to learn to be on their own. It is true that I was in National Service for two years, but that was a very limited experience, and even then I had a boyfriend, which is also its own kind of dependence. In my whole life, I have never had the experience of being on my own.

My husband now supports waiting longer to get married. He can now see in himself how much he never had a chance to mature and ripen. Not that he regrets anything, God forbid. He is not saying to wait too long, of course, but to find some sort of balance. But maybe if I had gotten married when I was older I would feel the other way around?

For us, it did not even occur to us to wait longer to get married. Also, my children came right way. Many couples get married young, and then they wait to have children. But if anyone had dared to suggest that to me, I would have swallowed them whole, without salt. I would have told them that bringing children to the world is the whole purpose of the family unit. But now I see that it would be better if some couples waited, that rushing into things is sometimes not good for the child and not good for the parents. And I know that Jewish law is flexible on this subject, and that each rabbi needs to look at each couple and see what its needs are. The Torah teaches us to "Educate the child in accordance with its way,"[4] and we should also educate each couple according to its way.

EARLY MOTHERHOOD

It is impossible for me to say now that it's too bad I didn't wait, but it really was a difficult time for me, since I was commuting to the university at the same time I was having my first children. I got pregnant after eight months of marriage. It was a little bit stressful and unpleasant, since we were

---

[4] Proverbs 22:6.

living with all the *kollel* couples, and the other wives were all pregnant and having babies, and they were looking at my stomach all the time waiting for me to get pregnant.

The first pregnancy was fine, except for all the strange symptoms. That was funny, and also hard. It is the first time in your life that you discover that you can be a totally different person: who is tired, who is weak, who throws up, who is heavy. It was a very difficult period. I was studying at Bar Ilan University, and we didn't have a car, so often it would take me two hours to get there, and two hours to get back while I was waiting for someone to drive by and give me a ride. Lots of times I would get to the settlement next to our own, and I would be ten minutes from home, and I would still have to wait another hour for a ride. In those days there were no cell phones, so I couldn't just call my husband and tell him to borrow a car and come to pick me up. Every night I had to decide whether I should walk into the settlement, and find a public telephone, and miss a ride in the process. Two or three times I just started crying from the stress of it all, since it was late at night and my baby at home was waiting to nurse.

Another problem with marrying young is that you don't enjoy your studies. I was just waiting for it to end. You cannot study if your heart is always at home. You have to get up in the middle of a lecture to pump milk. You're not here and you're not there. I also felt guilty, because I had to leave my second child when she was just a month old.

Now I think that all of this was just not normal. Everything was decided based on necessity, and not at all because of what I wanted. I chose what to study based on the need to find a practical profession that would enable me to start making money quickly. Also, I chose where to study based on the fact that we had a child, and we needed to be near my parents so they could help out. Lots of times I would skip classes. I would think, "I only have two classes. I'll just not go this morning." People have to understand that when they get married young they are getting into a cycle that is not so easy.

We are not the type of people who have ever lived in a city, and so we knew we should live in a settlement, and it was clear that if we would be on a settlement then we should stay near our parents in Enav. They also had an apartment where we could live, and this was very important, because where did we have any money from? Both of us were studying, and we lived there for years, near our parents, and we only left this year. Leaving Enav felt sort of like being born, like leaving the womb.

A DIFFICULT YEAR

After I graduated, for four years I was working as a math teacher in the high school where I studied as a girl, and for three years I enjoyed teaching, until last year when I had a very difficult year. I gave birth to my fourth child, and I had a group of students with whom I had a very, very difficult time. They were very rebellious. They all went against me, and I am not a strong person. I am a person who can flow with other people, but it's difficult for me to be so authoritative or something like that.

At the end, the students admitted that they had lost out, but by then the whole year was lost. It made me especially angry, because I had left a nursing baby at home. If you leave a baby at home and you enjoy your work, then that's fine, because you know that working is ultimately good for the children as well. When a mother comes home energized and in a good mood because things are good for her at work, and fun for her, then the children benefit from this as well. It doesn't matter whether the mother is home or not at home, the main thing is that she should be happy, and calm and tranquil for the hours that she is home. Last year, my situation at work damaged a lot of things, and affected the wholeness of our home.

Also, in recent years things have been difficult with the security situation.[5] A few years ago, my younger brother was stabbed by an Arab at the entrance to the settlement, and then last year people that we knew from Enav were killed, so that did not make anything any easier. And last year we decided that we would move to another settlement closer to Jerusalem. Moving apartments is very difficult. At least for me it is very hard. Also, even though I knew it was an intelligent decision, emotionally it was very

---

[5] The Hebrew expression for the recent Intifada in which over a thousand Israelis were murdered in terror attacks by Arabs between 2000–2004.

difficult. Enav as a settlement is losing people these days because it is in a part of Samaria where many of the terror attacks have been concentrated, and the fact that the ones who are leaving are even children of the settlement was very difficult. We saw that our leaving was very painful for our parents, and very painful for the community as a whole, and it was also painful for us. But I understand that we had to do it.

Itamar never found himself in Enav. Also, he had not found work that he liked, and then he started working in Jerusalem at a job he liked a great deal, and as soon as people smell Jerusalem, they just have to move closer. He said that for him to stay in Enav was like the binding of Isaac. He felt that being so near our parents was very limiting, and did not enable him to be himself. Our parents were fantastic. They gave us a lot of freedom. It was really us and what we were going through. In the end, Itamar said that we had to leave, and I'm happy he did because it was also important for me. All around us, people from the settlement were asking us how we could do such a thing. I was speaking with an older woman at a wedding, and when I told her we were leaving, she started to cry. People would say that we were traitors to leave when things were so difficult, jokingly of course.[6] But the truth is that for many years we had wanted to leave, and we had said, "This year we'll stay..." for this reason or for that reason. It was very hard for us to go, but it really was a turning point for us.

STAYING HOME

It's been very good for us in Kokhav ha-Shahar. It is very good for the children; there's a great school nearby for my oldest son. I am at home this year, and I am focused on the home. I am not the type to sit and talk with other women like we are talking now. I am usually home with my children. I had always said that I would not be able to spend even one month at home taking care of the kids, but now I see that it is very nice.

---

[6] The settlement they moved to was also considered to be in a dangerous location, and it suffered many casualties during the Intifada. Clearly, security concerns were not their motivation for moving.

From a financial point of view things are more difficult; since I don't work there is more pressure on my husband. Everything is fine. The ceiling isn't caving in, we still have money for rent and food. But it has been stressful, since everyone expects for me to be working. Last year my parents asked me, "So, what will you do next year? What job will you have?" When I told them I wanted to stay home, they said, "OK, so what will you study?" My husband asked me the same thing. They are all in shock that I am staying home for even one year. My parents have never even heard of the concept of a woman staying home to raise her children. Time spent at home with the children is not considered real time.

My husband understands that I have taken off this one year because I told him that it is too much for me to both move apartments and start a new job. But it makes him pretty nervous when he sees that I like being home, and that I am not studying to prepare for a different career. It would be easier for him if he knew that I will be studying for two years and then I will be a social worker, and the financial pressure will end. That would make him calmer. But I am not there. And this pressure has also affected me. Instead of being able to enjoy this year off, I have just felt this pressure all the time. It makes me feel like there is something wrong with me.

I have started attending a consciousness-raising group where we learn to accept ourselves with all of our failings and weaknesses. Once we had a class on money, and the teacher said that she was giving each of us an open check, and we could pay ourselves a salary for what we do in our lives. Afterwards, my husband couldn't even believe how little I paid myself – like 1500 NIS[7] a month. I told him, "Why should I get anything? I don't work." And he said, "Why don't you think you deserve a decent salary for taking care of the children, and taking care of the home?"

Anyway, I see that staying home is good for me right now, and that I really don't know what I want. I want to just not think about what I want to do for a while, and just flow with it and see where I end up.

The truth is that staying home has been awfully fun. You don't have to rush anywhere in the morning. I had always thought that when I was home,

---

[7] Approximately USD 350.

I was not doing anything, and I gave myself a hard time. But now I see that being home is exactly what I want to be doing. I realize that it is fun for me to stay home and watch my children, and that there is nothing that I need to prove to the world by working.

In the beginning of this year, I thought if I took a break from teaching I should be taking all of the courses and all of the classes in the whole world. So I signed up for a class but I didn't enjoy it, and I was so hard on myself for giving it up. But then I thought, "What? Who is saying that you are required to do anything?" I think we have been so influenced by the Western way of thinking that we must always be chasing after money or knowledge.

But in Kokhav ha-Shahar there are many mothers who stay at home. It makes it easier for me that I'm not the only one. I always knew that women like this existed. When I was in my last year of high school, they had a Career Day, and brought us all sorts of women to speak with us and tell us about their lives – a teacher, an occupational therapist, a stay-at-home mother. But the idea of being a stay-at-home mother did not speak to me at all.

In Enav, there were sometimes mothers who were home, but it was never because they wanted to be, but rather because they did not have a choice, because they could not find work, etc. In Kokhav ha-Shahar, it is very different. Many women stay home, and the ones who work are often women like my neighbor who works a bit as an assistant to the preschool teacher, so she can have fun and get out of the house, but it is also important to her that her kids have a mother at home.

I am not staying at home based on ideals. If it were not good for me, I would go back to work. A child with a working mother who likes her work might get less mothering hours on a technical level, but the mother he gets is a happy, energetic mother. I don't think it's the same for everyone.

TRANSITIONS

I do not have an interesting story. I have never done anything interesting in my whole life. I have changed my view of a lot of things – not from being National Religious to being Haredi, or something like that. But my view of what it means to be a couple has changed a lot. I used to think that the point of being married was to have children, and now I feel that to work on your marriage relationship is important as an end in itself.

My religious view has also changed. We used to be more connected to Merkaz ha-Rav,[8] our view of religion was more spiritual. Now we see that Judaism is not ritual, the gemara is not a dry, halakhic text. Today I see when I study gemara with my husband that it is so full of life and richness and color if you know how to read it. Torah used to be something peripheral to life, and now we see that the Torah is life itself.

DAUGHTERS

I hope that my daughters will be much more independent than I am. Of course, I want them to be married and to have children. But I also want them to be independent in their thinking, and that they will follow their dreams, that they will not be dependent on the reactions of others.

I want them to do good, to throw away the chaff, and to trust themselves. I hope that they will know how to stand up for what they want. Of course, I want them to be religious. That goes without saying. I want them to feel that *Hashem* is with them in their lives, and that the Torah is a way of life – and not just something marginal to life, or alongside it. I used to be critical of people who took a slightly different path from mine, but now I like it when people have more individual interpretations of Judaism. As a mother, I want to be able to accompany my children, but not to guide them – to give them all the tools to succeed, so that they can find their own way that will be good for them.

---

[8] The yeshiva in the Kiryat Moshe neighborhood named after the Rabbi Avraham Yitzhak Kook. Adi means that they were affiliated with the National *Haredi* camp rather than the more centrist National Religious camp, with which they identify now.

BLAH-BUSTER TIDBIT

Things I Have Learned in My Dozen Years of Marriage and Motherhood

by Rebbetzin Nechama Greisman[1]

Get as much help as you can! The physical work required in running a household can be overwhelming and, thank God, keeps on growing. But help is 100% necessary in the building of a "miniature Temple." Get as many labor-saving machines as you can afford; a large dryer and a dishwasher can help a lot. Hire help once or twice a week. If you have small children and are overtired, hire a girl to take them to the park in the afternoon and perhaps feed them an easy-to-make dinner while they're out (weather permitting). If you're behind on mending, hire someone every couple of weeks to help.

When my twins were home and I was an extremely overworked mother, I hired a high-school girl on Thursday evenings to peel and check all the vegetables for Shabbos. During my last pregnancy, I hired a girl for one hour every night to sweep the floors, wash all the dishes, and fold laundry. It made a world of difference. True, help costs money, but one has to get one's priorities into perspective. You might want to consider borrowing money or asking family members for help.

Make lists! There's so much that we have to remember and do! No wonder our heads are spinning and we sometimes feel like we are drowning, God forbid. I was always fascinated by the power of list-making to organize my mind and keep me from forgetting all the things I had to do. I am hooked on lists….

Every morning I make a 'To Do List.' That same list has phone calls for the day. (The secret is putting in the phone numbers right away.) The list includes regular chores, what I'm serving for supper, and special things. I try to check off the most important things first. The pleasure of list-making is the satisfaction you feel in crossing off the items once you've done them and watching the day progress purposefully.

Beware the phone! A few years ago, when I was beginning to feel that the phone was intruding too much on my mothering, I made a few decisions which, with hindsight, I can say were on target. First, I bought an answering

---

[1] *The Nechama Greisman Anthology: Wisdom from the Heart*, 138–139.

machine. I do not answer calls when I am involved with my children at suppertime, bedtime, or at any other time. I also tell people to call me during the morning or after-bedtime hours, and I refuse to get involved in long conversations when my children need me. How would you feel if as soon as you came into the house you saw your husband on the phone, and every time you had to ask him something or tell him something he told you to wait because the person he was talking to was more important? Beware of that phone!

SARA'S STORY

LEARNING TO VALUE OUR SUPPORTING
AND NURTURING ROLE[1]

SARA IS A 39-YEAR-OLD mother of eleven children between one year and seventeen years old. She grew up in an Orthodox family in Cleveland, Ohio, and since she married her husband eighteen years ago, she has been a kollel wife, living in the Haredi section of the Ramot neighborhood. I have known Sara for about eight years, and something that has always amazed me about her is her ability to deal with all of the challenges of managing a large family, including a special-needs child, with a smile on her face, dismissing setbacks with her quiet sense of humor. This is especially impressive considering the fact that as a kollel wife, she manages to keep this smile on her face without a cleaning lady, in a small three-bedroom apartment, and on an extremely tight budget.

---

[1] Recently, I heard a talk by Rabbi Yaakov Meir Sonnenfeld of Jerusalem's Ramat Shlomo neighborhood. He explained that the first tiny *kollel* or *yeshiva* for married men in the whole world was established only a hundred years ago by Rabbi Yisrael Salant in the town of Kovno, and, even then, only great scholars were expected to continue studying Torah after marriage. He described how only fifty years ago, girls from *Haredi* families were embarrassed to say that they would be marrying men who studied in yeshiva full-time. Today, in the *Haredi* community in particular, the situation has changed completely. Rabbi Sonnenfeld explained that young *Haredi* women today are embarrassed to say that they are marrying a man who will *not* be learning in *kollel* at least for the first several years of marriage. Because of this, today there are thousands of *kollel*s all over the world and tens of thousands of women raising their families with a tremendous amount of hardship and self-sacrifice while their husbands study Torah full-time, as we will see in this interview.

I think that much of her ability to deal so calmly and heroically with a potentially overwhelming situation comes from her sense of mission as a kollel wife, feeling that her husband's Torah study justifies all the challenges involved. I cannot think of any other couple I know that so demonstrates how living a life in accordance with the Torah can make someone into a kinder, more sensitive, and generally better person.

CHILDHOOD

Baruch Hashem [thank God], I grew up in a very happy and warm family as the youngest of four children. My father owned a clothing store, and when we were very little my mother stayed home with us, and then she became a teacher and taught for many, many years.

My mother was born in Germany and left for America in 1938 on one of the last boats before World War II. My parents met in Cleveland, where I was born. I went to a Bais Yaakov school and my brothers went to yeshiva. After school, I went to a seminary near my home for two years. I've never been such a loud, outgoing person, but I think I had a lot of friends, and I spent a lot of my time with family.

MARRIAGE

I had spent a year teaching, and then I came to visit my sister and my brothers who were in *kollel* here, and I enjoyed going to their houses and seeing how they lived their lives and raised their kids. That was the kind of life I thought I would like as well. I felt that *Eretz Yisroel* [the Land of Israel] was *Eretz Yisroel*. I saw that it was a place where I could grow, and that raising a family here would be a big bonus.

My brother and brother-in-law were learning in the same yeshiva where my husband was learning at the time. So they were looking for a nice *bochur* [yeshiva student] for me. My brother thought of the *shidduch* [match], and my brother-in-law worked on it very hard, so we got to meet each other, and we got married that year.

BECOMING A MOTHER

I became pregnant soon after we got married, when I was twenty-one. It's very special to be expecting, and to be expecting right away and to be bringing a new person into the world. Every stage of the pregnancy was very thrilling, even though at some points I did not feel so well.

Motherhood was definitely a new stage. There was a lot of happiness, and a lot of new challenges involved in bringing a new person into the world and raising him and having him grow into the person he should be. Recovering from the birth and nursing the baby are not so simple. It all takes a little bit of adjustment.

A SPECIAL CHILD

Aryeh Leib, our sixth child, was born during the beginning of the Gulf War. I was in the *bet hahlama*[2] in Telz Stone for the first siren. It was good that I was there, since I do not think I would have had the strength to deal with everything that was going on two days after giving birth. Many people in Israel missed the first siren, which was in the middle of the night on a Thursday night. A lot of people slept through it, but in the *bet hahlama* they woke us all up.

Usually the nurses wake up the mothers in a very sweet way: they have an intercom, and they call everybody to get their babies. But this time, it was different, since they were calling us at two in the morning. When we arrived at the *bet hahlama*, the woman in charge told us, "When *Moshiach* [the Messiah] is on the way, don't use the elevator." Meaning, if there's a missile attack, which is like *hevlei Moshiach* [the birthpangs of the Messiah], don't use the elevator. So all the mothers took their gas masks and went by the stairs to the Baby Room, which was set up as a sealed room. I think everyone was nervous during that time. Instead of people talking about their birth and

---

2 The *bet hahlama,* or "recovery home," is an institution where many religious women go after giving birth in order to rest and regain their strength before returning to their homes and other children. *Batei hahlama* are especially popular among *Haredi* women.

delivery experiences during the meals, everyone was talking about what was going to be during the war.

But, *baruch Hashem*, we all experienced many *nissim* [miracles]. With all the missiles that fell only one person was killed, and there were so many people who were out of the house, and then their houses got hit by missiles. So many *nissim*. All the mothers were all just hoping for *Moshiach* [the Messiah], for the *yeshua* [redemption], just like we are right now.

With Aryeh Leib, at the very beginning we didn't notice that there was anything wrong with him. He seemed just fine until I saw that he didn't seem to be reacting to his surroundings as my other children had at the same age. If we put him on the floor with a toy, or hung a mobile in his crib, he didn't play with them as a child his age was supposed to. Then, at the Baby Clinic they give regular developmental tests, and he did not react to sounds during the hearing test. He had always had problems with fluid in his ears, and we saw that he really had hearing loss, so we put tubes in his ears, and it helped somewhat, but not really. We were advised to take him to the Center for Child Development, and we took him for therapy, and they also told us that he was developing at his own pace, a little bit slow, but he's happy, and that we should not worry about it. This was when he was about a year.

I guess it was a *hesed* [kindness] from *Hashem* that we did not know right away, since it would have been a big blow at a difficult time, when everyone was so tense at the beginning of the Gulf War. Now we can see that Aryeh Leib really is very behind in most things, except that he is a very fast runner! A special-needs child always needs more attention in different ways, and that's fine, but since he's a bit frustrated because he can't communicate, and a bit jealous of younger siblings that are ahead of him by a lot, he takes out his frustrations on them and hits them, which makes it very difficult.

He needs to be occupied in a positive way. My children are very good with him. The big ones take him out, and they all give him a lot of love. Even though lots of time Aryeh Leib is not so nice to my five-year-old, she tries not to take revenge, and she is very proud of that. Even though you could say that at some times the interactions between them are not so easy, all the kids love him, and they *daven* that he should have a *refuah shlemah* [full recovery]. Even my littlest children have started doing this as well without my having to tell them.

It gives us strength to know that he probably has a great *neshama* [soul].[3] But it's also challenging. I can spend a whole morning cleaning the house, and in five minutes he can turn everything upside down again. The other day, my kids made a surprise for me. I had taken one of the children out to an appointment, and when I came back, they had cleaned up the house so nicely. Then Aryeh Leib came home, and within three minutes he threw the chairs down, and got onto the table, and took all the papers that they had worked so hard to organize into neat piles, and threw them on the floor. He could turn on the stove, and be so many places within minutes. But there are definitely gifts that he gives us as well.

Because of our experience with Aryeh Leib, I have certain anxieties, and I am anxious to see that every new baby is doing everything at the rate they are supposed to be doing it, but I just have to keep on being *mis-hazek* [spiritually strengthened] and know that *Hashem* has an endless supply of mercy. We have to realize that everything's in *Hashem*'s hands, and we just have to *daven* [pray]. Having a child like Aryeh Leib requires me to have more patience and to try to do what I can to help him progress. *Hashem* helps. *Hashem* should give everybody strength.

MOTHERHOOD NOW

Especially since we had one child who is slower, when a new baby starts doing things at the right time and going through the stages of development like sitting and crawling and walking, it has become more exciting for me than it was before. It always was, but now I feel it even more. As I get older, all the things that the younger ones do seem even more cute and sweet. It was that way as well with the older kids, but when you have bigger ones and smaller ones, the things that the younger ones do just seem so especially sweet. It's something about everyone enjoying everybody else together.

---

[3] Some rabbis teach that people with mental disabilities are the reincarnations of holy people who needed to return to earth in order to perform the few *mitzvot* that mentally disabled people can perform.

When the baby starts making sounds, I think everyone tunes in, because everyone's waiting for her to talk.

I think some of my younger kids started walking earlier because they got so much encouragement from their older brothers and sisters. My oldest started walking a bit later. I think we were a bit scared for him to just take off walking, even though he probably could have done it. But when you have a whole big crowd cheering you on to do it, then it really changes things. My littlest girls were walking before eleven months.

Every day is like a new beginning, and I know we're going to try to use the day to its fullest. I wake up and I hope that I will be able to send the kids off happily, and give them what they need. One of the best parts of my day is when everyone's come home, and they've had their good days, and they tell me about everything during mealtime.

Bedtime is a bit harder. It's not always just tucking them in; we have to fly around the house a bit first. Nobody really wants to go to bed that fast. We're living in a building with very nice neighbors with children who are close in age to my children, *baruch Hashem,* so the little ones have a very active social life. They want to start playing at 5:30 PM which is right when, in my mind, I would like to start giving them supper, bathing them, and getting them to bed. So sometimes bedtime can last from 7:30 to 9, and that's only the younger set.

You can get overwhelmed. For example, on the first day of *bein ha-zemanim* [summer vacation] right after Tisha be-Av, you have laundry from the nine days,[4] and you're sort of tired after the fast, and you have to put the house together after everyone's been playing the whole day and you were not on top of everything. And there's different things everybody needs. One child says, "What am I going to do during vacation?" and one needs to buy this, this, this, and this for yeshiva, and one says, "I need to go shopping because I need new shoes!" So, on the first day of vacation, I sort of feel like, "Help!" So I say to everyone, "Don't tell me anything. Just write down your list of what you need, and we'll try to get to everything" because I can

---

[4] It is forbidden to do laundry during the nine days before Tisha be-Av.

SEVEN SECRETS OF JEWISH MOTHERHOOD

feel like I'm getting bombarded. And on top of everything, this past year, on the day after Tisha be-Av, my washing machine broke down.

Raising a large family has forced me to learn how to keep my priorities in order. Sometimes a whole morning can go by, and I can be hard on myself and say, "OK, what did I really do?" But when you think about things that are really priorities, and you know that you have accomplished them, then that puts you in the right frame of mind so that you know that the other things will get done as well. I figure out what my priorities are by thinking about how women merit *olam ha-ba* [the World to Come] – by sending off their children and husbands to learn Torah and by waiting for their husbands to come home from learning Torah. So, if I've gotten all my kids out, and I've taken care of all of my babies, and my husband is learning Torah, then I know I'm doing OK.

I once heard someone ask a mother, "So, how are you managing?" and she said, "Who said that you have to really manage?" If you're doing the most important things, even if your cabinets are empty, and there are dishes in the sink, then you're doing OK. You always have to try to keep things in perspective. Sometimes there are very busy weeks. This week, for example, I had two appointments out of the house, and appointments out of the house are the thing that usually makes everything topple over, because then there isn't time to concentrate on the house. Aryeh Leib cut his eye this week, so I had to take him to get it patched up, and then he played with the bandage and the cut got infected, so I had to take him again to get stitches. But I have to remind myself that if I am doing the things that are most important, then I'm doing fine. And then you decide to slowly take one step at time, first making the beds, and then making some lunch, and working on it that way.

In all stages of pregnancy and birth and motherhood you see how much everything is from *Hashem*, and that we need help from *Hashem* in everything that we do. A normal pregnancy and a normal delivery, and all the *nissim* that are a part of them, are such a *hesed* [kindness] from *Hashem* that a person cannot even fathom it. It's mindboggling how *Hashem* is controlling the whole entire world right down to the tiniest little cell. That's definitely something to think about, just to thank *Hashem* for all the *hasadim* [kindnesses], and all the *"nissim she-be-khol yom imanu, ve-al nifle'otekha ve-tovotekha she-be-khol et – erev, boker, ve-tsaharayim."*[5]

HOPES FOR DAUGHTERS

I hope that, *be-ezrat Hashem* [with God's help], my daughters will find their *bashert* [soulmate] and raise a *Torahdike* [Torah-focused] family, and that they will follow the way that we would like them to go. I would like for them to marry men who learn in *kollel*. I think that's a very important way to start a home and to keep it on the right track. I think we've always raised our daughters to encourage their husbands to learn, and to know that Torah is what is keeping the world going.

---

[5] "All the miracles that are with us every day, and for Your wonders and Your kindnesses that are with us every day – evening, morning, and afternoon." From the standard prayer book.

BLAH-BUSTER TIDBIT

Creating Holiness

by Rebbetzin Nechama Greisman[1]

Jacob was buried in a holy place. Rachel was not buried in a holy place. But she made the place become holy by being there.

This, ultimately, is the difference between the role of a Jewish man and the role of a Jewish woman. A man serves Hashem in matters which are already holy, whereas a woman (for the most part) serves Hashem through everyday activities that she does for others – and in so doing she makes those activities holy. As the Lubavitcher Rebbe says: "When we do something for the physical well-being of others, it becomes a spiritual act."

When you do something for yourself, you only get to enjoy it for two hours or so. But if you go and do the same thing for someone else, that is a mitzvah. Everything that we do for somebody else is a mitzvah. While ironing clothes for our husbands and children, while bathing the children, while sweeping the floor and shopping, we are engaged in the holy task of running a Torah home and raising Jewish children who will grow up to bring Godliness into the world. It is all for a higher purpose.

---

[1] *The Nechama Greisman Anthology: Wisdom from the Heart*, 134.

DEVORA'S STORY

LEARNING TO VALUE OUR ROLE
IN THE HOME

DEVORA IS A THIRTY-NINE-YEAR-OLD mother of eight children who recently moved to the Haredi town of Kiryat Sefer from the centrist-Orthodox settlement of Efrat. She grew up in a non-observant family in Sacramento, California, and took a long and winding path to Orthodoxy over the course of her teenage years and early twenties.

Her interview focuses on the fascinating twists and turns of this path, which led her from a Jewish day school, where she decided at the age of eleven that the only way to avoid divorce like the parents of many of her friends was to keep the laws of family purity,[1] to a public high school and university where she clung to basic aspects of Jewish observance, to a hedonistic year spent in poverty and spiritual darkness in Tel Aviv before she found her way to a women's yeshiva in Jerusalem.

All through those years, her greatest dream was that she would be able to devote herself to being a mother and have a loving marriage fortified by a religious way of life. However, once married, she still found that it took her several years to reconcile her idealistic dreams about having an observant Jewish home with the day-to-day realities and demands of managing one.

CHILDHOOD

My father was the son of religious Hungarian Jews who fled Hitler and went to Argentina. He moved to New York when he was a teenager. My

---

[1] The laws concerning permitted times for physical and sexual contact between married couples.

mother's parents were born in America and my mother grew up in Kansas City, which is where I spent the first years of my life.

The home where I grew up was hot. My father is very South American, very emotional, strong, impetuous and a dreamer, and my mother is more mid-Western in the quiet, stable, and patient sense.

My father's attitude changed towards religion when, following his father's death, a respected rabbi told him his father would turn over in his grave if he knew my father was studying philosophy in college. Also, his father's business partners were very religious men who after his father's death totally ignored his mother and her three children. Because of this they went from being wealthy to being left with nothing, and that left my father feeling very bitter and angry towards the religious world in which he'd grown up. My father was like the rebbe's son in The Chosen.[2] He went to study psychology and philosophy in university, wanting to find and cultivate the good in all mankind, and disillusioned regarding his own religious upbringing.

My father was drawn to my mother because she was so giving and sweet and quiet and good, and also because she didn't know she wasn't supposed to turn on lights on Shabbos, and he thought that that was what he wanted. My mother, on the other hand, knew that my father came from an Orthodox family, and she had hoped that he would teach her more about Judaism. Before the wedding, they never discussed religion, and the first Shabbos after the wedding, my mother asked my father when it was time to light candles, and he said, "Light any time you want. Do you think lighting a few minutes earlier or later makes a difference to God?" And she started crying. She had wanted him to be the religious one, the leader. There have been ups and downs, but this is a constant theme in their relationship to this day.

When I was a child, my grandparents moved to Sacramento, and they told my parents they should move there as well, so we did. There was a Jewish day school there, and my parents asked me if I wanted to go to public school and go to Hebrew school on the afternoons and weekends, or whether I wanted to go to the Jewish day school, and have my afternoons

---

[2] Potok, Chaim. *The Chosen*. New York: 1967.

and weekends off, and, baruch Hashem [thank God], because of laziness I chose the Jewish day school. All the parents who sent children to that school were upwardly mobile first-generation Americans who did not want to send their kids to the public schools. They didn't particularly want their children to attend a school that was Orthodox, but they liked the idea of a private Jewish school.

But secretly, the children were learning Torah, and about kashrus and Shabbos. The teachers were amazing. They said to us, "Your parents never got a chance to learn what you are learning. It is a gift to you, and it is not to be used against your parents, and you should not judge them for their lack of observance. We know you cannot put this into practice now, but this is your tradition. Put this knowledge in your pocket for now, and when you are on your own, take it out and use it!"

For ninth grade, I screamed and yelled and cried until my parents allowed me to go to Los Angeles to yeshiva. I didn't even last one year because I was so homesick. Then I went to the public high school in Sacramento, but I still had a desire to learn how to develop a relationship with God. I was the girl who wore skirts, and if a boy bumped into me in the hall, I would actually feel my arm burn from the *avera* [sin].

It was very strange to be a *baalat teshuva* [newly religious Jew] with no support or direction in a public-school world. My father put up a lot of resistance. He said, "You think you know everything? I was raised this way!" A *baalat teshuva* who doesn't know anything is a scary kind of person to be around. I would shout out quotations from the Torah and preach, and my specialty was one-liners. When my sister would speak back to my parents, I would yell from my room, "Honor thy father and mother!" My sister and I didn't really speak to each other that year until I realized I had to mellow out. I started wearing pants. I spoke *lashon ha-ra* [gossip], since popularity in high school comes from cutting other people down. I was a clown, making funny observations about life and making people laugh. But I still kept kosher and Shabbat as well as I knew how.

In 1980, during my senior year, my father arranged a full scholarship for me to go to Israel for eight weeks with a study program. All the participants were secular, but my teacher was an Orthodox rabbi. I dressed like all the other kids, talked like them, had my jeans, lipstick, guitar, but they all thought I was so religious since I did not turn on lights on Shabbat. The trip was amazing, I fell in love with Israel. I was lovesick to the point that when it was time to go back to America I was nauseous.

Back in Sacramento, I was in mourning. One day, I went with my mother to the grocery store and saw the cucumbers. They were all the same shape and size and they were covered with wax, and it reminded me that during our first week in Israel, we'd come to the mess hall and seen these things that looked like twisted pickles, and they were yellow and green, and they weren't shiny, and we all laughed, "This is a cucumber?! This is a pre-pickle!" And then I bit into it, and it was the sweetest, crunchiest, and most delicious cucumber I'd ever had. So, at the store with my mother, I picked out the most perfect cucumber and walked over to my mother with tears streaming down my face, and said, "It's covered with wax!" I wanted to be real. I wanted to be a Jew. I wanted to be in Israel.

HITTING BOTTOM

A few months later I moved to Israel to study in university. It was a very rude awakening coming to Israel. I thought people would be dancing the hora in the streets welcoming me, a new immigrant from America who gave up everything to join her people! No. On the way from the airport, the cab driver made a pass at me. I went to Tel Aviv University and realized that I was the only Orthodox person in my whole dorm. I needed an advisor to plead with the dorm mother just to arrange one room for girls who would keep kosher.

Tel Aviv University had no synagogue, but it had a disco. I was in the cool European crowd. I still kept Shabbos, which meant that I would go to the disco on Friday night, and my friends would pay. If I would say I shouldn't go, they would say, "What? Why shouldn't you dance on Shabbos? Hasidim dance! Friday night is the perfect time to dance." No one offered to stay in the dorm room and have a Shabbos meal, so I would dance to Pink Floyd, and that was how I kept Shabbos.

I moved in with my two best friends, Becky and Mike. We were going to be a family for each other. It was "Three's Company." I dropped out of university to write a brilliant first novel that never made it past the tenth chapter because I got very depressed and would spend most of the day in bed. I discovered only later on that I suffer from Seasonal Affective Disorder, depression brought on by the reduced sunlight in the fall and winter months. By the evening I'd feel a little better, and my friends were able to convince me to join them on Dizengoff for some night life.

The next year I convinced my little sister to move to Tel Aviv to work as a waitress like me, and live with me in a rented apartment on Dizengoff Street. I worked at a Kentucky Fried Chicken sort of place, and my sister worked at a sleazy, low-life joint on the beach. Once in a while I would borrow one of her dresses and we would go out dancing. We were very, very poor and this was our way of forgetting our problems. One Friday, I realized that we had thirty-seven cents and no food, and my sister was so depressed that she just didn't know what to do, so I told her I would take care of the Shabbos shopping. I managed to buy a half a loaf of bread, some yoghurt, and two persimmons. We didn't starve, but that memory sticks out in my life as the ultimate low point. Of course, my parents would have helped us, but we were embarrassed to ask for money. There were still other children at home for them to raise, and we were adults and felt that we should be able to take care of ourselves.

I was feeling alone and really depressed at this point, and I went to speak with the rabbi who had been my teacher at the High School in Israel program. He asked me what I wanted to do with my life. I told him that I wanted to be a mommy, and that I wanted to marry a guy who wore a *kippah* [yarmulke], who realizes that God's above him. "Why can't I meet someone who wears a *kippah* and keeps Shabbos? I keep Shabbos," I whimpered. The rabbi said, "What messages are you giving with your appearance that let men know what you care about? Look what you're wearing." I was wearing a M*A*S*H t-shirt and tight, worn-out jeans. Anyway, when my rabbi said that, it made sense to me.

And then I had a very strange dream, and that dream changed my life. I had a dream that there was an Israeli man standing in front of me with his hands on my shoulders. It was the ex-boyfriend of a former roommate. He's a foot shorter than I am, and he looks up at me and says, "I want you to marry me." And I look down at him, and I think, "I don't love him, and he doesn't love me. He's not going to be faithful to me. We have nothing in common. But he knows that I will be a good mommy. I'll have babies and I'll make macaroni and cheese. We won't have any relationship, really, but he won't be bad to me." But I think, "Who cares anyway?" and I say "OK." And he says, "And I want you to wear this at our wedding." He's a lawyer, so he opens up his briefcase and takes out a wedding dress which is a sleeveless mini-dress with a low neckline, and it has black ruffles along the bottom. And I think, "It's hideous. And if anyone deserves to wear all white it's me, the last virgin on the planet. And I don't even get a long, flowing, princess dress, just this." And I think to myself, "Who cares anyway?" And I say, "OK." I look at him again, and he smells badly, and I know I will never be attracted to him. And I think, "Who cares anyway?" Then I go onto the street and I see a friend who looks and acts just like a brunette Marilyn Monroe, and she says, "We're going to Disney World! Want to come with us?" And I say, "No, I can't. I'm marrying Yossi." And she's so happy, and hugs me, and shows such ecstasy, and I think, "Who cares anyway?"

And I woke up sweating, and realized that this dream was the model of what I had been doing since I moved to Israel. The life I was living was not the one I had imagined, where I would be living in a holy land where everyone kept Shabbos and was into Jewish philosophy and God. If you want to do something and it seems attainable, then you will put in an effort until your dream comes true. But if you feel, as I did, that you will never be able to attain your dream, then you will just stop trying. My future had seemed so bleak that it had simply become too scary to care.

I wrote down this whole dream in a letter to my mother. I hope my mother burned that letter since then. And I had to get dressed to mail it. I owned one skirt, and I put it on, and going to mail this letter I said over and over again out loud, *"Baruch Hashem"* [thank God]. I was saying that because

I cared, and I couldn't remember the last time in life when I had felt like I really loved life, and cared about things. And then I realized it was when I was eleven years old, when I was in day school. And I promised myself to get back to that, to living a life that I was proud of. To start living a life that had a purpose, that was leading towards a good future, that was promising enough that I could take the risk of caring about it.

MARRIAGE AND MOTHERHOOD

I was nineteen years old, and I decided that I would go to study in yeshiva, at Brovender's.[3] I thought that was the closest thing to going to day school, and I absolutely loved it. At the same time, I was still yearning for the perfect relationship. One night, I leaned over the railing of my porch in the dorm and screamed as loudly as I possibly could, "Where are you? I want to meet you already!"

That same year, I went to an engagement party. In the end, that couple broke off their engagement, but that was where I met my husband. When I got to the party, I was talking with some friends about how crazy life is in America, and how priorities are so warped, and I don't remember why, but I said, "Remember 'The Dating Game'?" What was the name of the host? And across the room I hear someone say, "'The Dating Game' with Jim Lang," and he started singing the theme song. And I looked up, and I saw my husband. I started talking with him across the room, and then I went over to sit next to him to continue our conversation. I just remember sitting down and feeling a sense of immense comfort, as if I were sitting next to an old friend. We talked the whole night. We talked about how our parents had dealt with our move from university to yeshiva, and whether you had to be in Israel to be religious, blah, blah, blah. And I remember looking around the party. I saw no flirting, just young men and women talking together having worthwhile conversations, eating baked ziti and listening to a *devar Torah* [a short talk on a Torah subject]. I thought, "This is a wonderful world. I think I'll stay."

---

[3] Midreshet Lindenbaum, a Modern Orthodox yeshiva for women.

When we were engaged, my husband asked me whether I wanted to use birth control. I said, "God forbid. I'd rather have my little toe removed! I'm ready. I want children." Our parents were concerned. My mother said, "How are you kids going to make it? You don't have any money." But I said, "We won't die of starvation." I had read so much about the Holocaust, that financial stability seemed like an insignificant worry. I didn't realize that there are stresses involved in having this kind of attitude, and being immature doesn't help either.

Baruch Hashem, I was expecting within the first month of marriage. My husband was studying at Yeshiva University. I was twenty-two and he was twenty-four, and it was stressful. I was nauseous, and I would just lie on the couch whining, and then I would go to teach Hebrew school, and come home and pass out on the couch again. I had a convenient place to keep the dishes. I just kept everything unwashed in the sink. If you needed a spoon, you would just reach in and get one, and wash it off. This was not easy for my husband, one of two children raised in a spotless home by a working mother. She made three-course meals. He doesn't remember ever seeing a crumb or a speck of dust anywhere, ever.

One morning I woke up with a bellyache, and then I realized the bellyache was coming every five minutes, and by the time I got the hospital it was time to push, and our boy was born. My first day home with him, I was nursing him and I guess it was hormones, but I was crying. My husband said, "What's the matter?" I said, "I can't believe what I've just done. I am so selfish to have had this baby. He never asked to be born. I have no control over his health and happiness. I have no way of making sure that he will not be teased and tormented and suffer and be in pain. Why did I do this? How could I have brought this beautiful and pure and helpless creature into this cruel and terrible world?"

It was the first selfless thought that I'd ever had my whole life. It was also the first time in my whole life that I realized my limitations. My husband comforted me, and said, "Hashem commands us to have children, so we will do what we can and Hashem will do the rest." It was the perfect thing to say. It snapped me back into the proper mindset, to realize that taking care of children is not only up to me. My part is to try my hardest and to daven [pray], and the rest is not my responsibility.

To this day, this is one of the most important things that I've ever learned as a Jewish mother. For example, I have a child now who is having a hard time making friends since we moved. So I invite his classmates over to play after school, and I speak with his teacher, and I daven, but instead of being eaten up with worry, I know that Hashem is also a parent to this child, and He is looking out for his interests as well as me. It is amazing how effective this is, how well Hashem can take care of our problems when we let Him.

The year following the birth, I worked as a dorm mother. It was an ideal job for someone who had to be a working mother. Ideally, I didn't want to work. I wanted to have my baby and my home be my top priorities. But I wanted my husband to keep on learning Torah, because I felt that if people want to be learning Torah in our day and age, they should be able to, because there are not so many people who want to or know how to. I felt this was especially important after the great loss of Jews and Torah-knowledge during the Holocaust.

But in the end, working was very stressful. I was putting in forty hours for this job that I thought was supposed to be part-time. Let's just say that if there is stress at work, then it comes home. Also, I was overwhelmed by the housework, the meals, the laundry. What used to be one load a week for a single girl became five loads with husband and baby and sheets and towels for Shabbos guests. I was not happy that year. It was one of the most difficult years of my life. And my father-in-law was dying, and my grandfather was very ill.

After visiting my father-in-law, my husband said he wanted to go out to dinner to tell me something that would change our lives. This was very unique, because it's not my husband's personality. He's usually very solid and calm and patient like my mom, and I'm the impetuous one. He said, "I know that when we got married I said that it would take about five years until we saved up enough money to move to Israel, but after seeing my father I'm realizing that we don't have a lot of control over what happens, and we just need to be where we want to be. We're struggling here, we're not putting away any money. Why don't we at least struggle where we want to be?" I was thrilled. I was twenty-four, and by our second anniversary I was living in Israel and expecting our second child. My husband joined the kollel at Brovender's in Efrat, so we moved there.

HOUSEWORK

I loved being a mother, but I didn't want to do any cooking or housework. That meant that I was an at-home mother with a very messy house. My husband would say, "At least when I come home, could I come into one room that looks nice?" You see, he's the son of orderly parents out of Leave It to Beaver, and I was the oldest daughter of parents who were products of the 60s, with a "hey, chill out" attitude. I was indignant and self-righteous about the mess. I told him, "What's more important? Cleaning the floor, or playing on the floor with the kids!?"

And that was what he wanted, that was why he married me. He wanted someone more laid back. And he wasn't asking for spit and shine, he just needed a little bit of order. He wanted me to see that there was a value to this. But I wasn't listening. I wanted an excuse not to have a neat house, so a friend and I who were stay-at-home mothers and wanted to nurse forever decided to start a nursery school. We watched four kids in addition to our own. Again, it didn't make any real money, but it gave us enough of a basis to say to our husbands, "We're busy! It's the two of us, taking care of a bunch of kids. And we have to pray with them, and teach them beautiful songs like, 'Hashem is here, Hashem is there,' and go for walks with them. You can't expect us to be cleaning the house in addition to all this!" So I was definitely in denial. My definition of a Jewish woman was, again, whatever I wanted it to be. I wasn't willing to accept that a Jewish woman also needs to find a way to get dishes cleaned once in a while.

This was a cause of tension with my husband. He would come home after a long day of learning, and I'd hear him let out this huge sigh, which I interpreted as, "I hate coming home. My wife is useless." He never said that. He just came home to a total mess, no order, no food ready, and he sighed.

And I took his irritation with the mess as a personal attack on me, that he doesn't love me, and doesn't understand how hard it is. Doesn't he understand that I'm nursing, and my body has to produce milk? I'm lactating, don't bother me! I was very, very immature.

I'm not denying that it was hard. Everything that I was saying was true. It was hard. But after a few years of marriage, and many more sighs from my husband, I realized that I had to start getting to work. I realized that as a Jewish woman part of my responsibility was to take care of the house so that it could feel like home. Together my husband and I had always managed to have the house look nice for our Shabbat guests. So I decided to try to create a pleasant environment during the week as well. It helped me to think of the idea that my home is a *mikdash me'at* – a mini-Temple where God's presence dwells amongst the happily married couple and their family.

I also became more sensitive to my husband's feelings, and started feeling the same as he did about the cleanliness situation, because that is what naturally happens when love grows between a couple. I now understood that he wasn't brow-beating me, he simply had needs from me, just as I had needs from him in our partnership. The kids and I knew that twenty minutes before Abba [Dad] came home it was time to clear the table, sofa, and floor. We would sing the words "table, sofa, floor" over and over while dancing around. He still sighed when he saw the bedrooms, but at least I felt there was *"shelom bayit"* [marital harmony] when he was greeted by a neat living room.

MOVING TO KIRYAT SEFER

That was almost fifteen years ago. A lot has changed since then. My kids started out in the state-religious schools in Efrat, and last year we moved to Kiryat Sefer. We felt like the Haredi society was the more appropriate fit for our younger children educationally, and our older children pushed us to make this move. I am very early in terms of understanding the cultural norms of this community – for example, who buys the apartment when you marry off your children, or what kind of jewelry you buy your daughter-in-law. I don't know anything about that. And I honestly feel that my husband

and I aren't going to completely conform to these other-than-Torah aspects. But in terms of Torah learning, knowledge of Jewish law, and working to improve my *midot* [to become a better person], I feel I've been very frum [Orthodox] for a long time. For many years I've known that being connected with Torah is the only way I want to live.

In general, my greatest joy as a mother has been watching my kids get older and seeing who they've become. I think seeing this process of growing up is why I'm addicted to having babies. You know, when your first child turns two, and you're pregnant again, you say, "Wow, this little thing kicking me inside my belly is going to turn into a little two-year-old who smiles and laughs and says "No!" And then you see the kids getting older and more independent, and turning into human beings that you can speak with like friends. Seeing this happen makes my excitement about pregnancies become greater and greater. You would think that a mother of eight children would be burnt out, but the opposite is true. I was even more excited about the eighth pregnancy than I was about the first, and that's saying something. When you have a large family, and you can see what you've accomplished with all these wonderful kids, you really do feel your contribution to the world. Now more than ever.

I never used to like to call myself a *baalas teshuva* [newly religious], but now, looking back on my past, I think that best describes who I am. I feel like Hashem took me from an empty, directionless life to a place of Torah and caring and giving and goodness. Hashem gave me a wonderful, patient husband who learns Torah in addition to working, and he gave me these eight kids I love so much. It's like I became Miss America, you know what I mean?

HOPES FOR DAUGHTERS

What I would hope for my daughters is perhaps what I would change for myself if there was a way to go back to the beginning of my marriage again. I would encourage them to find the balance in their marriages between intimacy and separateness. When there is a conflict brewing, I have found that a bit of emotional distance enables me to respond in a more respectful way, while overfamiliarity can cause me to react in anger or without thinking before speaking. For years, I had such a temper and I felt that if I didn't say everything that was on my mind and if I wasn't completely heard and understood by my husband, then our love would somehow be fake or blemished. In recent years, I've witnessed what I personally feel are miraculous improvements in our marriage because I have learned that when I have important things to say to my husband, I need to say them only once, and in a calm and quiet tone. That doesn't mean that I'm fake or distant, it just means I'm showing a little respect to the person I love the most... even if he's wrong! And usually, his reaction and responsiveness to the issues I raise is better than I'd hoped for.

In all probability, my daughters will need to balance motherhood with a part-time job. That seems to be the reality in Israel, especially if they choose to marry men who spend as much time learning Torah as possible. I hope my daughters, as well as my sons, will be able to communicate their limitations to their spouses, and to come through difficult times even closer to one another. Thank God, I can say my husband and I have. I hope they'll kiss in front of their kids sometimes, and remember to pray for every little improvement they want in their relationships with each other. And one last thing; I hope they'll be able to make each other laugh.

Many Ways to Feel More Contented

from *Mother Nurture: A Mother's Guide to Health in Body, Mind, and Intimate Relationships*[1]

There are many ways to break the spell of sadness on your mind. Here are some suggestions:

Enjoy your children. It's easy to get so caught up in the tasks of daily life that you can miss opportunities to enjoy your kids. But there are always at least a few occasions each day when you can take the time for an extra cuddle or linger a few seconds longer when they're being extra lovable....

Accommodate the changes in your life. There's a kind of wishful thinking in our society that says a woman can simply graft motherhood onto her old life with nary a change.... You can help yourself by rethinking unrealistic expectations that still linger in your mind about somehow returning to business as usual.

Laugh away the tears. Sometimes it's so awful, it's funny. Perhaps imagine the weirder mothering moments in your day as if they were scenes in a sitcom with a laugh track.

Shine a light. Bright light, particularly sunshine, can lift your mood, especially if you get gloomy during dark winters.

Have some fun. Make a list of activities you enjoyed before you had children, and think about how you could start doing some of them again.

Make a contribution. Find some sort of community service. You'll feel good about yourself, spend time with other people, be distracted from your own pain, and even access a kind of self-nurturing source inside as you nurture others.

Look on the bright side. When you appreciate what you have, rather than longing for or grumbling about what you don't, feelings of contentment naturally fill you. One mother recalled straightening up her six-year-old's bedroom one night. The usual debris was everywhere and she was grumbling to herself about him. Then she happened to turn over a National Geographic magazine whose cover showed a famine-stricken mother holding

---

[1] Adapted from *Mother Nurture: A Mother's Guide to Health in Body, Mind, and Intimate Relationships*, 65–68.

an emaciated, naked child. In an instant her perspective changed as she compared her own life to that of the woman in the photograph. She suddenly appreciated the dirty socks on the floor because they meant her children had clothes to wear at all.

Sprinkling moments of thankfulness throughout your day is like taking sips of cool water while working under a hot sun.

Anat's Story

Choosing to Grow from Hardship

ANAT IS A FORTY-YEAR-OLD mother of four children who works as a freelance photographer and lives in Jerusalem's Old Katamon neighborhood. In her interview, she describes at length her idyllic upbringing in Sderot in the only secular and educated family in the whole town.

Anat speaks in a quiet voice, and there is something wonderfully calming and almost mystical about her. While births by cesarean section are a commonplace as well as an often life-saving procedure,[1] Anat was traumatized after her first birth by cesarean birth, which made it extremely difficult to take care of her baby and home. Her story of confusion and lack of direction during this time reminds me of a person falling from an airplane, twisting in the air without a parachute. Just as the birth brought about difficulties in parenting, sending her son out to day care for several hours a day and a positive second birth enabled her to return to herself and function as a mother. Anat discusses how taking care of her four small children has given her a great inner urge to invest in Torah learning and spiritual growth.

[Translated from Hebrew.]

GROWING UP

The Sderot that I grew up in was very different from the Sderot of today. It was a very small development town. People used to joke that if you had a really long time to get somewhere, then you would take a bus, since the bus

---

[1] To read more about connecting spiritually while giving birth by C-section, read the article "Holy C-Sections" on my site www.JewishPregnancy.org.

would come by only once every few hours, and it would circle around and around before it would take you where you needed to go.

People always thought of Sderot as a backward place, and the government was always bringing in people from the outside to work with the youth movements and with the schools to strengthen the population. But as a child and also now I would say that Sderot was a healthier place than the big cities I saw later on. In Jerusalem, for example, there is a huge socioeconomic gap between people living in Old Katamon and in Musrara, but as a child I remember all of the families being pretty much of the same class, and all of the children playing together outside. There were no separations between Sephardim and Ashkenazim; we didn't even know what that was. As a whole, the people earned low salaries, but as a community there were no areas of extreme poverty, at least as far as I knew.

I was exceptional in the surroundings where I grew up. First of all, as far as I know, my parents were the only educated people in all of Sderot. My mother was a school principal and my father was a teacher and then taught at Ben Gurion University in Beer Sheva for twenty years, and that was considered very strange. Also, we were probably the only secular family in the whole town. My father had lived in Tunisia until he was twenty-two, and he was exposed to French philosophy, which is very secular. At the age of twenty he stopped keeping mitzvot, not because he got tired of them, but rather based on principle and secular ideals. He decided that in accordance with reason and science and intellect the entity that we call the Holy One Blessed be He does not exist, and he stopped observing Jewish law entirely. My mother came as a child from Tunisia, and she grew up going to a religious school, but when she married my father, she gradually accepted his direction in life.

Everyone else in Sderot was at least traditional, meaning that they kept Shabbat partially. They would say kiddush and go to synagogue, but they would also go to a soccer game or drive to the beach on Shabbat. This combination was very natural. The religious distinctions that we see now did not exist then, at least as far I knew. I did not know what Haredim were, and the differences between religious and secular were not so strong. This was a continuation of the way life had been in North Africa, where most of the residents of Sderot were from. When my father was growing up in Tunisia, for example, whether the people went to synagogue three times a day or once a year, they weren't considered more or less religious because of this. Maybe religion was something less external then, more internal. I don't know. I always mean to ask my father these things.

So I grew up with exposure to all sorts of people. My family was secular, but we had many neighbors who were Haredim, even though at the time I did not know that, and my neighbors and my extended family who lived nearby were traditional. We had some neighbors across from our house that you would call Modern Orthodox, and there was a girl in that family who was my age. All of the neighborhood children were always outside playing together in the courtyard, and I remember that when the sun started setting on Friday she would go inside and when she would come outside again she would be dressed in Shabbat clothing. On the holidays and many times on Shabbat I would go with her to synagogue. I was very drawn to this. I would tell my mother all the time that I also wanted us to go to synagogue and to have Shabbat. I liked the order of it, and the ritual of getting dressed up and lighting candles, and I liked the songs from synagogue. My parents did not take these comments seriously at all. They thought I was a little girl, and they did not say anything to me about it one way or another.

For all of the holidays we would go to my grandmother's house next door, and there I would also see how the holidays should be kept. But in our house it was different. On Yom Kippur, my father would eat and smoke. I remember trying to fast when I was eight, and my father explained that he thought fasting was not necessary. There wasn't anything coercive about it, he did not try to force me to eat, but he said that he did not want to. But I really respected my father, and when I was older, let's say when I was fifteen, I was very influenced by him, and that was in conflict with my natural tendency towards religion.

But, despite this, I was always looking for something deeper. I remember, for example, that most of the families in Sderot would watch TV, program after program after program until the shows stopped at midnight.

Once, when my parents were not there, my brother and I were watching TV. We watched program after program, and then we watched the program in Arabic, and then we saw that it was dark outside. I said to myself "How could I do that?" Three hours had passed by, and I had not done anything. I saw the emptiness of time when it doesn't lead to anything. It really shocked me. From that moment on I stopped watching TV.

In that way, I was strange in my surroundings. I do not think that other people thought about this kind of thing at all. Maybe I also liked to be home more than other children. In Sderot, after Shabbat all the kids would get all dressed up and go to the town center, to meet girlfriends and to meet boys. That was something I never wanted to do.

HER TWENTIES

Then I went to the army. Afterwards I started studied photography at Bezalel, and then I switched to study education. I finished my bachelor's degree and started a master's, but I saw it was not for me, so I went back to Bezalel to get my second bachelor's degree in photography.

It was as though in my twenties I went through a second adolescence. I had a lack of direction ideologically. I was searching for myself. My father had really wanted me to study, but he never pushed me so that by the age of twenty I would have a profession, and get a job, and get married quickly. At the age of twenty, I felt like the whole world was open to me, and that I had all the time in the world, as though I would never reach thirty. I allowed myself to study and study and then study something else, and I worked as a tour guide, and I traveled. But my parents saw that I was unhappy, and they wondered why their daughter wasn't managing, why I couldn't find myself.

I merited to have good parents. All parents are good, but I merited to have parents who provided me with a great deal of freedom and all of the opportunities that I could have asked for. They gave me everything I ever wanted, to study what I wanted, to travel where I wanted, to meet whomever I wanted. They gave me such a strong feeling of home that for many years I felt no need to build one for myself. If anything happened, I always felt that I could go home. It gave me an emotional base, an intellectual base in the world. But those few years were a period that we did not understand one another. There was a real distance between us. They did not understand what I was looking for, and I did not understand why they did not understand.

BECOMING RELIGIOUS

There are people who become religious after going to a lecture or a seminar, and that is the turning point for them. I did not have a moment like that at all. When I met my husband at the age of thirty, I was completely secular. My husband was a new immigrant from Mexico and he became religious while getting his doctorate in biochemistry at Hebrew University.

When we were dating, one Shabbat we went to Yemin Moshe, and a couple asked my husband to photograph them. My husband had a beard, but he did not wear a yarmulke yet, and he said, "I take photographs very well, but I do not take photographs on Shabbat." The man said, "Oh, you're religious?" He said, "No, I'm Jewish." [tears come to Anat's eyes]. And those words entered my heart like an arrow. To this day remembering this moves me, and I don't know why. You know, in Israel the divisions are so sharp. Either you are religious and you wear these clothes, or you are secular and you wear a tank top and jeans. This idea that you could have Jewish identity, whether or not you walk around with a yarmulke, really struck me. It reminded me of my roots.

My husband's family was also Sephardic, and had come to Mexico from Turkey and Syria. It impressed me that he managed to become religious while maintaining his own independent personality. I had a very good friend who had become religious, but her whole personality was swallowed up into the Haredi system. She started looking like them and talking like them. She totally got lost within that world. I thought it was fantastic that someone could become religious but still maintain his individuality.

When we first got married, two years after I met my husband, I did not yet cover my hair, but I knew that Shabbat, kashrut, and going to the ritual bath[2] were the admission requirements without which I could not marry him. By that time, I was not wearing pants, but I did not know how low my neckline could be or how short my sleeves could be, since I was not coming from the place of someone who had studied, but rather from a place of emotion. My decision to marry my husband also came from a place of emotion. I felt that I must marry him, and that I could not lose him.

THE FIRST CHILD

After I gave birth to my first child, Yitzhak, parenting was very difficult for me. The pregnancy was excellent, I felt very good, but the birth by C-section was very traumatic because I had really wanted to have a natural birth, and I had even planned beforehand that I would not take an epidural during the birth. But then, they saw that he was breech and started preparing me for the C-section, and they gave me a few epidurals that did not take. I do not know if they did not work because I was so opposed to it. They tried three times, and then they saw that he was progressing down the birth canal, so they gave me a spinal, which took right away. But I cried the whole operation, since I was so disappointed.

During the operation, it was as though I could see myself from above. I saw myself dying on the operating table, and I saw my mother outside, and my husband standing next to me, and that after the operation they took my body away. Before the birth I had not taken conventional drugs for at least ten years, and when I spoke with my homeopath, he explained that a person who does not take drugs for many years can be negatively affected by a large amount of medication. He also explained that the anesthetic they gave me contained a bit of the power of death, which is what it uses to anesthetize the body, and that was why I had this vision of myself dying.

I think all of this, the disappointment and everything all together, affected my functioning as a mother. Yitzhak would cry a lot and he would

---

[2] According to Jewish law, married women are required to immerse in a ritual bath one week after the completion of their menstrual periods in order to resume physical contact with their husbands. To learn more about the laws of *mikve*, visit the excellent site www.yoatzot.org.

not sleep at all, and I was very tired all the time because I held him all the time, and because I held him so much he did not develop physically, since he was not on his stomach. By the age of six months he was barely sitting up. I remember this as a period that was not good at all. I gave birth at the end of my next-to-last year at Bezalel. I did not intend to take a break from my studies; I always thought that after the birth I would turn in my final project and work on it, but that did not happen.

Maybe this was part of becoming a parent late in life, at thirty-three. There is something about late parenthood that brings about extreme opinions and convictions. Before I gave birth, I had thought I wanted to be home with my children and raise them. I had already studied and traveled and taken a full portion of what could be done in life, and I decided that once I became a mother, I was going to give everything to motherhood. So the whole year following the birth I stayed home with Yitzhak. I did not work and I did not study and I did not leave the house. And I can say now that this was not a good way to do things.

I put everything into taking care of the baby, but I did not do it naturally. I wanted to do too much. For example, I did not have enough milk, but I did not want to supplement with formula because I was afraid that my milk would dry up. And I did not listen to what my mother said, because in the baby clinic they said something else, but I did not trust what they said in the baby clinic, since my head was full of homeopathy and the natural approach. Everything was a big confusion, because I was terrified about making a mistake. The beginning of parenthood was not good at all.

Part of the problem was that I think I came out of the C-section a bit imbalanced and every action connected to the baby or to the home was difficult for me. The house was always upside down. I would clean up, and it would turn upside down, and I would clean more, and again it would turn upside down. I could not overcome the mountains of laundry, and taking care of Yitzhak seemed so difficult. He was a difficult child, but a mother who is having a difficult time can also create a difficult child. A mother who has an easy time can help a child to get some order in his life, but I could not. I was too disconnected from myself to do this.

When he was eight months old, I became pregnant for the second time. The beginning of pregnancy exhausts me and I was nauseous, and I did not know I was pregnant at the beginning, so I was still nursing Yitzhak. There was a little improvement when I was in the sixth month of pregnancy, and I felt better. I went back to Bezalel and I left Yitzhak at a babysitter for four hours every morning. And then suddenly, when I had a bit of separation from him, everything worked out. He started eating a regular lunch and got onto a bit of a schedule, and I regained my sense of order and direction.

I began figuring out how much to give him and when, even though it was still difficult. He almost never slept. I would sit in the chair and read him a book, and when I would finish, I would say, "OK, bring me another book from your room." And in the time that he was going to get a book I would close my eyes and rest. Then I would send him for another book, and I would rest again. I remember this as a long period of tiredness and difficulty.

REGAINING HER BALANCE

Then I gave birth to my daughter, and I underwent a big recovery. She was breech, and I was very afraid that I would have another C-section. I had a friend in the neighborhood who was a homeopath, and she told me to come to her when labor started. I went to her on Shavuot[3] at five AM, and I told her that I had not felt the baby turn around, and that I did not want to go to the hospital and have another C-section. So she asked me to sit down and we talked and talked, and she asked me questions about the pregnancy and about myself, and she noticed several symptoms, but she wasn't sure.

It was a critical situation, since we knew that if I had another operation, then I would have little chance of ever having a vaginal birth in the future. The homeopath gave me medicine and she prayed. She asked me how I felt, and I felt right away that the contractions had changed. Before, they had started in my back and gone to my stomach, and she said this was not good, and now I had one contraction in my back and one in my stomach, and she

---

[3] The festival celebrating the anniversary of the giving of the Torah at Mount Sinai.

told me that I could go to the hospital, and that everything would be OK. I went to the hospital and the midwife said that the head was down, and I had a natural birth.

It was a long birth, but I felt during the contractions that my whole mood was changing, and my emotional reaction to the birth was changing. My mother-in-law and sister-in-law were in Jerusalem, and they came in during the birth, and they told me later that they felt that my whole way of relating to them had changed, that somehow my whole approach to the world had changed. That was how I felt too.

When they handed Ruth to me, she was in distress because the birth had been so long, and I held her and stroked her in such a natural way, unlike the awkward way I had always been with my son. When I changed her diaper, it felt very natural, and the first time around it had felt so difficult. With the birth of my daughter everything in my approach to motherhood changed, and I think it was connected to the homeopathic treatment I had received. My friend told me later that the treatment she gave me works on issues related to home and motherhood. She took the breech baby as a sign that on a subconscious level I was not able to accept motherhood, and because of that I was not letting the baby get into the right position in order to have a natural birth.

From then on motherhood was very good. When Ruth was six months old, I suddenly started getting offers for work projects, to photograph freelance for several magazines. I sent my older son to day care and I had a babysitter come to watch Ruth so I could work in the morning. At that point I felt like the house and I were coming into harmony, after feeling so unharmonious before.

Since then, I have had two more children and things have just gotten better and better. First of all, I have developed an arrangement in the house so that there is room for me as well. I mentioned before that at the beginning, I decided that I wanted to be a total mother and to lose myself within the household. After I found the daycare and babysitter for the morning, I felt I had some time for myself. And this meant that when I took the kids home in the afternoon I had the emotional energy to play with them, talk with them, read them stories, and make things with them. It ended up being a very good balance for me.

The third birth was excellent. It was so quick and easy. Also, that child is so easy. He eats well and sleeps well, and everything's OK. Even when he is teething, he does not cry at all. I felt that by the time he was born, he came into an organized household, so he was able to thrive.

The fourth birth was even better than the third. I gave birth here, at home, in my bedroom. It was not something I had planned, but the Misgav Ladach birthing center had just closed down, so I went for a test at a regular hospital, and the midwife said, "OK, this is a big baby, and you're in your fortieth week. I advise that you stay here, and we'll break your waters, and we'll give you some pitocin, and it will all be over by the morning." I was so shocked by this approach. I felt like I was a machine going onto a hospital conveyor belt so that I could come out with a new part. That really was not what I wanted. I knew that labor is painful, but that it can also be an incredible experience.

Then I consulted with the midwife who had delivered my third child, and she told me that since they closed Misgav Ladach she can only attend births at home, so that was what we did. It was a magical experience, in the atmosphere of the home, and afterwards the children came in and there was a baby. There was something so natural and warm in that experience. My mother came afterwards and made me potato soup. I know it's nonsense, but there was some magic to it. I'm already forty, so maybe I will never do this again, but I'm happy that I experienced it this way at least one time.

CHANGE IN PERSONALITY WITH MOTHERHOOD

Since I've had children, I have become much more focused. Having children has brought me down to reality. I used to have a tendency to do too many things, and it caused me a lot of stress. When I became a mother, I could no longer spread myself so thin. I needed to use my energy in a more focused way and concentrate on fewer things, and because of this, since I am a mother, I am more successful in the things I do. I am getting a Masters now at the university, and I am doing very well. I even won a departmental prize for a paper I wrote, even though I have a limited amount of time. Before I was a mother, I did everything well, but I never excelled at anything.

When I was single, I used to lead hikes at Wadi Kelt in the Judean Desert, and there is a beautiful spring there with a lot of water, and sometimes after a rainstorm the water can just spread out and flow away, but if the water gets channeled into the aqueduct it can flow with a great deal of force. I often feel the same way about the strengths of a person. Before a woman has a child, her energy is very spread out, but afterwards when she has to channel her energy, it has a lot more power. It won't just shoot off in all directions until it disappears without making any impact.

RELATIONSHIP WITH PARENTS

I think that since I've become a mother my relationship with my parents has softened. I understand them and they understand me without my having to explain. They understand the stage I'm going through, because they went through it themselves as young parents. Nevertheless, there are still things they wish I would do differently. I think my father would be happier if I had work that was more stable, with a pension and benefits, and my mother would be happier if I had a more career-oriented job. And my becoming religious has been very difficult for my father as well.

When we come for Shabbat my mother makes sure everything is kosher and puts the food on the hotplate, and they don't watch television when we are there. When my husband makes kiddush, they participate. But my father is always challenging my husband, "Why did Rabbi Ovadia Yosef say this?" and "Why did Shas do that?"[4] as though my husband is the representative of the religious world for my parents. But our relationship has softened, and now I think our relationship is very good. We have recovered from the tension that existed between us during my twenties.

---

[4] The leading rabbi and political party affiliated with the *Haredi* Sephardic community.

SPIRITUAL GROWTH

Since I have never studied Judaism formally, I learn a lot with my children from reading with them. When I first became a mother I did not know anything at all. And then I learned with them, for example, that Shabbat Shira is the Shabbat when we read the Song at the Sea, and that Shabbat Shuva is the Shabbat between Rosh ha-Shana and Yom Kippur. Slowly, slowly I learn these things, but I know them at the level of a child.

Recently I have been thinking about how I need to go to study Torah on a more serious level. At the last birth, the labor was not progressing because the baby was very big, and I was crying and crying, and then I heard the word "purification."[5] I heard this coming from inside me. I was saying it. Since then I have had this desire, this inner aspiration to add more holiness to my life, if I can define it that way. I feel a great need to deepen my understanding of what it means to live a life in accordance with the Torah. That's also part of why I want to send my children to more religious schools.

Judaism helps to fill our lives and the lives of our children with holiness. It is because of the Torah that I know that the purpose of my life is motherhood and not the other things I do. If I raise children who are good and kind people who study Torah, then I will feel that I did what I needed to do in my life.

HOPES FOR DAUGHTERS

I hope that when my daughter is my age she will be able to enjoy the kind of life that I have, that she will be able to enjoy family and children and things that interest her. But I hope that she will get married earlier than I did, and start everything earlier, so that when she is twenty she will not waste her time like I did. I feel that I got married ten years too late.

---

[5] *Hitaharut* in the original Hebrew.

BLAH-BUSTER TIDBIT

Tears over Torah

There is a famous story told about the first two rebbes of the Lubavitch dynasty, the Alter Rebbe and his son, the Mitteler Rebbe. For many years, both father and son occupied different floors of the same house. One night, the Alter Rebbe and the Mitteler Rebbe were both learning Torah on their respective floors when the Alter Rebbe heard his grandchild crying inconsolably from downstairs. He assumed that somebody on the lower floor would comfort the baby, but when nobody did, the Alter Rebbe himself descended from the top floor and saw the baby crying in a bassinet right next to his son, who was fully focused on his Torah learning. The Alter Rebbe walked over and picked up the baby himself, stroking him and singing to him until he stopped crying.

The next day, the Alter Rebbe asked his son why he had not picked up his screaming child. The Mitteler Rebbe responded that he had been so fully focused on his learning that he had not even heard the baby crying. The Alter Rebbe rebuked him, saying: "You must never be so preoccupied with learning Torah that you do not hear the cries of a child."

NILI'S STORY

DON'T WORRY, BE HOPEFUL

NILI IS A TWENTY-SEVEN-YEAR-OLD mother who is my neighbor in Jerusalem's Nahlaot neighborhood, and is about to give birth to her second child. She grew up in Haifa as one of five children in a National Religious family, and in recent years she and her husband have been drawn more and more to Hasidic teachings.[1] In addition to mothering her daughter who is just over a year old, she teaches Torah in a yeshiva for women associated with the National Religious community.

Before she became a mother, a large part of Nili's identity came from the hours she invested every day in prayer, Torah study, and teaching. During her first months as a mother, caring for a colicky baby meant that she was unable to continue teaching or studying, and it even prevented her from taking care of her most basic physical needs. She recalls waiting days to take a shower.

Nili discusses the relief that came when her daughter's colic ended at the age of six months. Suddenly, she was able to focus on her teaching again, and to spend part of the day getting housework done without carrying her daughter around in a sling. Nili's description of her abrupt release from the traumatic months of taking care of a high-needs infant reminded me of the

---

[1] The Hasidic movement began in eighteenth-century Poland and spread to the Ukraine and Hungary. The Lithuanian (also known as the *"Litvishe"* or *"misnagdishe"*) approach, which predominated in Lithuania and White Russia, was opposed to the new movement. The most obvious distinction between these two groups in terms of outlook is the Lithuanian approach's emphasis on intellectually-focused study of Talmud compared with the Hasidic movement's more spiritual, emotional approach.

seventh secret of mothers who thrive – the faith that difficult times can pass in the blink of an eye.

[Translated from Hebrew.]

CHILDHOOD

My parents are the children of Holocaust survivors, and they both came to Israel with their families when they were two or three years old. I think that my parents are very typical of the children of survivors – I mean, with all the worries and the problems of the children of survivors. They are both people who are highly intelligent but also with emotional blocks. I did not grow up in a happy, flowing family. My mother is a very critical person, very intelligent and very critical. My father actually brought the warmth. He was the accepting one, the spoiling one. School was very important, and we always had to be the best students in the class. And we were, by the way. My father is the director of a community center and my mother is a child psychologist.

In other ways, my family is very strong, very connected, very close. It was not always an easy family to be a part of, but it was a good home.

MARRIAGE

From my point of view, from the age of eighteen, I had wanted to get married. I had the sense that every year I was not married I was losing out. In my mind, I was always waiting.

Ofer and I got married when I was 23. Many people had tried to get us to meet, and then we went out for half a year, and we got engaged and got married. Classic.

When I got married, the changes were simple – security, a home, tranquility, less of a sense of disconnectedness. Being single had been very hard for me. It's hard for me to describe to you how hard it was for me to be single on an existential level. Not because my friends were getting married, but because I could not suffer through it any more. It was not as though I was so old, but I felt that I was not connected to anywhere, that I was not creating a home like I should be. It was as though my life was on hold. When I was still single I studied a great deal, and I also taught, but I felt that I was in a place that was incomplete.

I got pregnant after a year and a half of marriage. The pregnancy was amazing. Of course, the first four months I had horrible nausea, and I was climbing the walls, and I felt terrible. But after the nausea passed, I blossomed in a way that is impossible to imagine. What a time of my life! It was amazing. I got insanely swollen. I was like a balloon. It was difficult for me physically. But emotionally, it was the best period of my life. No comparison. The only possible competition is this pregnancy. It's clear to me that these two pregnancies have been the best periods of my life. Really. It's a period of growth, and blossoming, and manifestation of all of my feminine powers.

Suddenly, you don't need justification for your existence. You are justified. Period. I'm making a child grow and I could just stay home the whole day and eat and sleep, but the baby is still growing inside me. It's the peak of life, and I don't have to do anything to make it happen. No one's going to measure and test to see if I did it well or not. It's a fact, it's good for the baby in there. Also, I love how my body looks when I'm pregnant. I don't have any complexes about being fat. I think I am most beautiful when I'm pregnant.

MOTHERHOOD: BEGINNING DIFFICULTIES

My first birth was very, very difficult, but thank God, it was a regular birth. It was very long; I was two days in the delivery room. At one point, they had wanted to do a C-section. But thank God, then there was the pushing, and the moment she was born, everything I had just gone through was erased from my mind.

My daughter is only a year and three months old, but I've already been through two stages in motherhood – up to six months and after six months. For the first six months, I think motherhood for me was primarily suffering. I am sorry to say this, but for those months I did not recognize myself. I lost the image of a human being. And from six months on, gradually, everything switched. Motherhood got easier, and then more wonderful, and then even more huge and great, and then even more than that. In the beginning, motherhood was an experience that was 90 percent negative, and now it's an experience that is 99 percent positive.

What I felt at the beginning was that the baby was an *or mekif* – a great strong, light that takes you over and doesn't give you any room. I am a person who lives in extremes, you see. I wanted to correct all the mistakes that my parents had made with me and I was over-aware of all the mistakes that it's possible to make with babies. I wanted to give her all of the warmth and love in the world.

I was an obsessive mother. I was very much into *The Continuum Concept*.[2] I would always say, "No, I'm not really like that. I'm not extreme." But, in actuality, I was even worse than extreme. Aviya was a very difficult baby from the start. She suffered from terrible stomachaches. I tried all of the approaches to preventing stomachaches – changing my food, changing her food, trying these medicines, trying those medicines, the natural ones, and the not natural ones. Nothing helped. It made nursing very difficult. She would nurse and then she would start screaming and spit up.

I'm exaggerating, but for four months my husband and I could not sleep for more than half an hour straight at night. She could only fall asleep inside the sling, and only after walking around, and after an hour and a half or two of crying. She could not fall asleep in the house, so we would walk around with her outside at night. Then, of course, I would have to sleep with the sling on. She slept very lightly, so if I would take her out of the sling, she would wake up. For months and months I could not sleep well because of this.

Until she was six months old, she was in my arms one hundred percent of the time, and any time I would put her down for even a moment she

---

[2] Liedloff, Jean. *The Continuum Concept: In Search of Happiness Lost.* London: 1975. This is a book that is popular today among many young religious Israeli mothers. The writer describes an indigenous tribe in which mothers carry around their babies for the first years of life. She believes that these babies grow up to be happier people.

would scream, and I could not let her scream. I thought, if someone is screaming, that means that he is in need. I could not cook, I could not clean, I simply did not function, you understand? I did not have a life.

And all the time, I was working and teaching with her. I would teach while I was carrying her in the sling because I was not willing to let anyone else hold her. Until she was five months old, she slept very well as long as she was in the sling, as long as I did not sit down. So I taught from a standing position, with a little bit of bouncing around. This was physically very difficult. Also, it was emotionally draining, since I never knew when she would start crying. I would have to stop classes or cancel classes if she started crying, but I did not have a choice. I had promised the program director that I would come back to teach.

I was supposed to run the program as well, but after a month and a half, I gave up. It was a very difficult program, teaching girls with a lot of problems, and I realized that either I was going to have to invest myself in them totally or fail with them, and I failed. How could I invest in them when I was totally focused on Aviya the whole day? I would come to teach, but the truth was that for me during those months, besides Aviya and myself there was no one else in the world. We were the only two people on the planet.

NURSING

In addition, I had many difficulties with nursing from a spiritual and an emotional point of view. I know that this is not a popular thing to say, but I felt like I was a slave, as though my body was enslaved. She would nurse in the beginning every hour and a half. That meant that I could never leave her alone, even to go by myself to the doctor. And after nursing she would always cry, and I would want to go to sleep, and I couldn't. It was as though my body was not my own.

My husband worked insane hours that year, and I gave birth on the day he started his new job. The whole day I was alone at home. I would wait for a shower sometimes for two days, and my whole body stank and was filthy. I would wait for a shower like I was waiting for a drink of water after Yom Kippur. I felt very heavy, something I had never felt during the pregnancy.

Also, nursing at work did not suit me at all, that a body part which is very hidden and intimate suddenly became public property. I know that this is something that is very easy for most women, but for me it was not. A woman who happens to walk by you absolutely must look at your baby while you are nursing, even though this is the reason you are covering yourself. I couldn't stand it.

I felt horrible with nursing. But, on the other hand, I could not let myself stop. Because, what? Was I going to be the worst mother in the whole world?! She needs it! Until she is six months old! And I would pump milk to feed her when I was in front of the class teaching. I would pump at night after my husband went to sleep. And I was looking for a better breast pump, this pump or that one? I felt like a cow. The whole day centered around my milk! Enough!

When she was five months old she started teething, and she would start biting me like crazy when she was nursing. She did not bite to make me angry; she bit me because she was in pain. But this broke me. I said, "Enough." So I stopped nursing and right away all the screaming and colic ended. It was a bit hard for me to stop, but then my body returned to itself, and I felt great again, like I was petite and light.

MOTHERHOOD GETS BETTER

At around that same time, Aviya started crawling. By nature, she is a very energetic and free-spirited girl, very much so. The moment she began to crawl, our lives totally switched. All of a sudden she was able to move around and get everywhere she wanted. So when she turned six months old her colic ended, and she started crawling, and then she started sleeping. She was still in the sling for most of the day, but when she learned how to crawl well, there were stretches of time, fifteen minutes, half an hour, when she was not on me, when I could do something, when I could chop up a salad for dinner. Slowly, slowly.

And since she started walking, she is really like a mature human being. She is also very happy. I had fears that a girl who screams non-stop for so many months could be emotionally damaged. Not at all! I'm the only one who sustained emotional damage from the experience. I love being with her so much. So much.

Everything got better also because I was able to send her to a babysitter when she was eight months old. She would go for two or three hours, the hours I was teaching, since she was already too big to stay in the sling. Now she goes to day care for many hours, from eight to three every day. I pick her up at three instead of four because of my own craziness. I will not pick her up at four, I don't want her to have to wait for us for so long. This morning, Ofer said he would take her at 7:30, which would have made it much easier for me, since it's far for me, and it's difficult with the carriage. But I said, "No, I don't like for her to get there too early."

I am compensating now by working a lot because I know that, God willing, there will be another baby in a few months and I will have to cut down my hours again and it is important for me to know that in the meantime I have been doing something that is not raising children. I also feel that I need to compensate emotionally now for last year when I was with Aviya one hundred percent of the time. Last year, an aspect of the period when I felt like I was a cow was that I thought I was not accomplishing anything at all. I was mostly at home. I spent the whole day with a person who does not know how to speak. OK, she says, "Ga-ga." But is that me? I did not recognize myself.

I was also isolated. I think that was the strongest feeling I had. I was teaching, but I would go twice a week, give a class, and come home. I did not have any connection with anyone at all. Even if friends came every now and then, it did not make up for the loneliness. Ofer has a very full life with his work, and even if he came home and did everything to help me, he still did not understand what I was going through because he has a very full life outside the home, and because he was not nursing, and he was not with her all the time at home.

But today I feel differently. Now that I have space for myself it means that when I am with Aviya, I am with her completely, and if I do anything else when she's with me, I do not feel good about it. This week a student told me that a teacher had said to her, "At a certain point a mother learns to pray while she is handing out apple slices." But that is not my personality. Whatever I am doing, I have to be doing it with my whole self. I am not embattled over this. I do not have a struggle with Aviya, and I do not have a struggle with work. When I am with her I am one hundred percent with her, and when I am at work I am one hundred percent at work. Otherwise, I feel as though I am doing something wrong – that I am wronging Aviya, or that I am wronging my students.

CHANGE IN RELIGIOUS OUTLOOK

I could not manage or feel at peace with the kind of Modern Orthodoxy that I grew up with, since I am a person who is very strong. I needed truth, and to keep the strictest standards. I felt it was so mediocre. It was clear to me that I would not remain there, but the question was where I would go. And the truth is, I went to a place that was not so far away. We are still connected in many ways to the way we grew up. It's not so terrible. I could have ended up much further away.

I met Rebbe Nachman[3] through books, and it was clear to me that my spiritual home is Breslov, not that I have studied so much in any sort of formal framework. For years I have been studying bits and pieces of Likutei Moharan on my own. And I broke my head trying to figure it out until I found that my truth was there. I worked very hard.

I also grew closer to Hasidism when I was near the end of my first pregnancy. Even though I felt great, I also felt on a certain level as though I was spiritually descending, and I realized I could not give birth that way. For years I had studied Torah in programs that were very textual, very

---

[3] Rebbe Nachman of Breslov, the grandson of the Baal Shem Tov, the founder of the Hasidic movement, was born in 1772 in the Ukraine. He became a prominent *tzaddik* [holy man], Torah sage, mystic, teacher, Hasidic master and storyteller.

intellectual, and I was searching for something totally different from that, and during my first pregnancy I found a center for baalot teshuva near Tel Aviv that gave classes in the evening. It was connected with Breslov and other kinds of Hasidism as well. It was a very special place, very spiritual.

It was the middle of the summer, and I would take the bus three hours there and three hours back almost every day. We did not have much money and I did not have much energy, since I was at the end of the pregnancy, but going there gave me something tremendous. I knew that I had to work on myself spiritually so that I would have the confidence to give birth. You know, all of your life you are jumping up a step, and then you take time to digest what you jumped. I knew that before I gave birth, I would have to jump up a step, since I knew that I wouldn't have time to invest in learning Torah when the baby was small.

CHANGES WITH MOTHERHOOD

When I was single, I did not dream about becoming a mother. I did not dream about having a child; I dreamt about having a husband. I certainly did not imagine that motherhood would be so all-consuming. That I would not go to synagogue for a year, or that I would not pray. Who, me?

I think that the biggest thing that marriage and motherhood have done is soften me. My spiritual foundations used to be so extreme and total. I was fire, very total in everything. You could even describe it in terms of masculine and feminine. I was very masculine. Even in my observance, I was very masculine. My religiosity was on fire, very extreme. And then I softened, even in the way I learn Torah, or in the way I pray. When I was single I would pray with such intensity that it was almost strange, and I always prayed three times a day. My connection with God was so intense, so strong. Also my Torah study. Even the rabbis I was connected to were very masculine, very extreme. Now, not at all. Now I open up the books of those rabbis, and think, "What did I ever find there?" Now I'm much closer to spiritual sources, much more into the psychological approach. My husband says you can even see the change in my face, in my movements. Really in everything.

I changed after the wedding, and then again when I became a mother. And now I've become a mother in the most traditional sense. I almost never perform positive time-bound commandments at all.[4] This is not a struggle for me in the least. It's not that I try to, and don't succeed. It's just that I don't feel connected to that anymore. What I'm doing is being a mother.

This isn't related to a lack of connection with God. On the contrary, I feel more connected with God now. Performing commandments in the way I used to is just less appropriate now. I'm not always looking for a way to get away from Aviya to say *Minha* [the afternoon service]. If I'm with Aviya, I'm with Aviya. I don't feel a need to say *Minha*. I'm not required to say *Minha*, thank God. That's the way it should be.

RELATIONSHIP WITH MOTHER

Having Aviya has really improved my relationship with my mother a great deal. We got along well before, but it was good with struggles. And now it's good with far fewer struggles. I really wanted for my parents to help out after the birth, and they really did, my mother especially. My mother is the type of person who is always busy. It's even difficult to get in touch with her. But even with her crazy schedule she did a great deal to help me out.

And they love Aviya, they love her in a way that is impossible to imagine, and that's very important to me. Very, very important to me. And she is not the first grandchild, she is the sixth grandchild. I do not know if she is the grandchild they love the most, but they clearly love her more. They have a great time with her, even when she is difficult or in a bad mood. If I could explain it in a psychological way, I would say that becoming a mother made my relationship with my mother easier because I received from Aviya what I had always wanted from my mother – unconditional love, simple love. My mother loves, but it is not simple love.

---

[4] Women are not obligated to perform time-bound commandments such as shaking a *lulav*, lighting Hanukkah candles, or laying tefillin.

301

DREAMS FOR DAUGHTER

My dream for Aviya is that when she is my age, God willing, she will have a husband and two children, you understand? Of course, I want that! I hope that she will be happy, that she will feel that she has a secure place in the world, that she will feel loved, and that she will be healthy. I don't care if she works, just that she does what is good for her. I just want her to be happy and whole and good.

As a summary, since I talked a lot about the difficult period, I think that it is impossible to imagine the extent to which motherhood has made me a person who is more whole, happy, and balanced. But this did not happen immediately, and it was not easy, in part because I am a person for whom nothing comes immediately or easily. Everything with me is a struggle. I have never been as happy as I am now. I am smarter than before – more balanced, more forgiving, I see things in perspective. And I am just at the beginning.

GLOSSARY

aliya – Immigration to Israel

Ashkenazim – Jews of European heritage.

davening – Prayer

Eema – Mom

Gemara – Talmud, the main collection of the Oral Law compiled about 500 CE

Haredi – Ultra-Orthodox

Hashem – Literally "the Name," God

Hasidim – Jews who follow one of the many traditions that arose within the Hasidic movement in Eastern Europe beginning in the late eighteenth century

huppah – The Jewish marriage ceremony; literally, the canopy under which the ceremony takes place

hutzpah – Nerve, gall, obnoxious behavior

kashrut – The Jewish dietary laws

Kiddush – Prayer said every Sabbath night and morning over wine. Also a buffet celebration on Saturday mornings to mark various events, including the birth of baby girls

kippah – Yarmulke, skullcap

Kollel – Program for intense religious study for married men

Mazal tov – Literally "good fortune," congratulations

Midrash – Collection of legends/commentaries on passages from the Bible

mikve – Ritual bath

minha – Afternoon prayer

minyan – Prayer quorum composed of ten men

mitzvot – Commandments, good deeds

nachas – Pride

Passover Seder – A ritual meal on the first night of Passover during which the story of the Exodus from Egypt is retold

Rebbe – The leading rabbi of a Hasidic community

Rosh ha-Shana – The Jewish new year

Rosh Hodesh – The first day of the Hebrew month, traditionally a women's holiday

Rosh Yeshiva – The director of a yeshiva, an institution for Jewish religious study

Sephardim – Jews of North African and Middle Eastern heritage. They were among the Jewish exiles from Spain in 1492.

Shabbat – The Sabbath

Shiva – The seven days of mourning observed following the death of a family member

shul – Synagogue

siddur – The Jewish prayer book

streimel – A fur hat worn by Hasidic Jews on the Sabbath and holidays.

Talmud – The main collection of the Oral Law, compiled about 500 CE

Tefillin – Phylacteries, leather boxes containing Biblical verses worn by men during prayer

Torah – The Pentateuch; also Jewish religious texts

tzaddik – A righteous or holy person

yeshiva – Institution for Jewish religious study

Chana (Jenny) Weisberg is the author of *Expecting Miracles: Finding Meaning and Spirituality in Pregnancy through Judaism* (Urim). She is the creator of the popular website www.JewishPregnancy.org, and her widely-read articles on parenting and Judaism have appeared on Aish.com, Chabad.org, and in *The Jewish Press*. Originally from Baltimore, she lives with her husband and five children in Jerusalem.